Price Guide to Majolica

L-W Book Sales
P.O. Box 69
Gas City, IN 46933

ISBN#: 0-89538-080-3

Published by: L-W Book Sales
P.O. Box 69
Gas City, IN 46933

Please write for our free catalog.

TABLE OF CONTENTS

Acknowledgments 4

Pricing Information 4

Prologue 5

Introduction 6-7

Baskets 8-9

Bowls 10-12

Centerpiece 12-14

Cheese Keepers 15-19

Compotes 20-21

Figural 22-33

Game Dish / Sardine Box 33-38

Lamps 39-41

Pitchers, Cups & Saucers, Ewers & Jugs 42-55

Plates, Platters & Trays 56-70

Serving Dishes 71-74

Sets 75-88

Strawberry Servers 89-91

Teapots, Cups & Saucers 92-98

Tobacco Related Items 99-106

Vases, Urns, Jardinieres, Candlesticks, Etc 107-123

Wall Hangings 124

Miscellaneous 125-143

ACKNOWLEDGMENTS

A very special thank you to Michael G. Strawser, the top Majolica Auctioneer in the country, for all of his help and photos of these wonderful pieces.

Majolica Auctions by Michael Strawser
P.O. Box 332 • 200 North Main Street
Wolcottville, IN 46795

PRICING INFORMATION

The values in this book should be used only as a guide. These prices will vary from one section of the country to the other. All prices are also affected by the condition as well as the demand of the piece.

Neither the Author nor the Publisher assumes responsibility for any gains or losses that might be incurred as a result of using this guide.

ABREVIATIONS

h = Height, d = Diameter, w = Width, l = Length

PROLOGUE

The styles of majolica, past time and contemporary, have varied from one extreme to another. From the onset of what is known as "majolica" in England in the 17th Century to the studios and potters who continue this tradition in modern times, there is a very broad base of styles and techniques in the production of these wares. The variety of appearance, shapes, and textures are even more diverse considering individual tastes of the creator and those of the customer. Elegant serene pieces are difficult to compare with some of the gaudy "novelty design" items, and as such the figural and textured art pottery wares seem to have even less in common. The all encompassing family of majolica seems to have at least some pieces that appeal to each individual, if not more, thereby leading majolica to its esteemed title as one of the most popular genres of pottery today.

What collectors today refer to as majolica is different from the original majolica that appeared in Italy within the 14th Century. The contemporary styles of majolica are attributed to Herbert Minton of Stoke-On-Trent, England. He debuted his series of "majolica" in 1851, soon to be followed by many others who appreciated, imitated, and attempted to improve upon the precedent set by Minton. Both European and American wares sprang upon the public, and majolica began a new legacy of appreciation which continues to this day.

Majolica is typified as having lead glaze which provides a deep vivid coloration and the soft bodied pieces are figural, textured, or emblazoned with high relief designs. Various producers of majolica often have their own characterized "trademark" styles which aid in identification (such as color preferences or consistency of similar design) yet as some newer potteries tend to duplicate these measures as well in an attempt to increase sales, you should only regard this as a rule of thumb.

Majolica has gathered an impressive following of collectors and enthusiasts. Some desire pieces by a particular pottery or studio. Some prefer either the high end items (or due to finances, may be limited to newer lesser known wares), while many are led by impulse and gather any item which catches their attention. Old English wares in the style of majolica are guaranteed to bring higher prices than newer pieces done in an imitative fashion, however, this may lead to an occasional problem with reproductions.

To the amateur pottery enthusiast, majolica by fashion may seem to cover a broad, vague base of classifications – and this is true. However, once they have achieved more than an occasional glimpse of these wares, it will all become clear. When this happens, they may intermix their knowledge and personal tastes in order to truly appreciate the realm of pottery we call *Majolica.*

INTRODUCTION

Majolica is an extremely popular field of pottery, which seems to gather in almost all antique shows and dealer shops. It is still obtainable at reasonable prices, and while most American collectors will desire to specialize in American wares, there are also many foreign (particularly European) majolicas available.

As collectors increase in volume, it is often a chore to discover a hobby to suit a reasonable pocketbook. Whieldon, Palissy, Delft, 15th Century Italian Majolica, and old Chinese, Egyptian, Persian, and Peruvian items are far too steep in price for most individuals (which is why these in particular are usually only seen in museum holdings or amongst a collection owned by the wealthy.) Facing such insurmountable obstacles, it is fortunate one can gain appreciation from almost any collection, regardless of what it can bring in as far as majolica is considered, many collectors specialize in a specific design, a mark such as Etruscan, or possibly figurines of animals.

As opinions of collectors and dealers meet (and often conflict), the true standards of collecting majolica are left to the individual. Almost all antique dealers feel that perfection in pottery is of utmost importance, yet many collectors and dealers alike feel that majolica is worthy of collecting even in slightly damaged condition. The value of non-mint pieces can only be estimated, but certain facts can aid in evaluating worth. A low-end item such as an ironstone plate which in good condition would rank under $25 would be worthless if cracked or repaired. However, a piece which is rare and worth hundreds of dollars in an undamaged state would still be worth a hefty fraction of that value as it is far rarer and a more worthwhile acquisition – possibly just over half of the original value in some cases. The relationship between condition, rarity, and value is exemplified further by the fact that almost all museum quality pieces still bear the ravages of cracks and restoration. As restoration is a very vague term, this can mean a slight repaint over a hairline crack or, at the other extreme, a piece completely reworked from an assemblage of scattered remnants.

Another fact to consider is that certain collectibles were used in day to day activity, whereas others were created from the onset to be purely ornamental. Obviously, those items which encountered even occasional usage will have developed more structural damage over the years than those which served a more aesthetic purpose. Majolica can be found in both categories – useful and decorative - and this is something to consider when judging the current status of a majolica piece. Furthermore, as Majolica is composed of a soft pottery base coated with a hard glaze, it could easily develop age cracks and sizable abrasions.

Majolica has increased in both demand and value over the last few decades - thus making it a scarce collectible in an era of many collectors. Therefore, new considerations may be necessary for the collector and dealer to appropriate items slightly damaged or repaired on occasion, obviously with such considerations taking into account the price.

"True" Majolica coined its name from the fact that this particular type of tin glazed pottery was made in Spain and ushered to Italy from the Balearic Islands – of which the main island was known as Majorica or *Majolica.* Majolica was originally decorated in gold luster and blue, later to be followed with four basic colors - dark blue, purple, green, and yellowish orange - to cover the white tin enamel. Most often these early pieces bore designs derived from the art of ancient civilizations such as Egypt, Syria, Turkey, and Persia.

This Italian majolica arrived at a name in a roundabout way, therefore we shouldn't be very concerned with misusing it when we refer to 19th Century and contemporary majolica. The original name arises from the fact that the imports came from the Balearic Islands, specifically Majolica. Even when the products were produced elsewhere, such as Barcelona, they were brought in by a ship from Majolica and became known as majolica. They were later produced in Italy.

American majolica is not the majolica as referred to in the above paragraph, and its general appearance is altogether different as well. Transparent lead glazes have replaced the opaque tin glazes. The old majolica was made by the use of an opaque white tin enamel which conceals the off-white pottery base and provides a white surface upon which to paint vitrified ceramic colors. This was originally developed in Spain and Italy between the 12th and 17th Centuries. The same ware in France was called *Faience.*

Most experts make the distinction that French Faience is 17th Century and a tin glaze, yet 19th Century so-called Faience is a lead glaze and should not be referred to as Faience any more than modern Majolica should be called Majolica.

In Holland the opaque tin enamel undercoat was used in combination with cobalt blues, and while the technique is that of majolica, it is known as *Delft*. This is proof that the name of a certain type of ware may not describe its physical characteristics and that the same processes of enameling, glazing, and coloring can use different names – although this is not always perfectly understood.

Actually, American type majolica ware is associated more with Palissy, Whieldon, Wedgwood, and Staffordshire than it is with Italian majolica. These are potters and potteries which used transparent lead glazes rather than opaque tin glazes. In the 19th Century and today the title majolica is used as a trade name. This is shown by the fact that one of the most significant potters in the United States – Griffin, Hill and Smith in Phoenixville, PA – used as their mark ETRUSCAN MAJOLICA for no other reason other than sales. It had no Etruscan characteristics, and it had no tin glaze. The name, however, was in use during the era in which majolica and Palissy were so popular and is still in use with both collectors and the antique market. Therefore, the decision has already been arrived at to refer to all of these wares, old and modern, as majolica whether historically correct or not.

The current stylings of majolica owe a great debt to a handful of artisans of which provided designs, color schemes, and styles which have been copied and imitated time after time, creating many beautiful wares by many different hands. A few of the more prominent craftsmen are portrayed below.

Bernard Palissy was born about 1510 and died in 1590. He is of interest to enthusiasts of majolica because he made the earliest and finest lead glaze pottery and developed the technique of "applique", and according to the New York Metropolitan Museum of Art, it was he who invented the mottled glaze used so prevalently in the 19th Century for majolica pottery.

Palissy was born to a poor family, and managed to secure an apprenticeship in glass painting while in his teens. He later established himself and his designs after settling in Saintes, France. His designs of vivid animals in blues, greens, and browns later turned into relief and applique figures of shells, flowers, fish, and other organic scenery. The underside of his pieces were often more eye-catching than his more sedated surfaces, as his technique with strong colors within smeared streaks provided contrast with his detailed textures and patterns – often relating to tortoiseshell or tree bark.

Palissy's wares were unmarked, and in the 19th Century were among the most revered ceramics. The result was innumerable forgeries and imitations from both England and France. Genuine pieces are believed to be the minority when considering Palissy's work – therefore many pieces on display may read "In the manner of Bernard Palissy" so as to avoid the argument as to whether or not it is a genuine article.

Thorn Wieldon is a potter from England with an interesting history, and an impressive legacy left behind. His pottery churned out wares from 1740 to 1780. He employed Wedgwood only to later enter into business with him and had employed such reknowned artists as Spode. Whieldon's works are credited as being among the finest of lead glazed pottery.

Whieldon is a lead glazed ceramic, a forerunner of 19th Century American majolica, which it resembles closely. In its customary appearance, Whieldon is a speckled or mottled brown and yellowish glazed pottery sometimes referred to as tortoiseshell ware. Sometimes, rarer pieces may be found with blue, gray, yellow, white, and green hues blended together marvelously on a variety of shapes. The difference between Whieldon and Etruscan is easily noticed: Whieldon paste is much thinner, lighter, and with differing designs.

Herbert Minton was born in 1792, his family already bearing an impressive reputation for pottery manufacture and design in the Staffordshire area. In 1836, Herbert assumed direction of the Minton works in Stoke-on-Trent. A Frenchman, Leon Arnoux, began designing for Minton in 1849 and brought about many new changes, techniques, and materials to be used. Arnoux enabled the pottery to rework designs inspired by older wares and mutate them into new and fresh ideas. When majolica gained worldwide attention in 1851, Minton was prepared and contributed greatly to this movement. Continuing the evolution of his wares rather than resting on his laurels, the wares to come forth would provide a glimpse of the future as new trends were set. By the late 1850's, Minton was so reknowned of a pottery and in demand that other producers of pottery followed in suit, creating similar styles and designs. Some of the greatest competition, such as Joseph Holdcroft and George Jones, had already gained their experience working for Minton themselves.

Wares produced by Minton are often in pastels, such as blue, green or pink. The Palissy inspired wares were in a collage of dark mottled blues and browns, while a few others appeared in mottled yellow and green. Deep green bottoms are common to many of the wares, along with a few that appear in turquoise, pink, or other pastels. Interiors of Minton wares are in these pastel colors as well, with a vivid reddish pink being the most common.

The change from opaque tin enamels to clear transparent lead glazes was a great advance in the general technique of pottery. More accurate glaze colors were permitted by using various metal oxides, more definition was allowed, and it was altogether cheaper to provide. It was quite natural, consequently, to copy the lead glaze techniques as well as the designs of Palissy and his successors, Whieldon and Wedgwood. On this subject and on the question of one pottery copying another, it is understood by some that Wedgwood occasionally encouraged duplicates of designs so that spare cups or saucers or even rush orders might be filled through Wedgwood by other potteries.

One characteristic of 19th Century majolica is the inside coating of many vases, pitchers, bowls, and cups. They have a characteristic tint of lavender, blue, pink, or red. Another characteristic is a mottled effect in the center on the face of the plates. While occasionally flat, 19th Century majolica is more often molded to form, for example, with the leaf design and the many raised configurations after Palissy and others. It was also made in a great variety of shapes (such as shells, animals, and flowers) in the form of pitchers, compotes, teapots, or bowls, with appropriate background in relief.

The older pieces were frequently painted by young girls, some efficient and some careless, which accounts for the "sloppy" work seen within some pieces. This is particularly true of American majolica where low wages were prevalent and cast against the demand of the markets at the time.

Modern majolica made currently or within the last fifty years can be as beautiful as their predecessors, but most of the "reproductions" have a discernible "new look". Those of European origin must bear the country of origin stamp. More marks and signatures on the new pieces would help future collectors identify majolica, as we have encountered this very problem with items of old. Classification and age will always be a difficult but interesting chore for the collector of majolica.

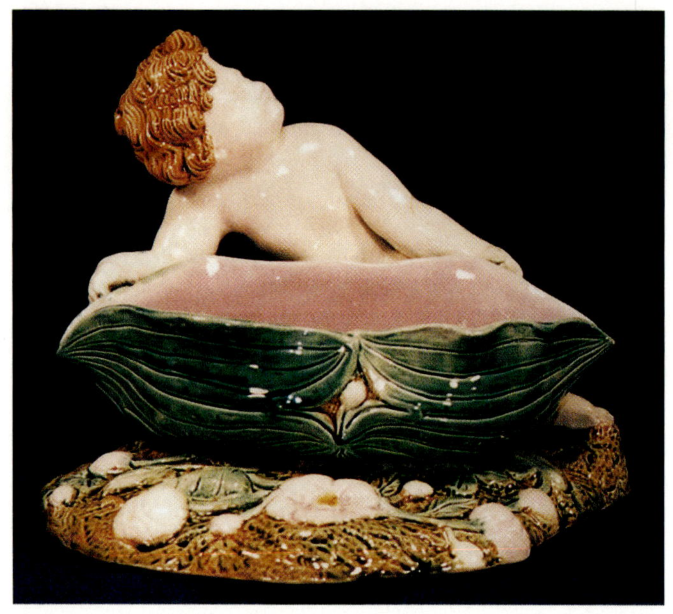

Minton Cherub with a Leaf Basket, bright lavender interior with green leaves on base which is mottled with lavender flowers and green leaves, 7 1/2" h x 11" w x 10 1/2" l.
$800

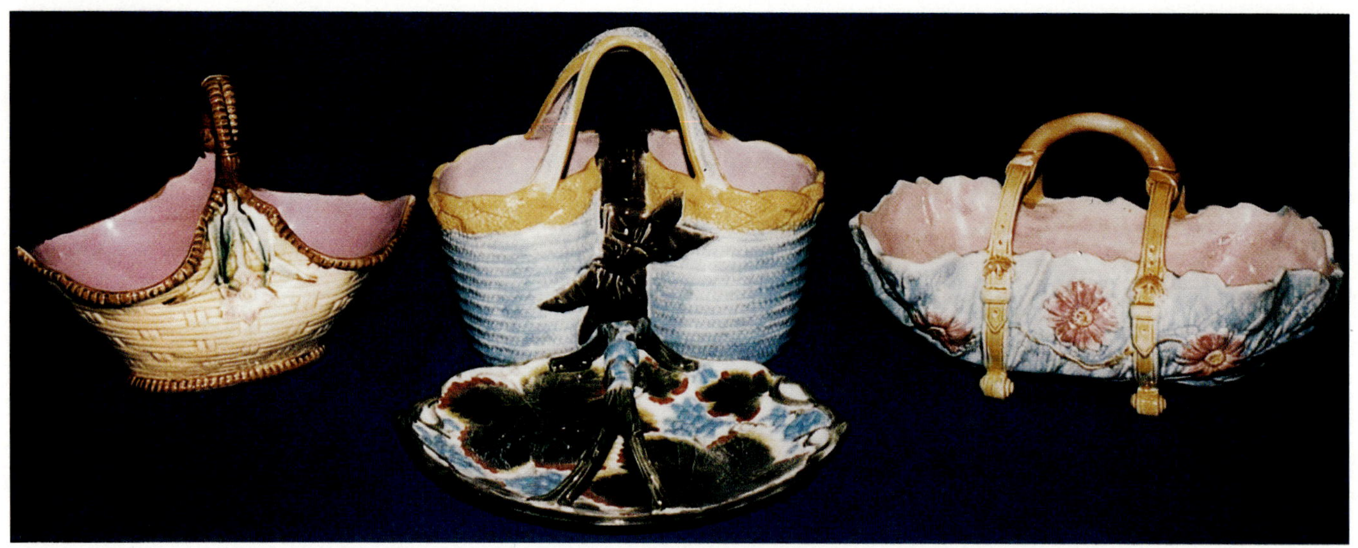

Front Row
Wedgwood Basket Handled Platter, grape pattern, 9 1/2" x 11 1/2" – **$225**

Back Row – Left to Right
Basket with brown handles and flowers, basketweave, with a bright pink interior, 11 1/4" – **$400**

Turquoise Basket with yellow rim and a black ribbon and bow, and a bright lavender interior, 11 1/2" l – **$400**

Cabbage leaf and daisy basket with luggage strap handles – **$375**

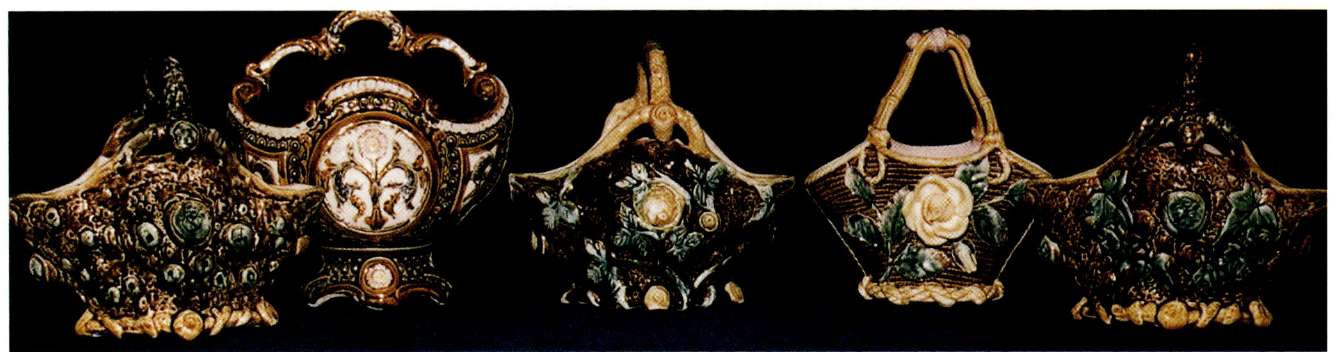

Left to Right:
Bird's nest basket, 9 1/4" w – **$225**
Green German basket, 9 1/4" h – **$250**
Bird's nest basket, 9" l – **$350**
Basket with applied flowers, 8 1/2" – **$175**
Bird's nest basket, 8 1/2" h – **$225**

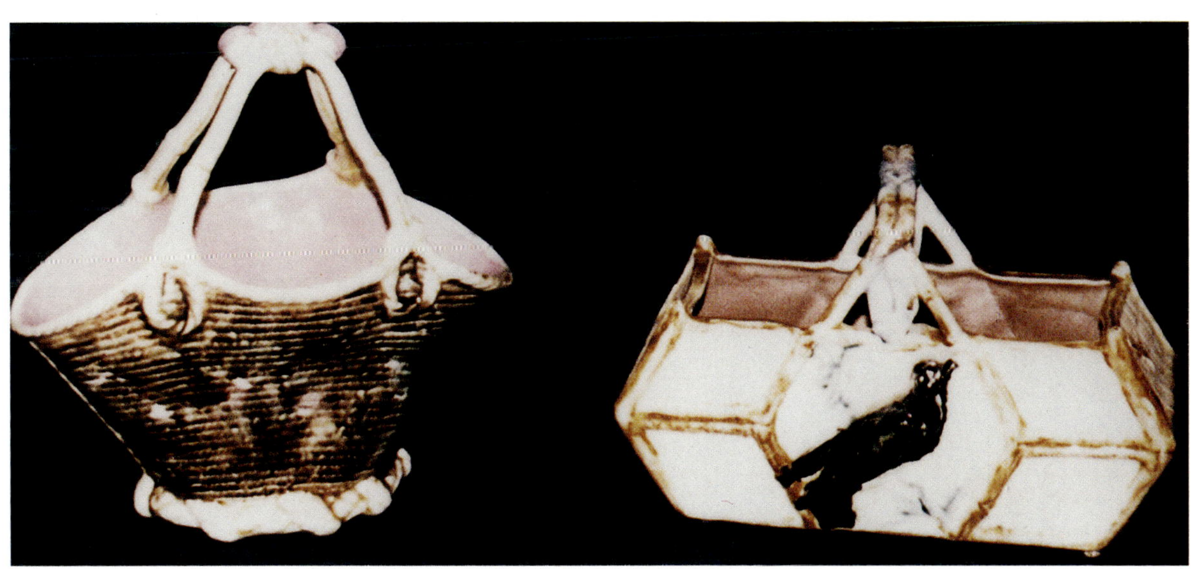

Mottled basketweave basket with pink bow handle – **$150**

Basket with bird on a branch. – **$100**

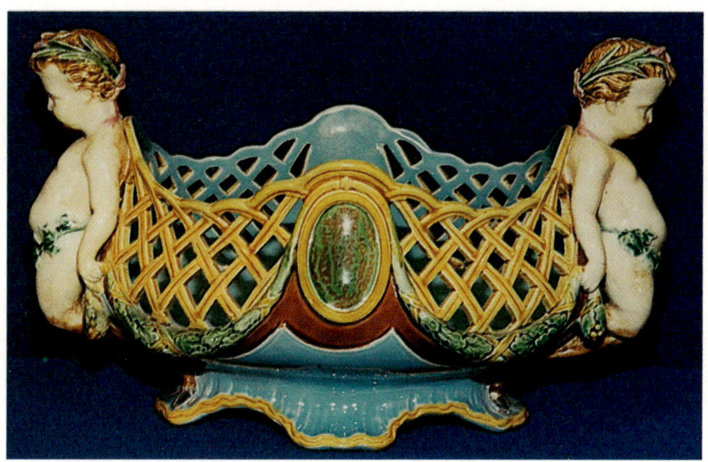

A Minton bowl with open lattice sides and two cherubs, one on each end. A turquoise base and interior, 6 1/2" h x 7" d x 11" l.

$1400

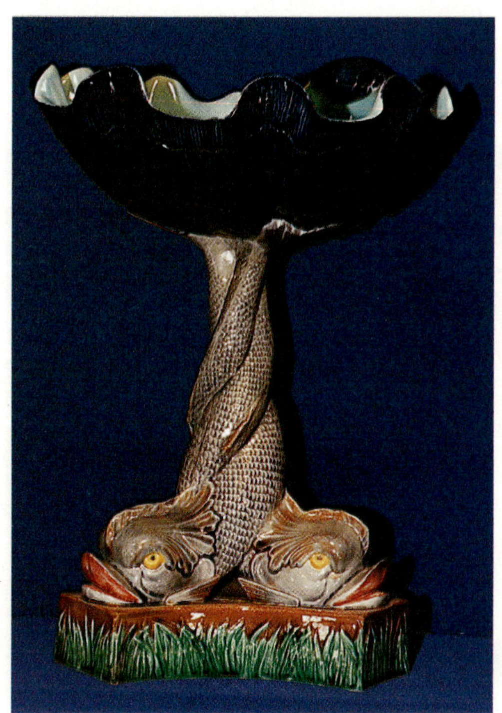

Cobalt blue shell bowl with two dolphins, holding up the shell bowl with their tails. By Holdcroft, 14" tall.

$1000

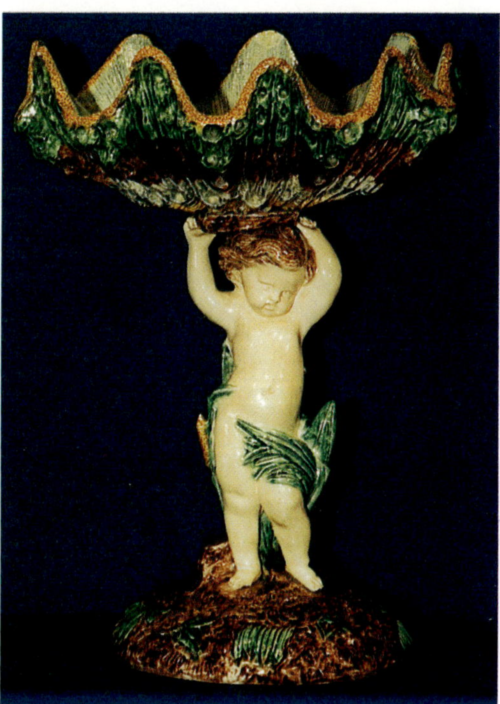

Portuguese shell shaped bowl with a cherub holding it above its head, 9 1/2" d x 14" h.

$350

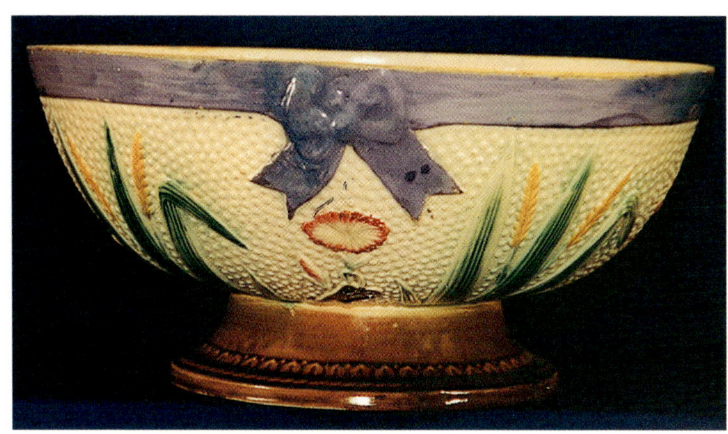

Samuel Lear wheat and ribbon footed punch bowl, 6 1/2" h x 13 1/2" d.
$775

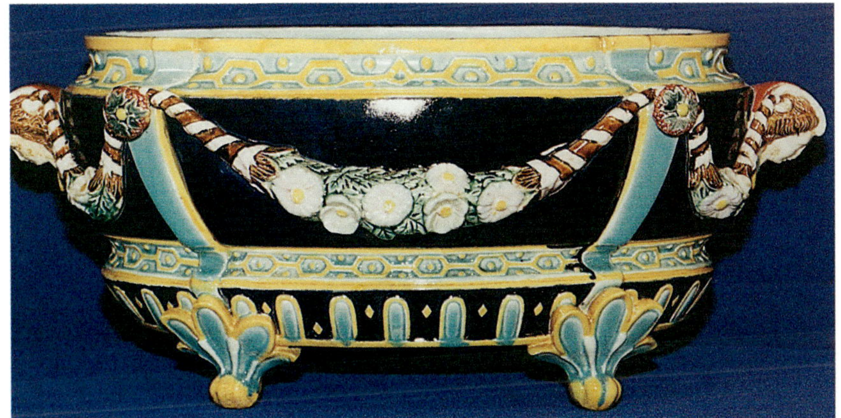

Holdcroft cobalt centerpiece bowl, trimmed in turquoise, yellow, brown, pink, red and green. Ladies head handles, 7 1/2" h x 9" d x 18" l.
$2,200

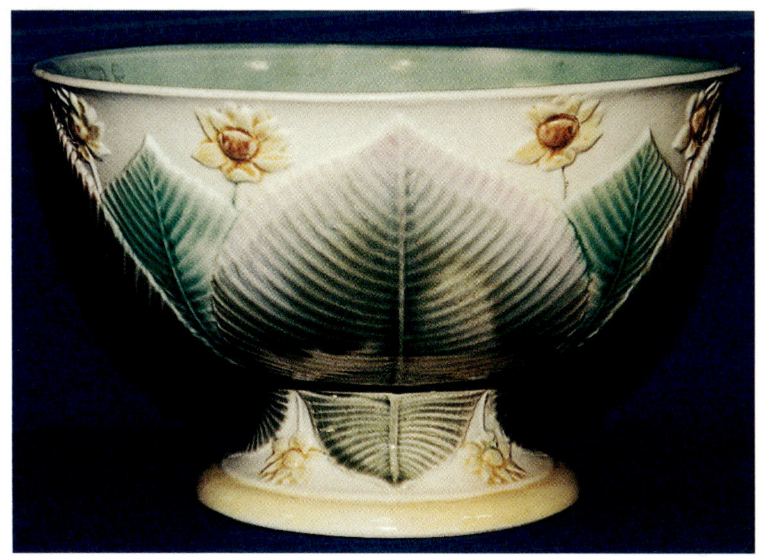

Etruscan lily punch bowl of Griffen, Smith & Co., 5 1/2" h x 9 1/4" d.
$850

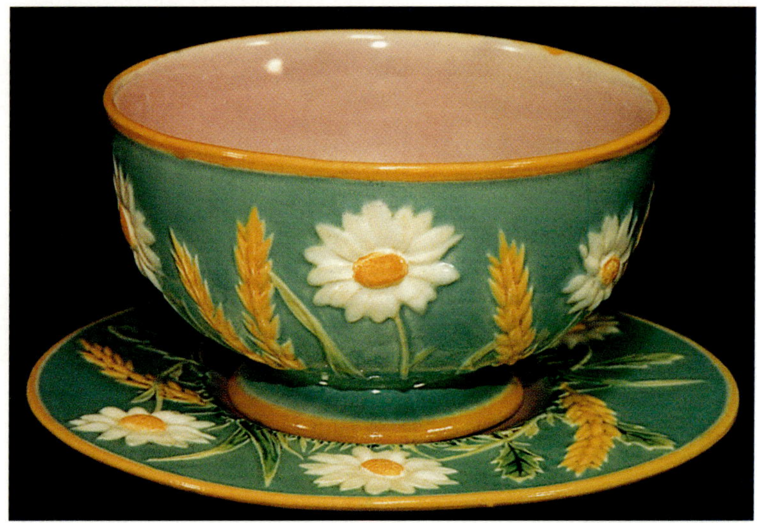

George Jones wheat and daisy bowl with an underplate. The bowl is 6 1/2"d and the plate is 8 1/4" d.

$1800

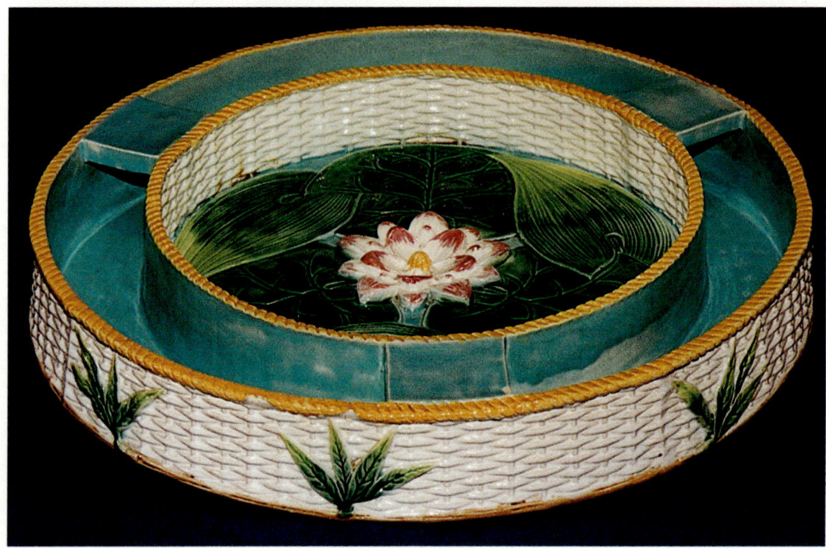

George Jones water lily centerpiece with a floating flower ring border and a lily in the center. The centerpiece is white basketweave with a turquoise interior, 2 1/4" h x 14 1/2" d.

$2,100

Egg Spoon Warmer by Brown-Westhead, Moore & Company. The robin's egg is sitting amongst cattails, 5" h x 8" l.
$850

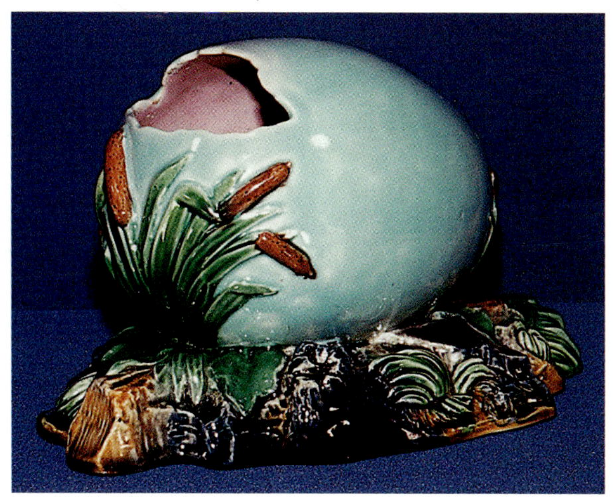

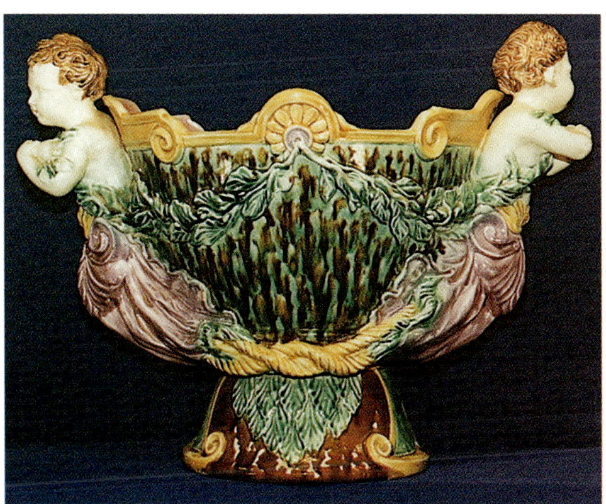

English Centerpiece with two large cherubs on each side with lavender skirts. The piece has a mottled ground, and a pink interior, 15" h x 20" w.
$1800

Minton Rabbit Centerpiece, 41/2" h x 91/2".
$5400

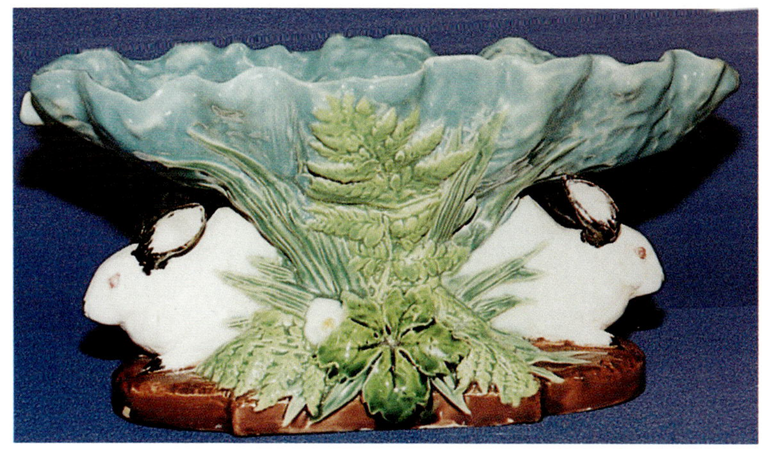

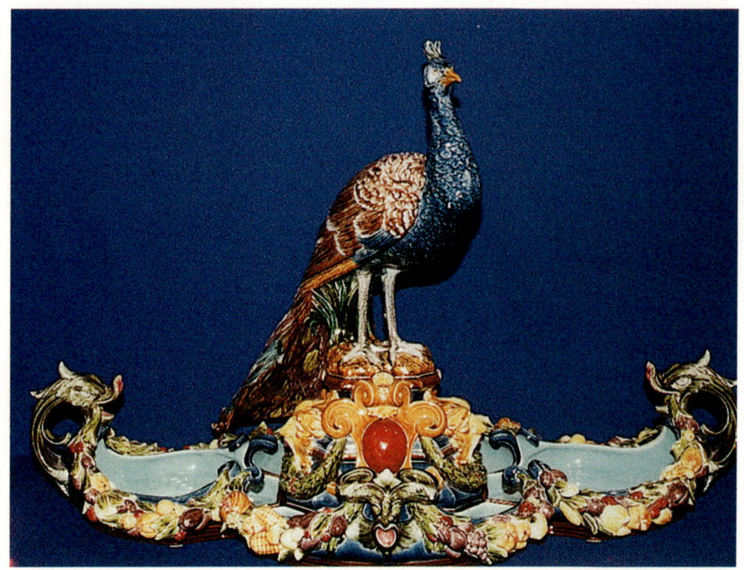

Sarreguemines six piece Peacock Buffet Centerpiece Server with gargoyles, della robia and laurel swagging. It has four serving dishes around base. (Rare)

$8500

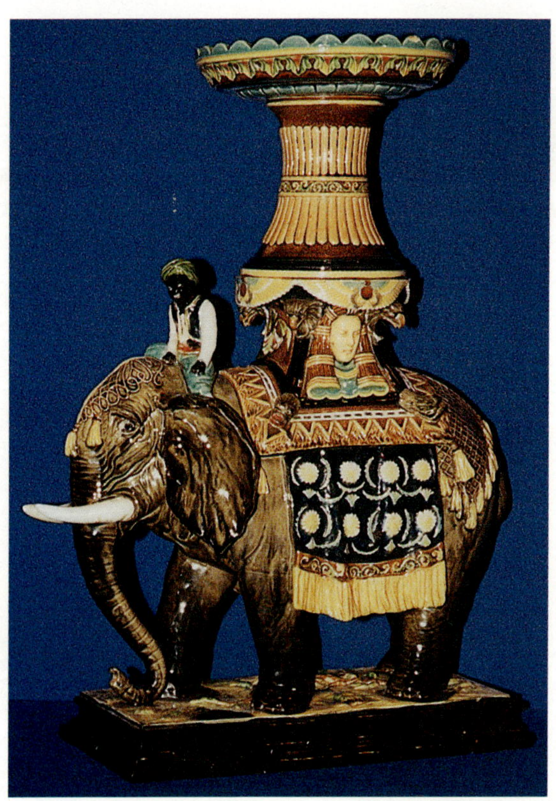

Elephant Centerpiece with Indian man riding the elephant, Egyptian style, 21" h x 16" l. by Wilhelm Schiller & Sons. (Rare)

$4500

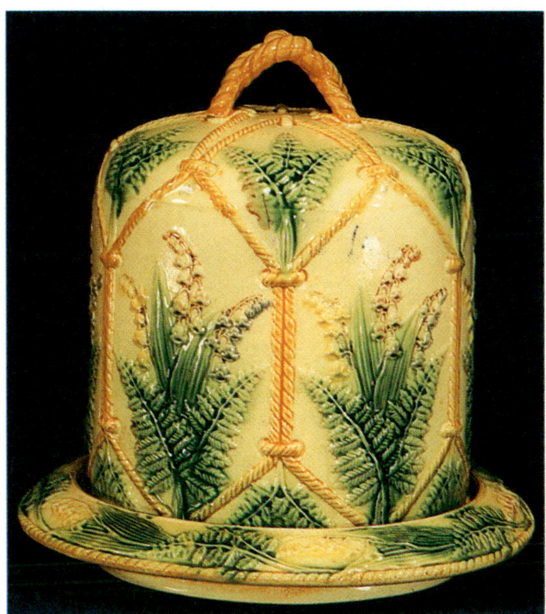

Rope and Fern Cheese Keeper, 8 1/2" high. This is an example of Samuel Lear's "Lily of the Valley" Pattern.

$3000

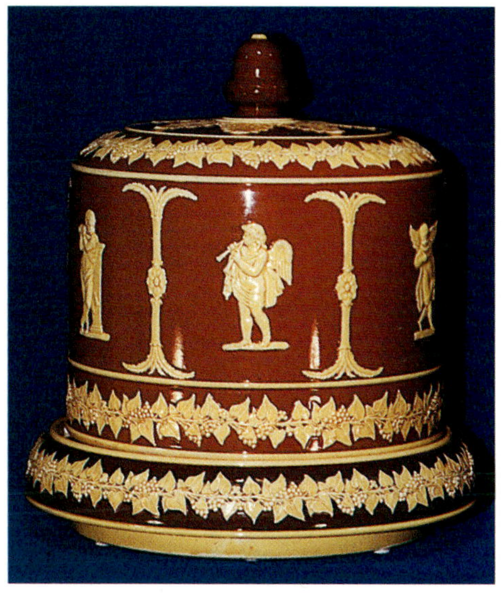

Cheese Keeper by Samuel Lear, 11 1/2" tall.

$300

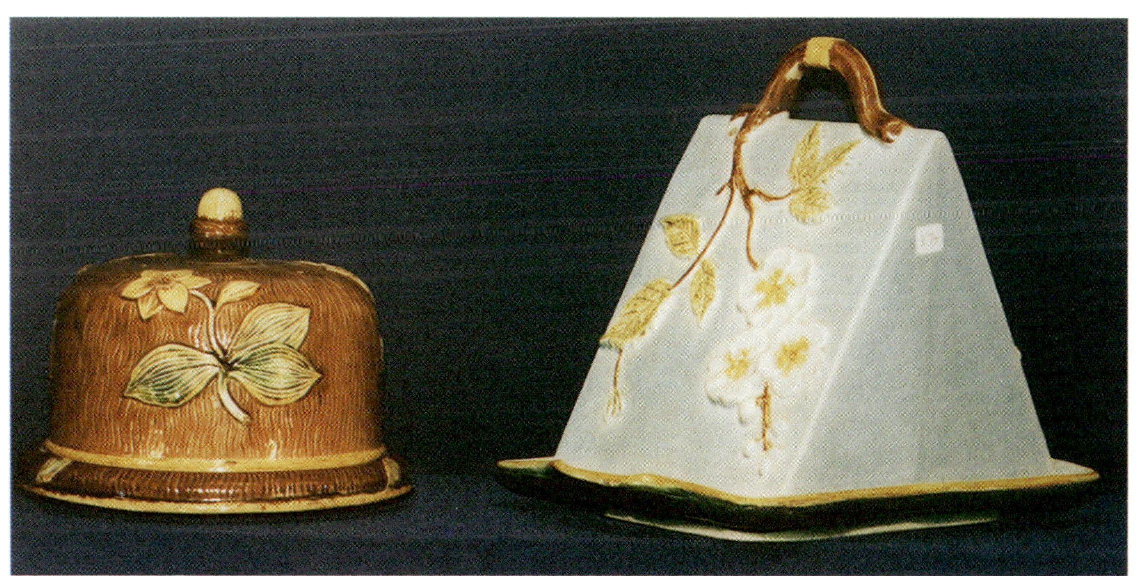

Left to Right:

Brown Cheese Keeper with a floral design and an acorn handle, 6".

$200

Holdcroft Wedge Cheese Keeper, turquoise with lavender flowers, and a stem handle, 9 1/2" h.

$775

CHEESE KEEPERS

Cheese Keeper, yellow background with a bird on a branch and a water lily flower handle, 7" h.
$1200

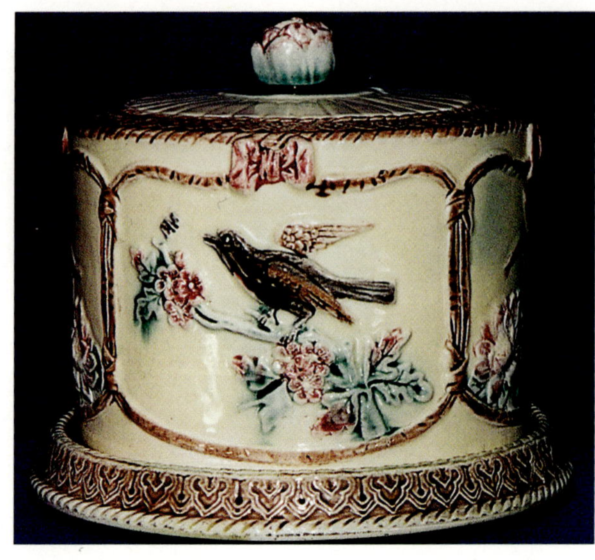

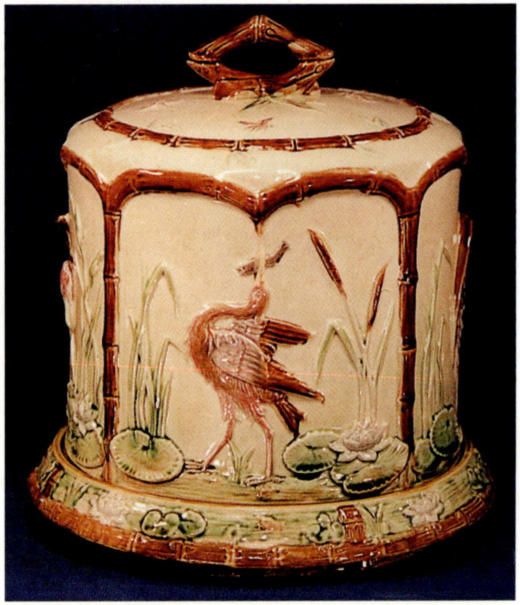

Cheese Keeper with a Heron standing between the lily pads and cattails, 11 1/2".
$3200

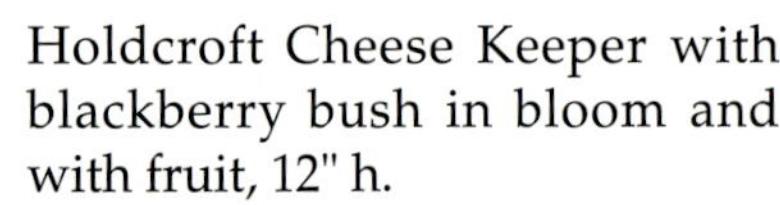

Holdcroft Cheese Keeper with blackberry bush in bloom and with fruit, 12" h.
$1050

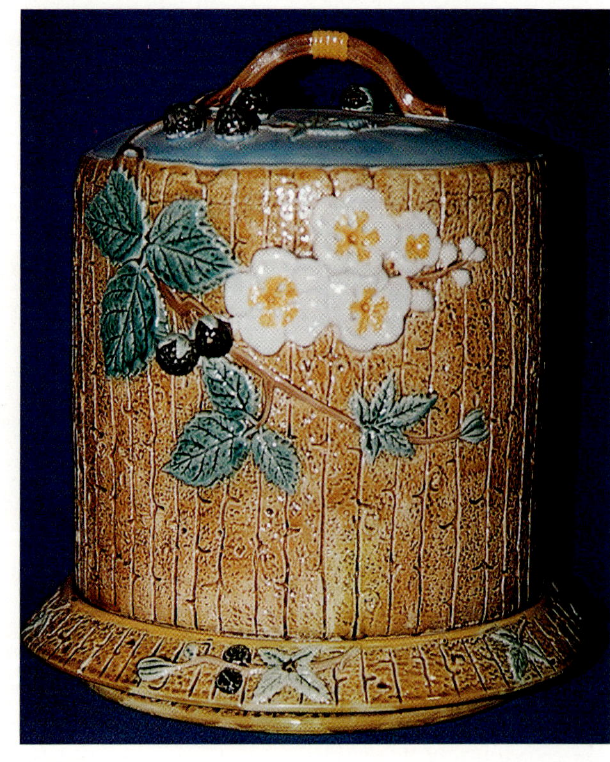

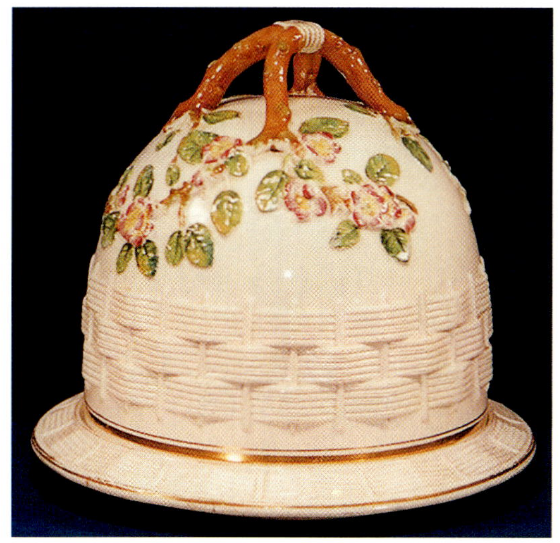

Apple Blossom Cheese Keeper, by George Jones. White with a woven fence pattern, with two stems for the handle, 10" h x 11 1/4" d.
$1300

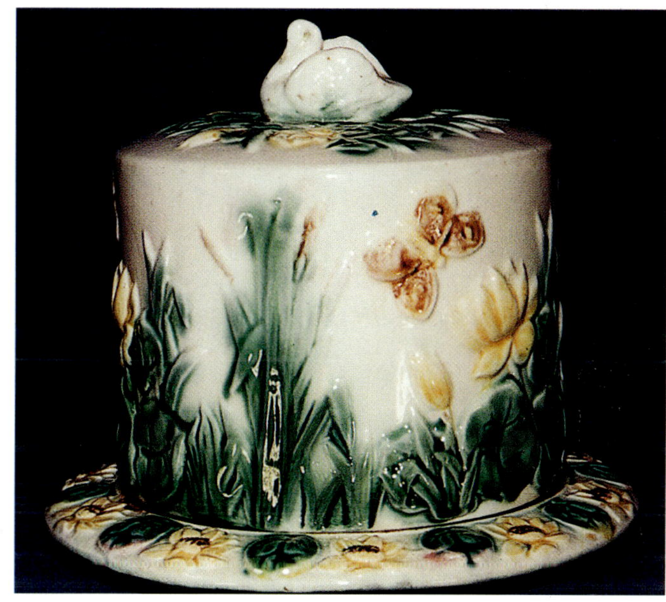

Etruscan Cheese Keeper, with butterflies, lilies, and cattail design with a swan as the handle on the cover, by Griffen, Smith & Co., 7 1/2" h.
$3100

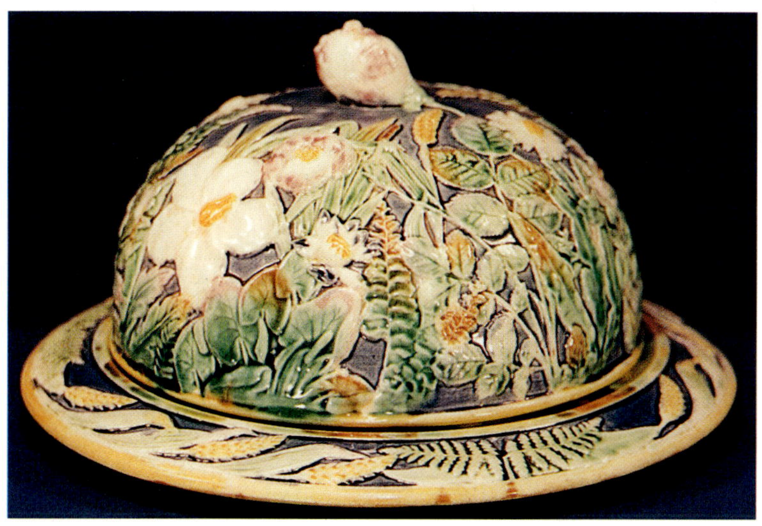

Etruscan Cheese Keeper, cobalt background, with lilies and ferns covering the keeper, 6" h x 11" d.
$3300

CHEESE KEEPERS

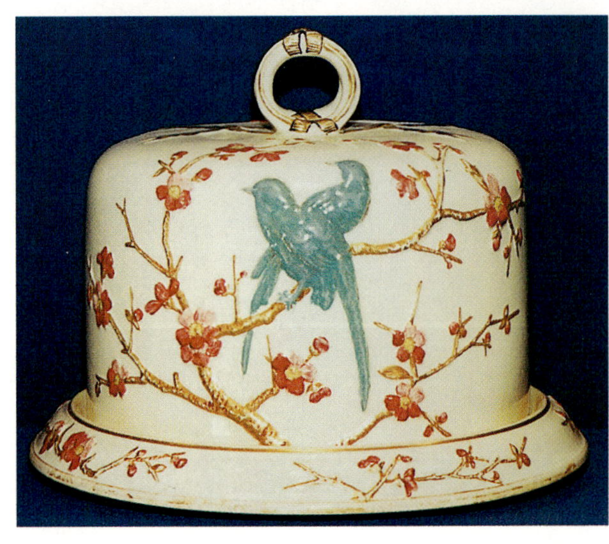

Cheese Keeper with love birds and dragonflies on a prune tree, by George Jones.
$525

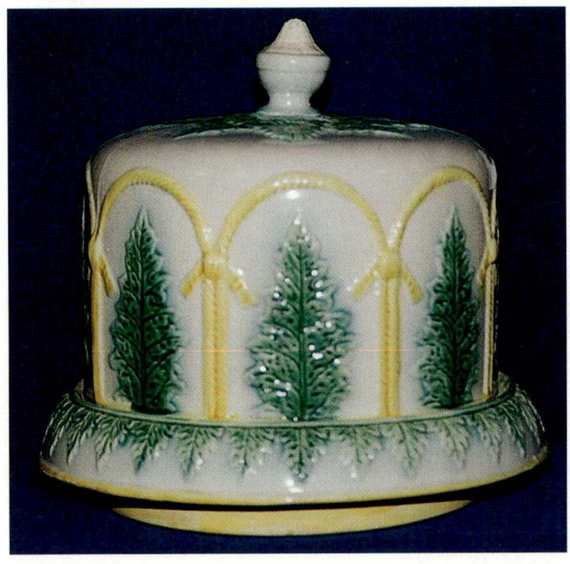

Rope and Fern Cheese Keeper.
$1000

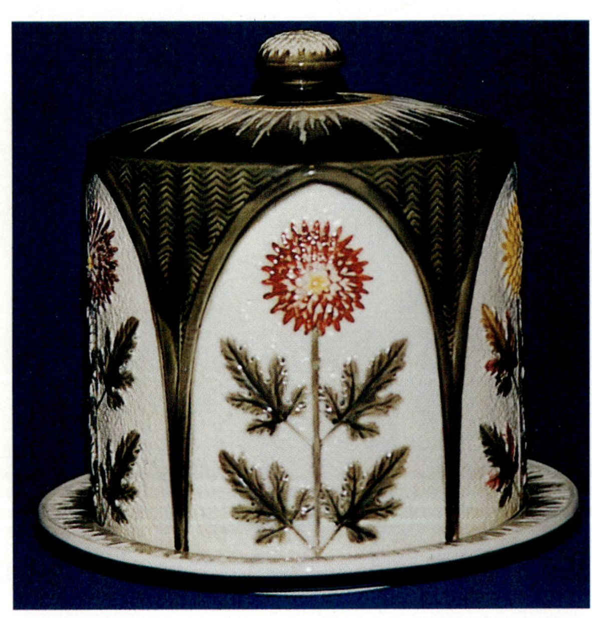

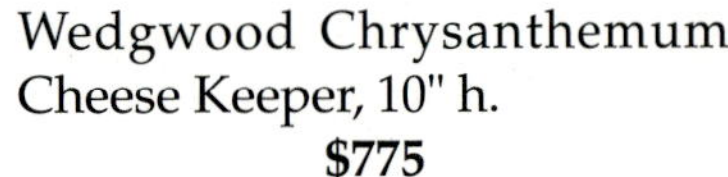

Wedgwood Chrysanthemum Cheese Keeper, 10" h.
$775

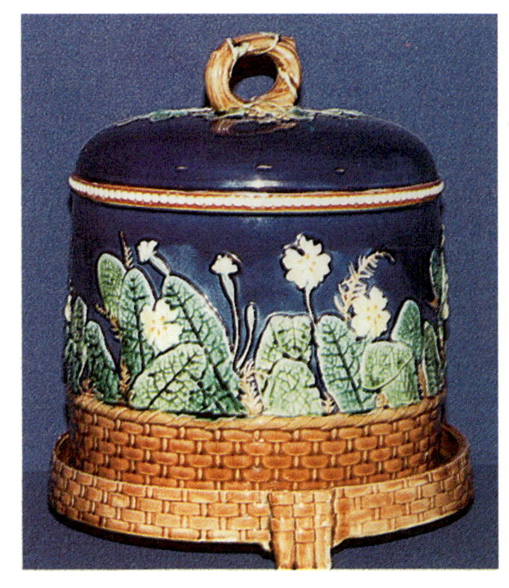

Wedgwood Cheese Keeper, cobalt blue primrose and basket , 10" h.
$4000

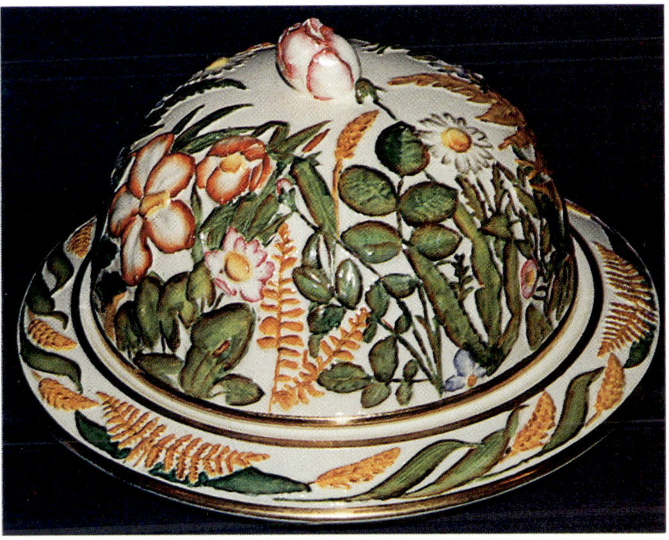

Etruscan Cheese Keeper, albino lily.
$1400

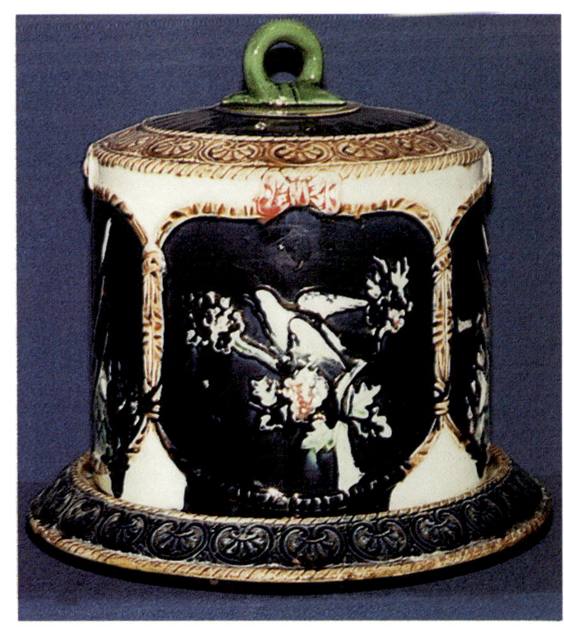

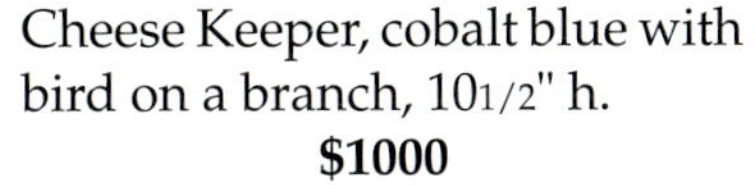

Cheese Keeper, cobalt blue with bird on a branch, 10 1/2" h.
$1000

COMPOTES

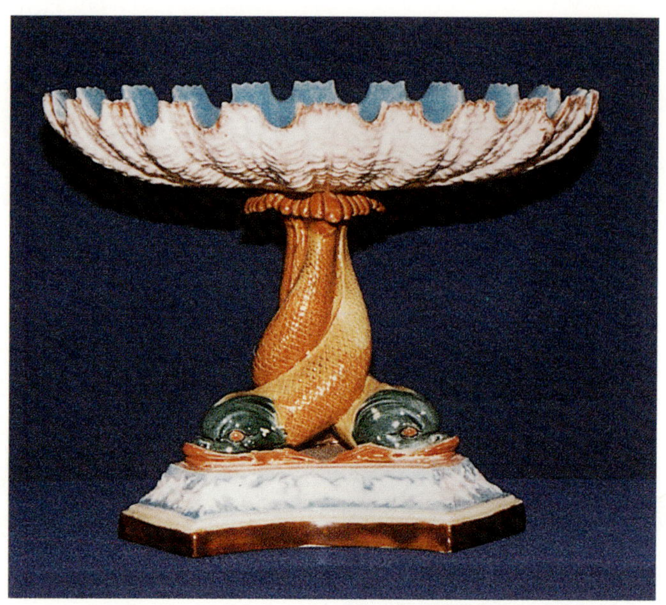

Royal Worcester Dolphin Compote, 7" h x 9" d.
$650

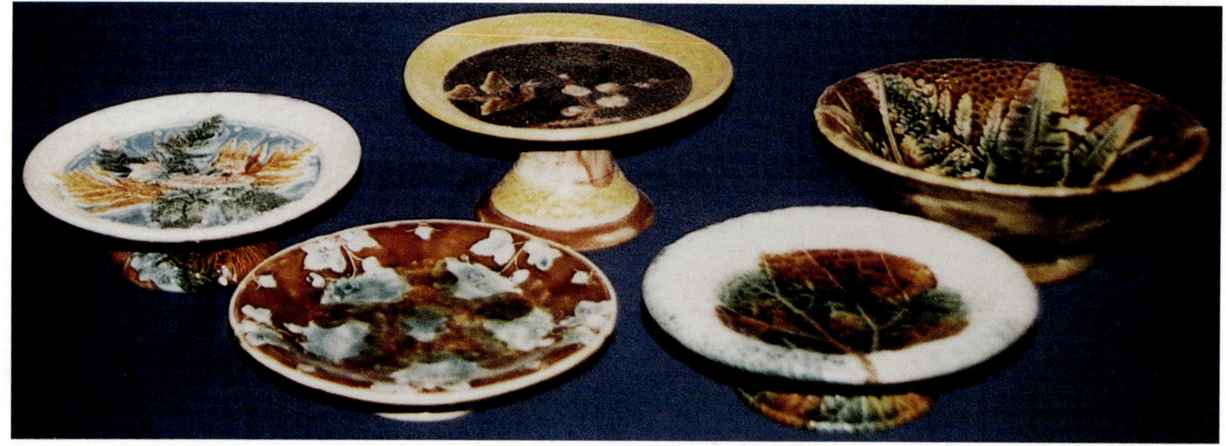

Front Row Left to Right:

Footed Cake Stand, mottled brown and green strawberry leaves and blossoms, 21/4"h x 91/2" d – **$75**

Begonia low compote, 3" h x 91/2" d – **$175**

Back Row Left to Right:

Fern and floral low compote – **$150**

Footed Cake Stand, eureka bird in flight with branch, cobalt center with yellow rim, 41/2" x 91/2" – **$175**

Deep Bowl, brown leaf and fern design, 101/2" d – **$175**

Etruscan Footed Compote Bowl, shell and seaweed pattern. By Griffen, Smith and Company, 6 1/2" h x 9 1/4" d.
$1000

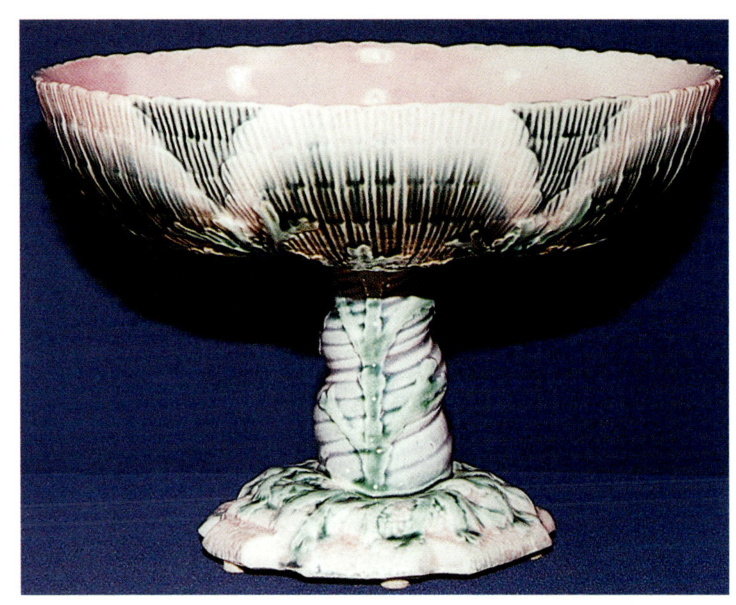

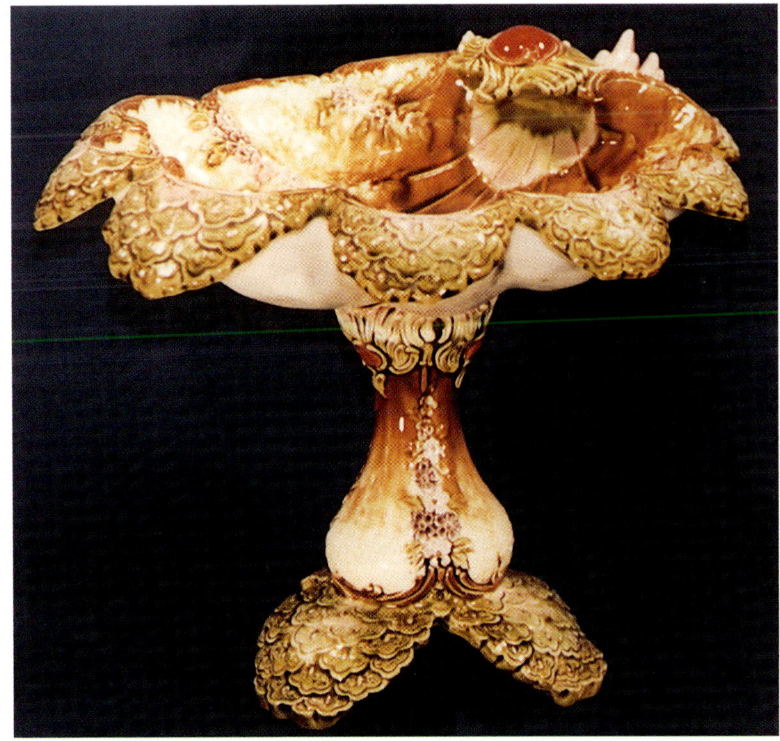

Large Shell Compote with pink and purple flowers, 13" high.
$550

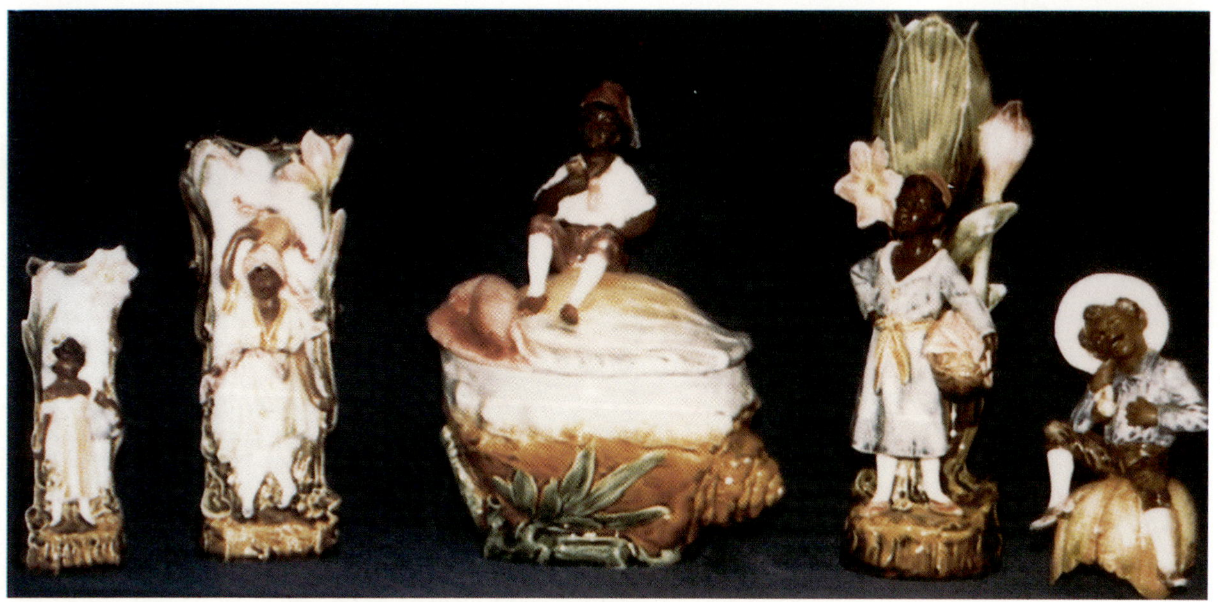

Left to Right:
Figural Vase of a black girl holding a pot, 6 1/2" h – **$175**
Figural Vase of a black girl, 9" h – **$175**
Shell Humidor with a black man sitting on top, 10" h – **$1000**
Continental figural vase with a black man holding a basket, 11 1/2" h – **$400**
Continental figurine of a black man with a pipe seated on a melon, 6 1/2" h – **$150**

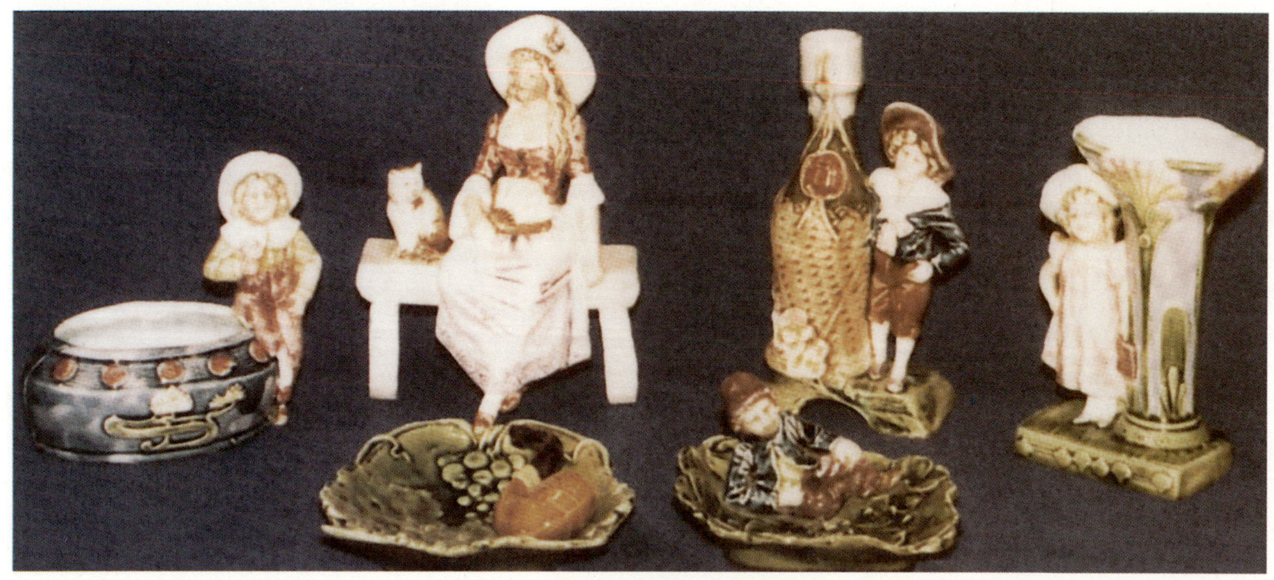

Front Row – Left to Right:
Pipe on a leaf dish. – **$50**
Boy on a leaf dish. – **$50**

Back Row – Left to Right:
Boy seated on planter. – **$150**
Lady and a cat seated on a bench. – **$150**
Continental figural candlestick with a boy standing by a bottle. – **$150**
Continental figural lady standing by a vase. – **$75**

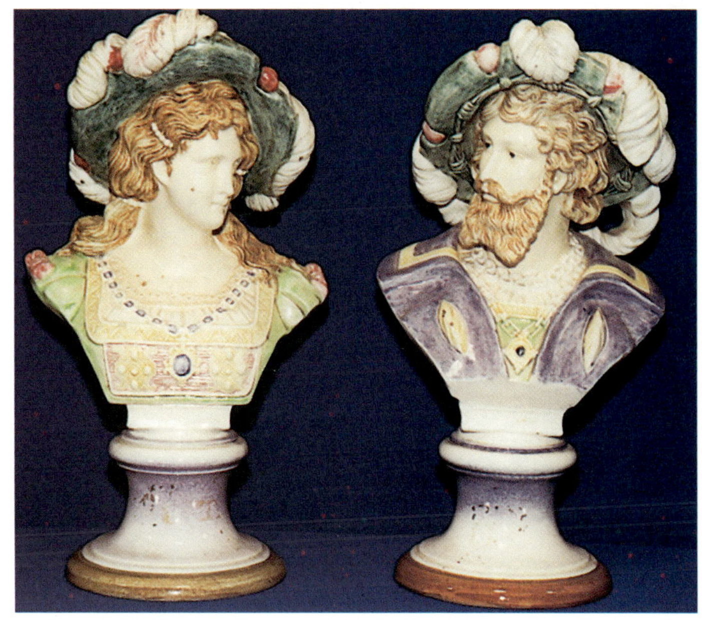

Man and Woman Victorian Busts, 14" h, very colorful.
$350

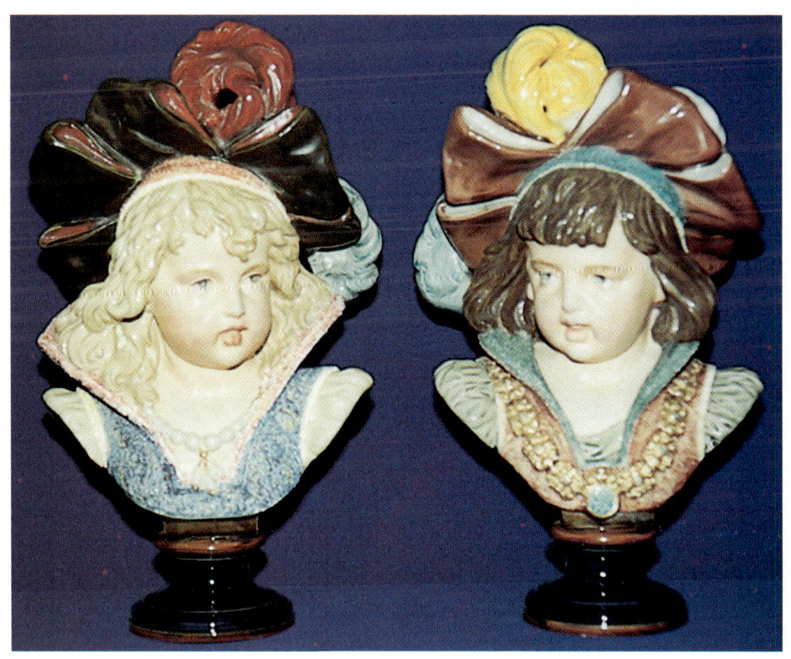

Boy and Girl Busts, multi color, some sand finish, 14" h.
$75

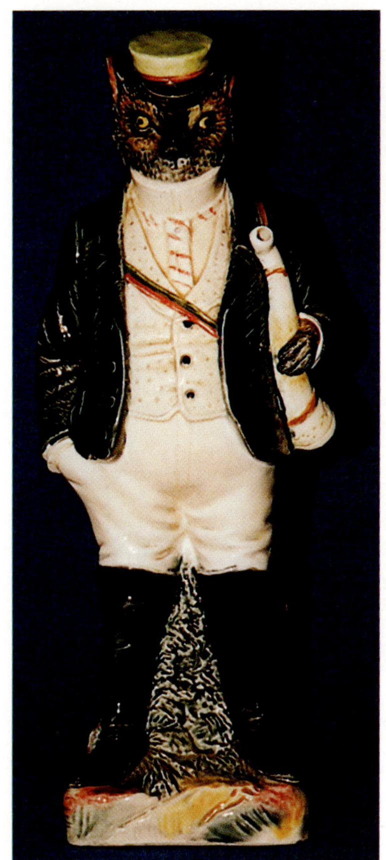

Fox figural bottle with pour spout. The fox is leaning back on a barrel with books on top, dressed in a suit, 12 1/4" h.
$550

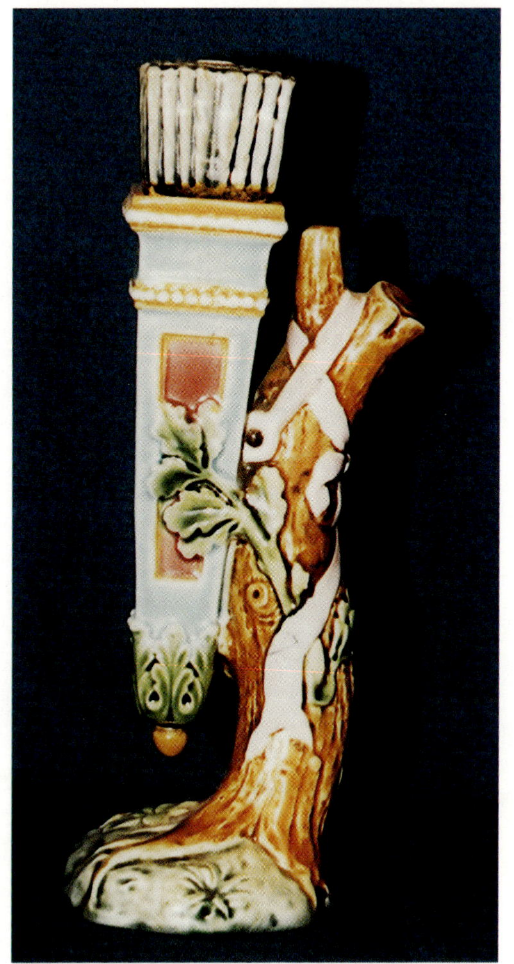

Minton tree trunk with lavender ribbon and bow holding a square vase with lid.
$1100

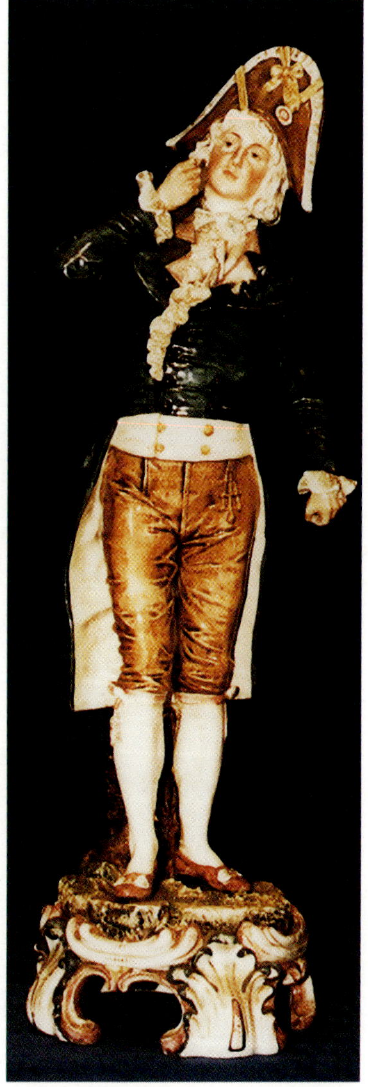

Continental Victorian Man figure, 25" tall.
$225

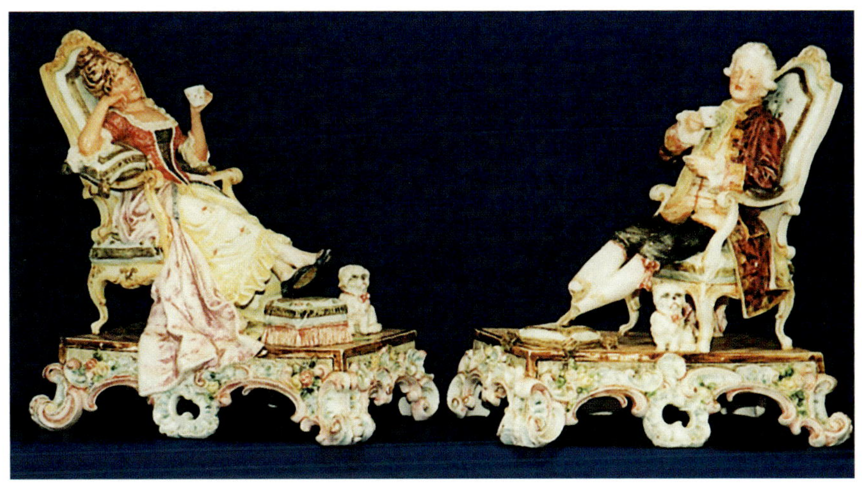

A pair of Victorian figurines of a man and woman seated in arm chairs, drinking tea with their poodles at each of their sides, 13"h.

$175

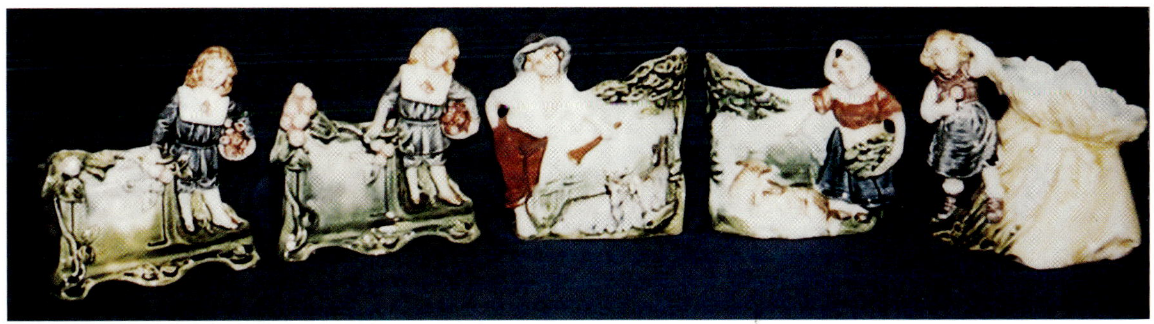

Left to Right:

A pair of figural boy planters – **$50**

A pair of boy and girl with sheep planters – **$75**

A planter of a girl beside a wheat stock, (mate not shown) – **$175**

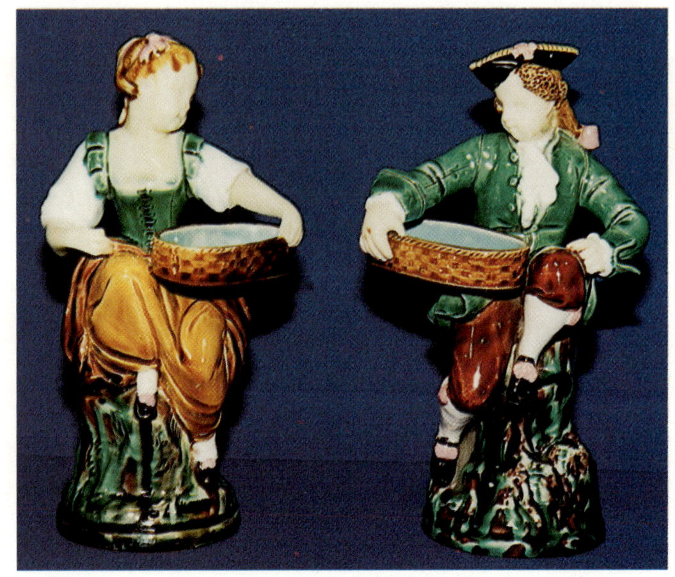

Minton Harvester Girl with basket, 7 1/2" – **$600**

Minton Sailor Table Salt, 7 1/2". – **$600**

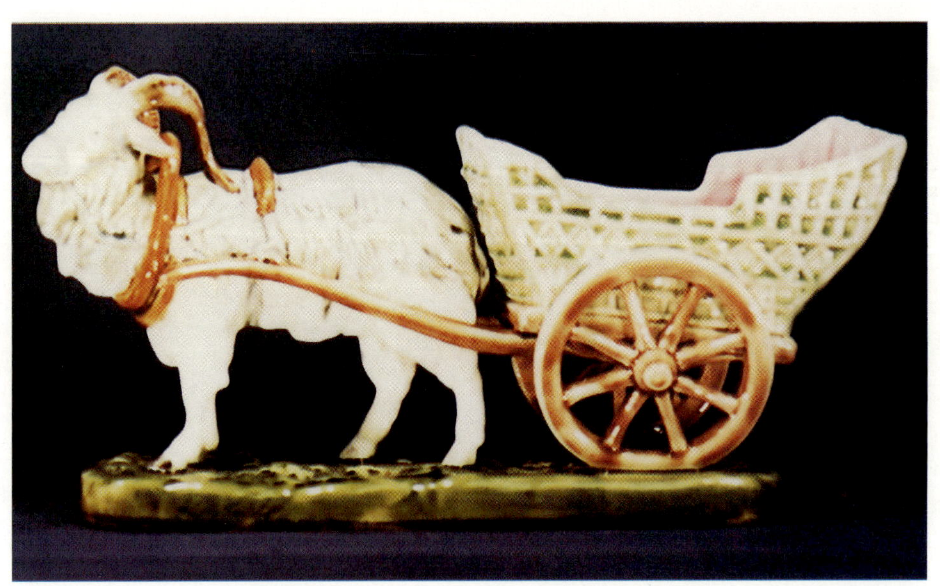

Royal Dux, Czech. goat and cart, 7" h x 14" l.
$500

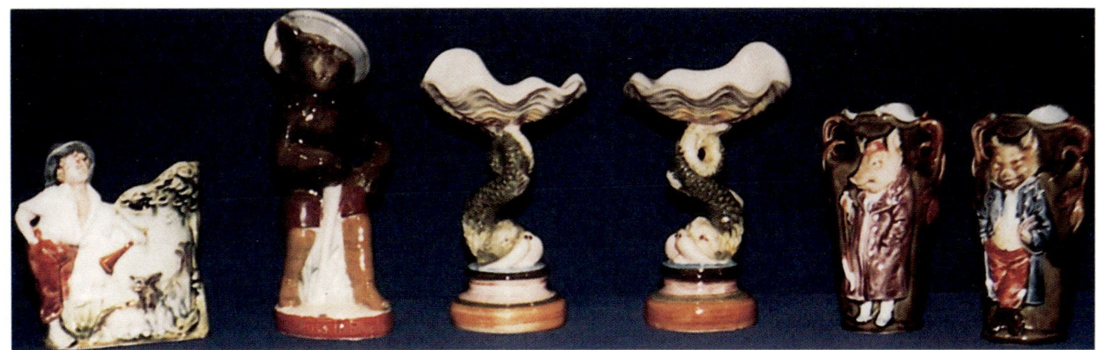

Left to Right:

Boy with rams on a planter, 43/4" – **$25**

Puss in Boots figural shaker bottle, 71/2" – **$225**

A pair of dolphin footed shell compotes, continental, 61/2" – **$25**

A pair of continental pig vases, 51/4" – **$350**

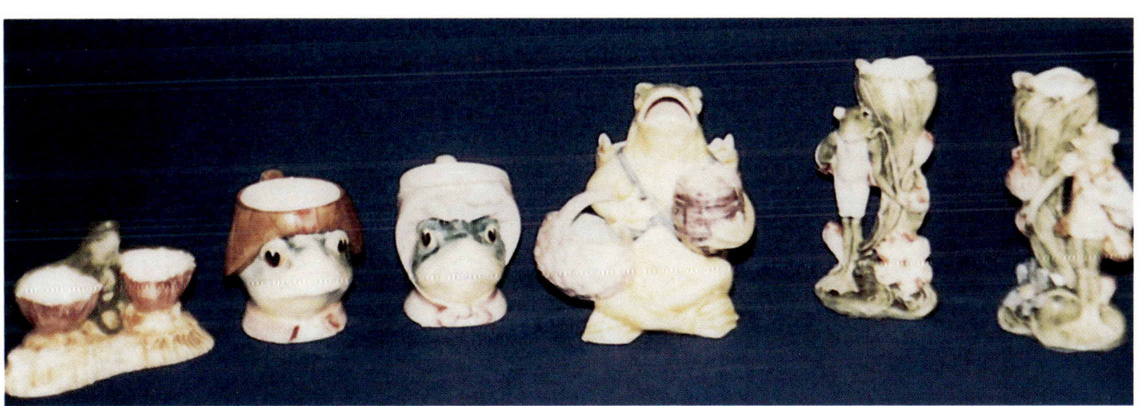

Left to Right:

Continental frog figural salt cellar, 31/2" x 5"l – **$350**

Man and woman frog mugs, 31/2", signed "R. Tallin, Majolica".
$100

Match holder with striker, frog with two baskets, 6" – **$575**

Two frog vases, on 6" and the other 5" tall – **$400**

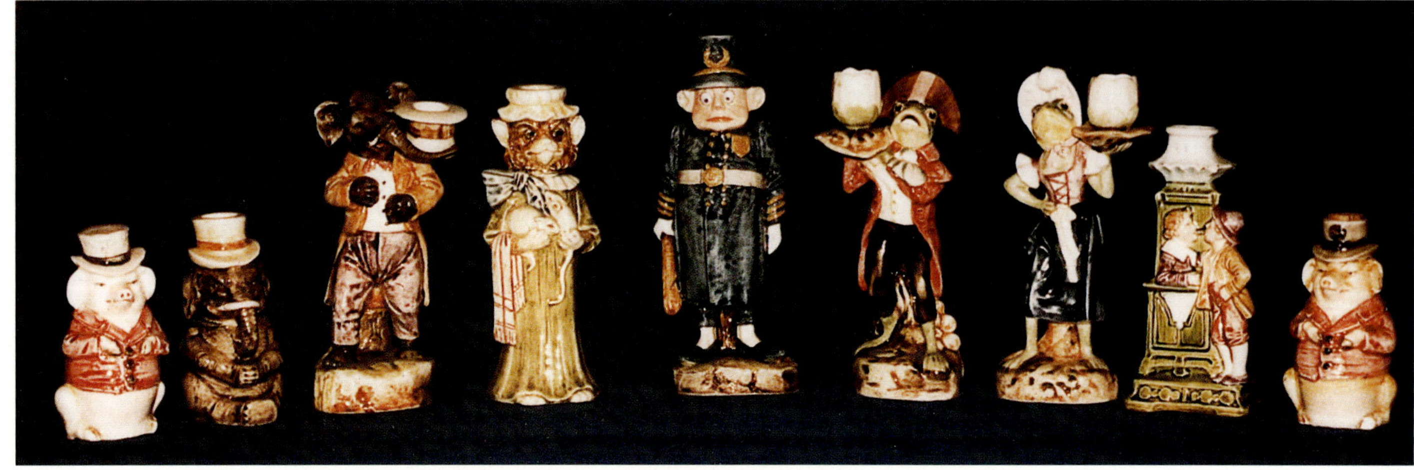

Left to Right:
Pig piggy bank with red coat, 5" tall – **$475**
Seated elephant candle holder, 5" tall – **$250**
Elephant candle holder with a top coat and a hat that he is holding in his trunk, 8" tall – **$475**
A lady cat holding two mice candle holder, 7 1/2" tall – **$600**
Brownie candle holder in a blue police uniform holding a billy-club, 9" tall – **$575**
Pair - a male and female frog candle holders, signed "R. Tallin, Majolica", 8" tall – **$110**
Figural candle stick of two boys with cigars, 6 1/2" tall – **$55**
Continental figural pig bottle, wearing a red jacket – **$200**

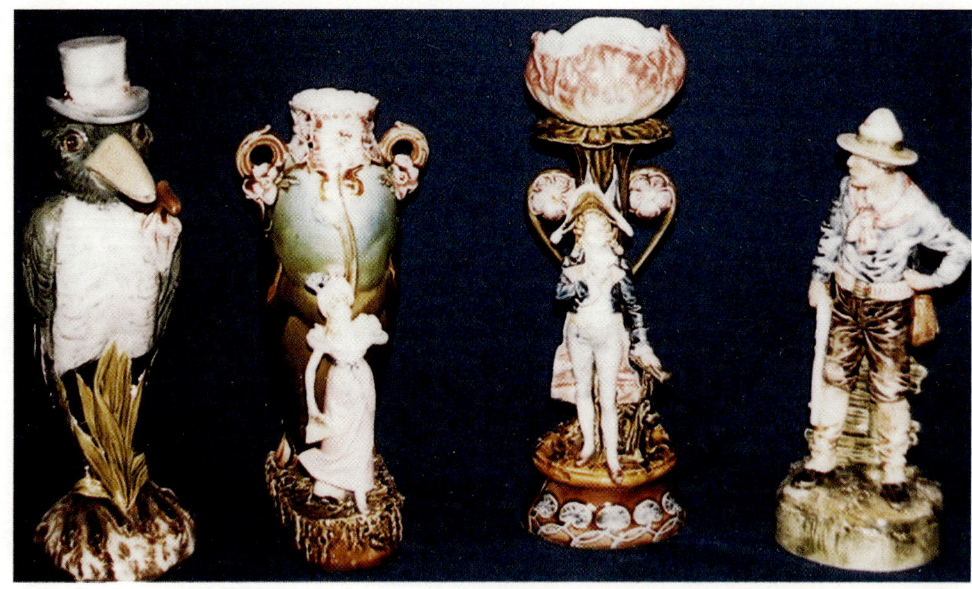

Left to Right:
Continental bird figurine with umbrella and top hat – **$250**
Lady figural vase, 9 1/2" – **$150**
Continental man figural vase (art noveau style), 11" tall – **$75**
Man standing holding a rifle at his side, 10" tall – **$450**

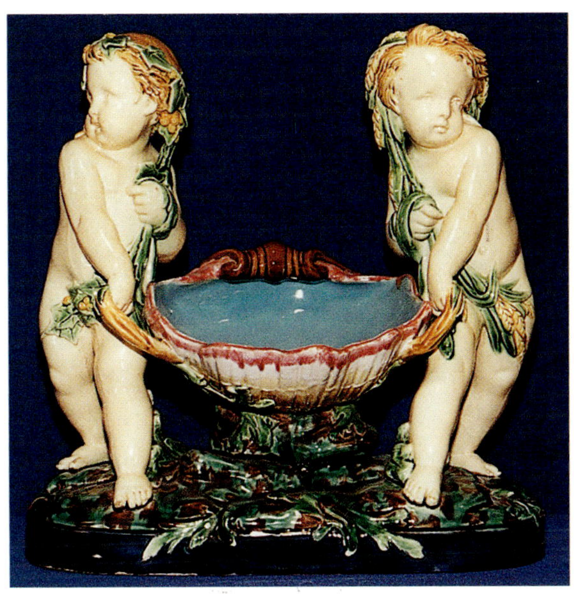

Two cherubs carrying a shell, Minton,
11 1/4"h x 11 1/4"l, cobalt blue vase.
$2250

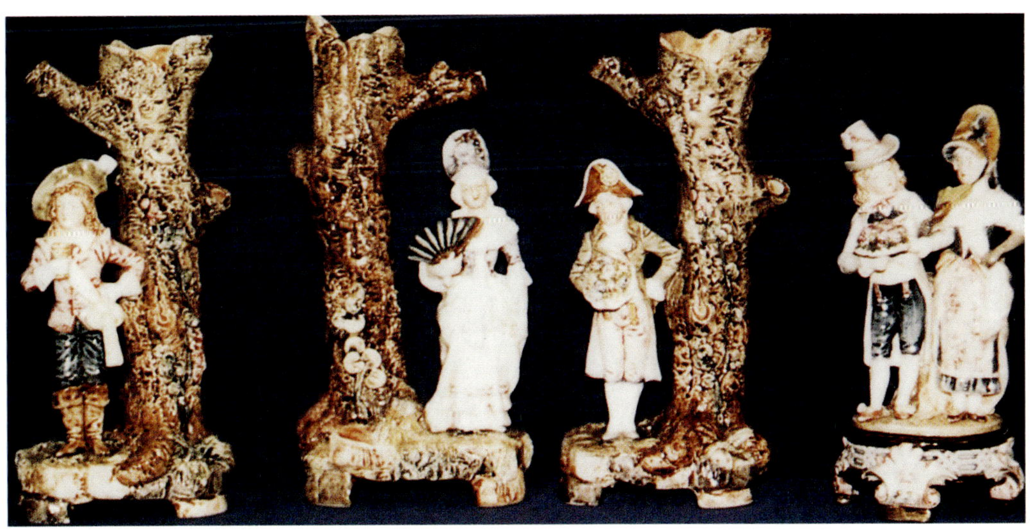

Left to Right:
Man beside a tree in a red coat with wine goblet, 11 1/2" tall– **$100**
Pair- Continental figurines, a man and a woman standing by a tree,
she has a fan and he is holding a basket – **$175**
A man and woman figurine, 10" tall – **$100**

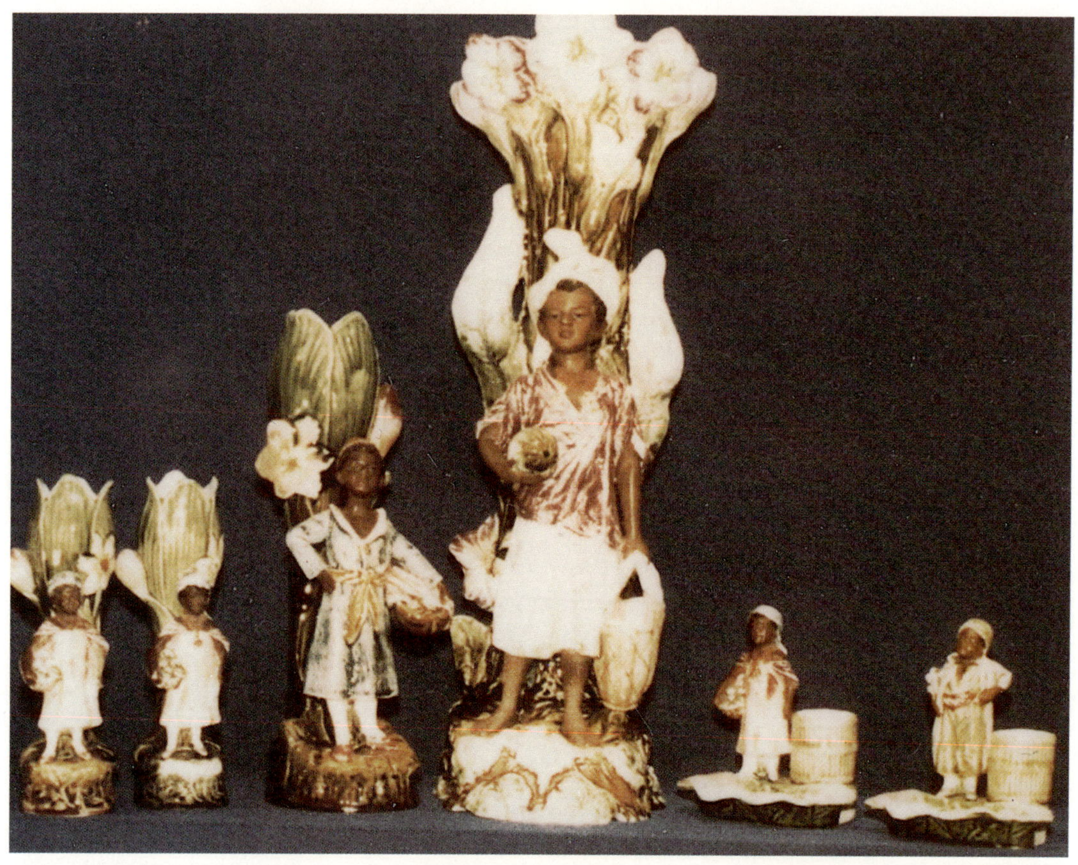

Left to Right:

Pair of figural vases with black women holding baskets, 7 1/2" – **$125 each**

Continental vase with black woman holding basket, 11 1/2" – **$175**

Large continental vase with black lady carrying a melon and a basket, 19" tall – **$950**

Two match holders and strikers, one has a black man the other a woman, 5" tall – **$175 each**

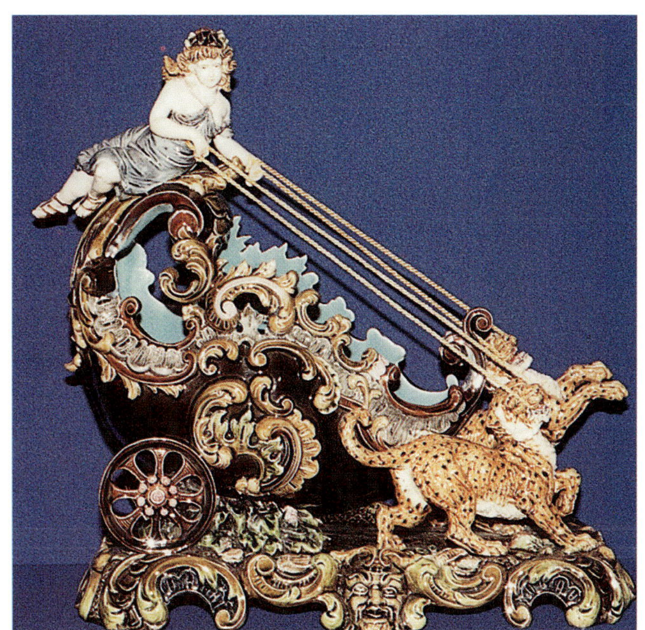

Lady riding a chariot pulled by two tigers with Northwood faces on base, circa 1892. Made for Leipzing World's Fair in 1892 and won first prize for ceramics.

$3500

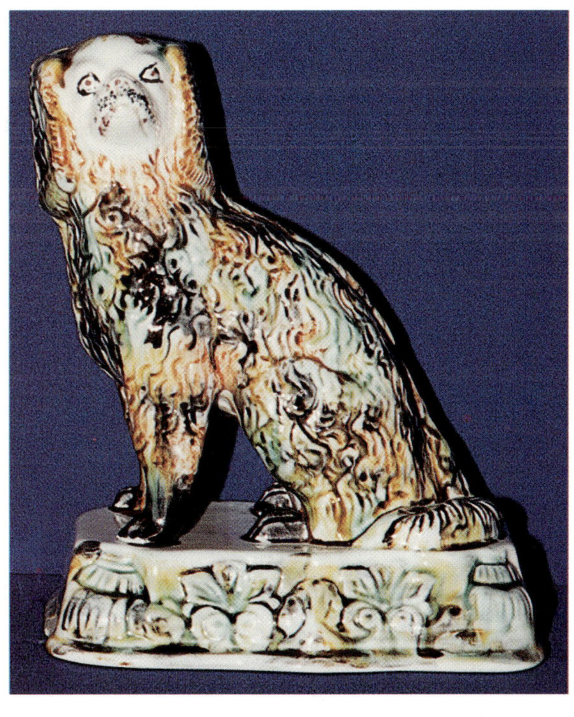

Doorstop hearth dog, 10", signed Morley & Co., Majolica, Wellsville, Ohio.

$3500

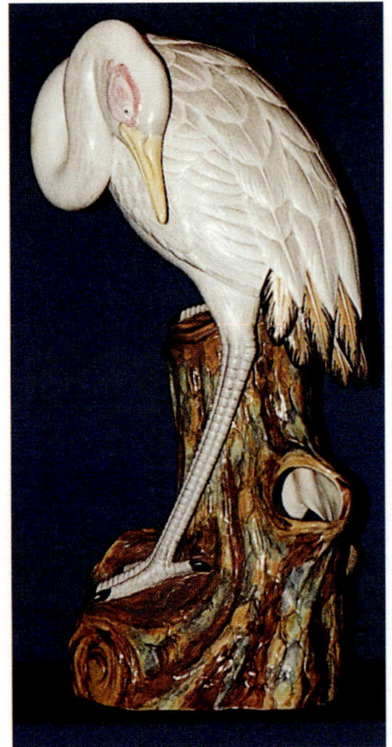

Royal Worcester heron on tree stump, 18".
$1000

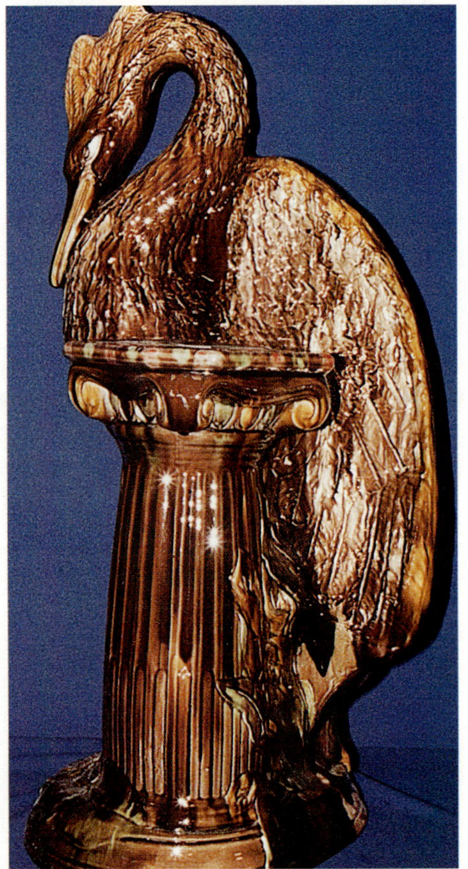

Heron garden seat, with heron behind pedestal, mottled, 38" h.
$2500

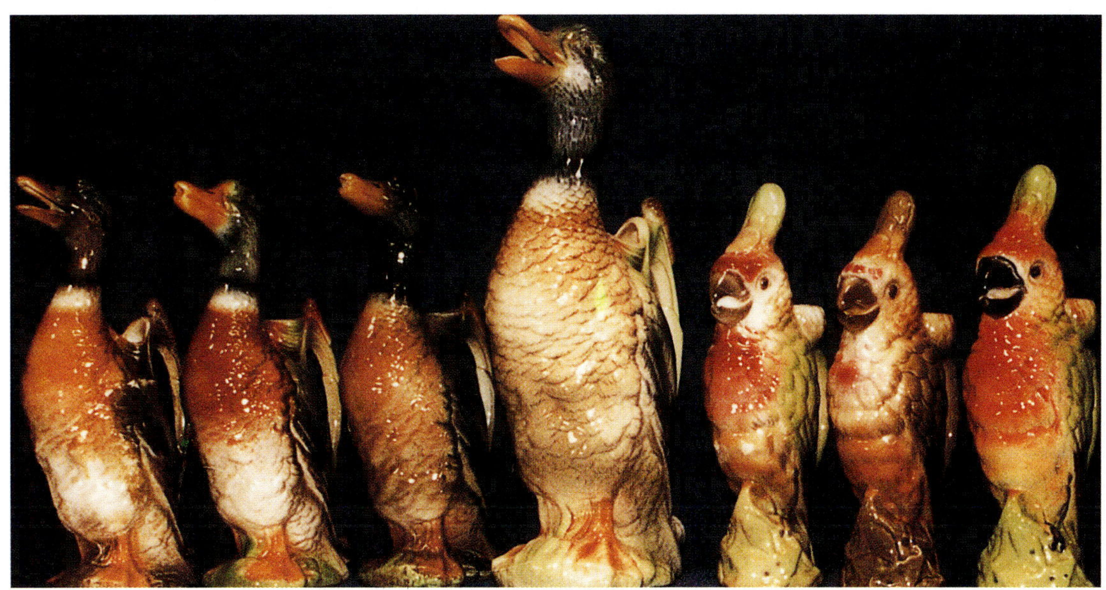

Left to Right:
Duck pitcher, 12 1/2" tall, marked "St. Clement" – **$100**

Duck decanter, 12 1/2" tall – **$175**

Duck decanter (glaze imperfection) – **$75**

Figural duck pitcher signed "St. Clement, France", 17" high – **$500**

Three parrot decanters, all 13" tall, marked "St. Clement" – **$50 each**

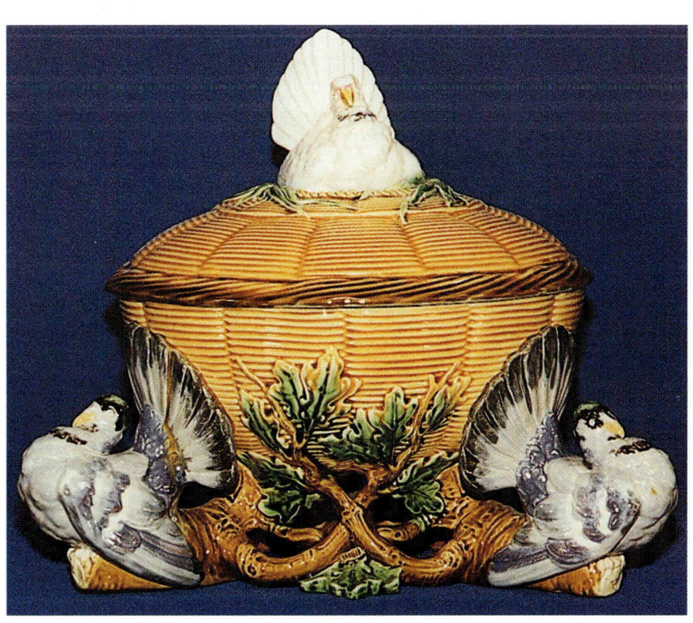

Minton pigeon game dish with liner.
$8800

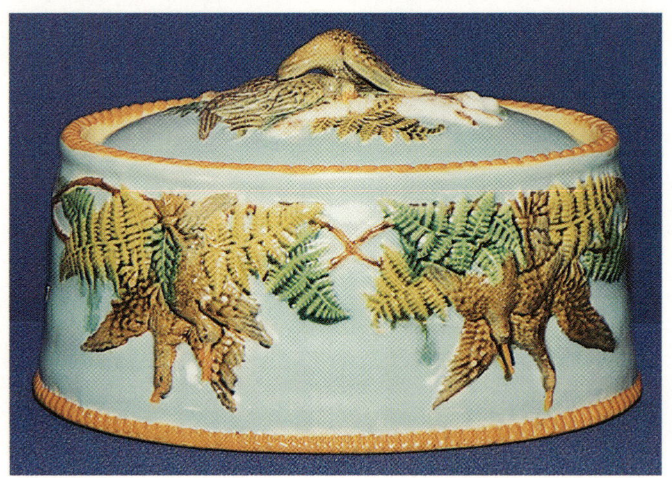

Brownfield Game Dish, 9" tall, turquoise with yellow rope trim, game and ferns cover the lid and sides.
$1800

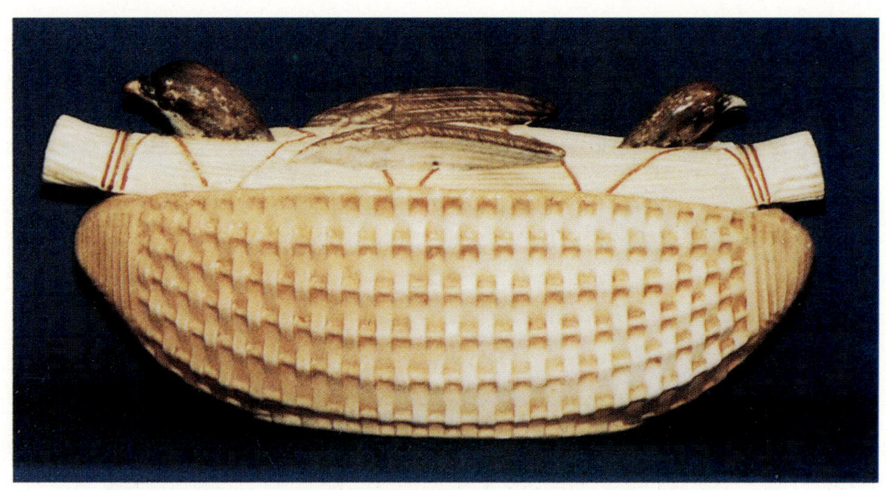

George Jones type creamware game dish with insert, with an English registry mark. The two quail in a wheat basket, tan and brown, 13 1/2" long.
$2200

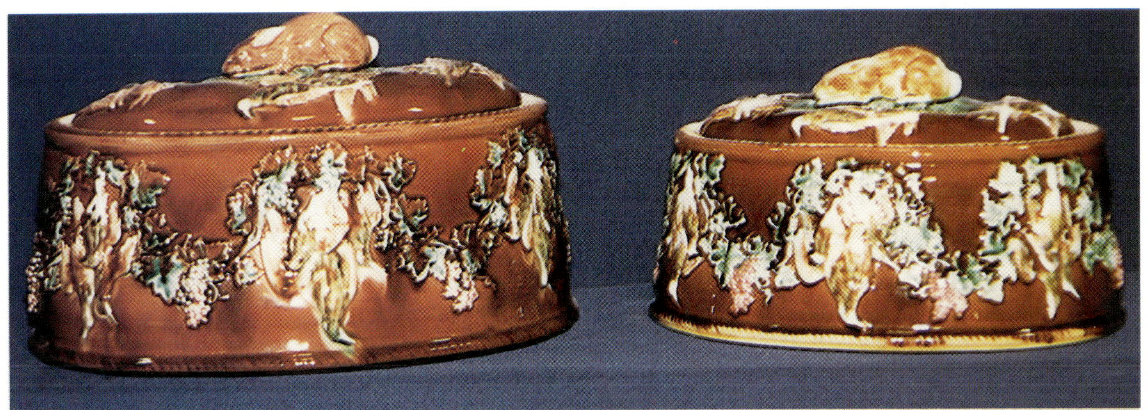

Wedgwood game dish with rabbits on the lids and game around the sides. (Two sizes shown).
$2200

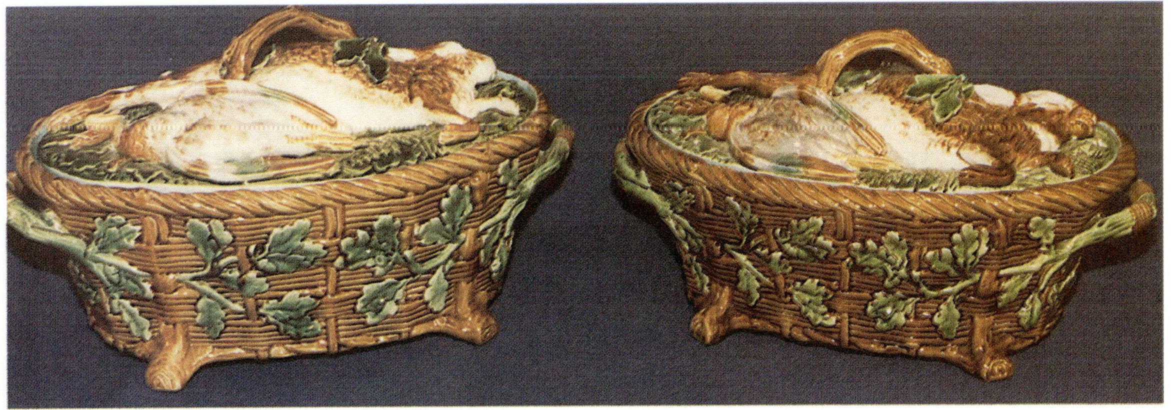

Two Minton game dishes with inserts, with a large sculptured hare and a mallard duck on both lids.
$3000

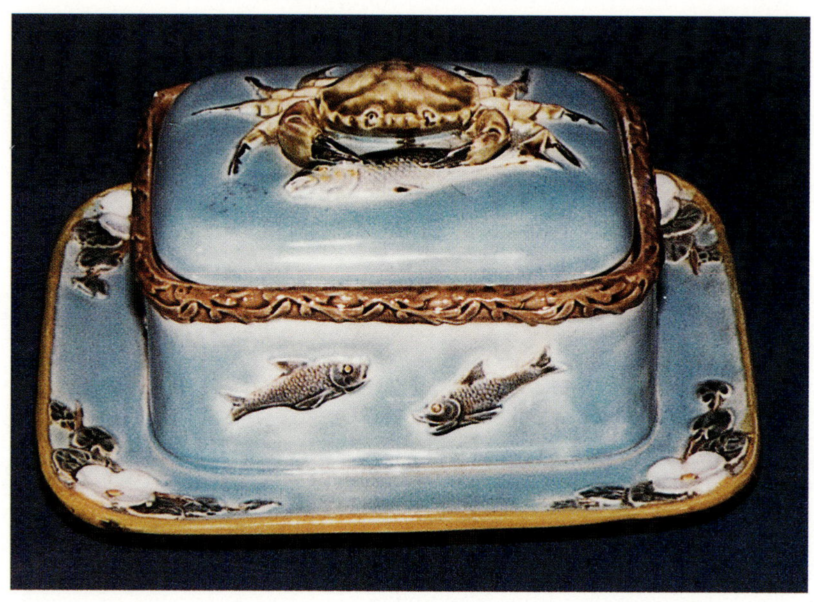

Holdcroft sardine box with a crab on the lid and fish on the sides, turquoise with brown border.

$2200

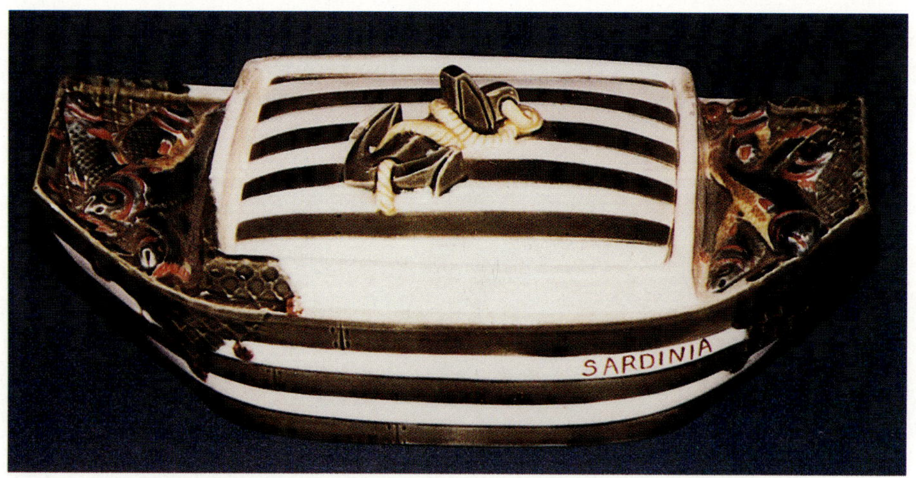

Wedgwood sardine box shaped like a boat with the name "Sardinia" on the side and an anchor on the lid, 9 3/4" tall.

$1050

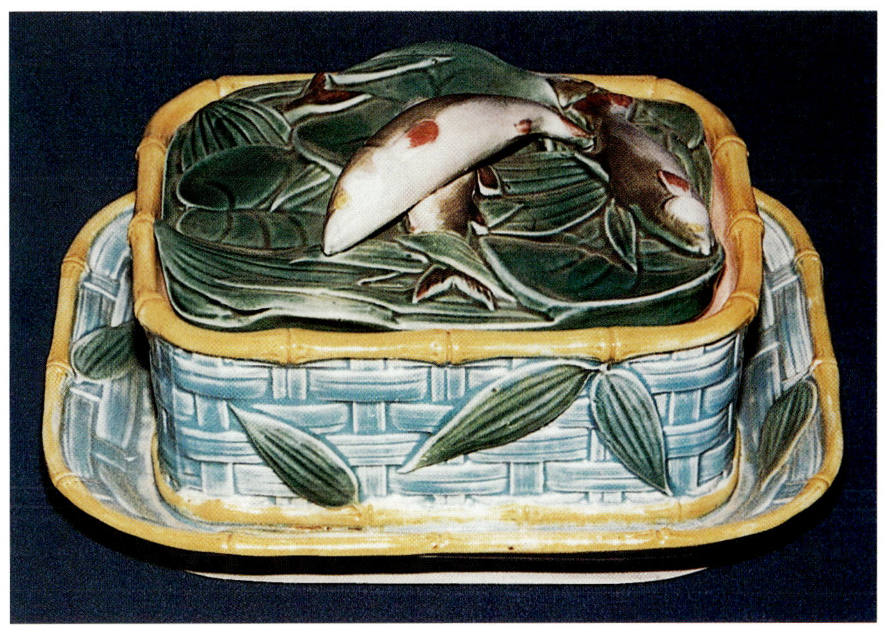

Pond lily and bamboo sardine box, basketweave with three fish on the lid, 9" long.
$450

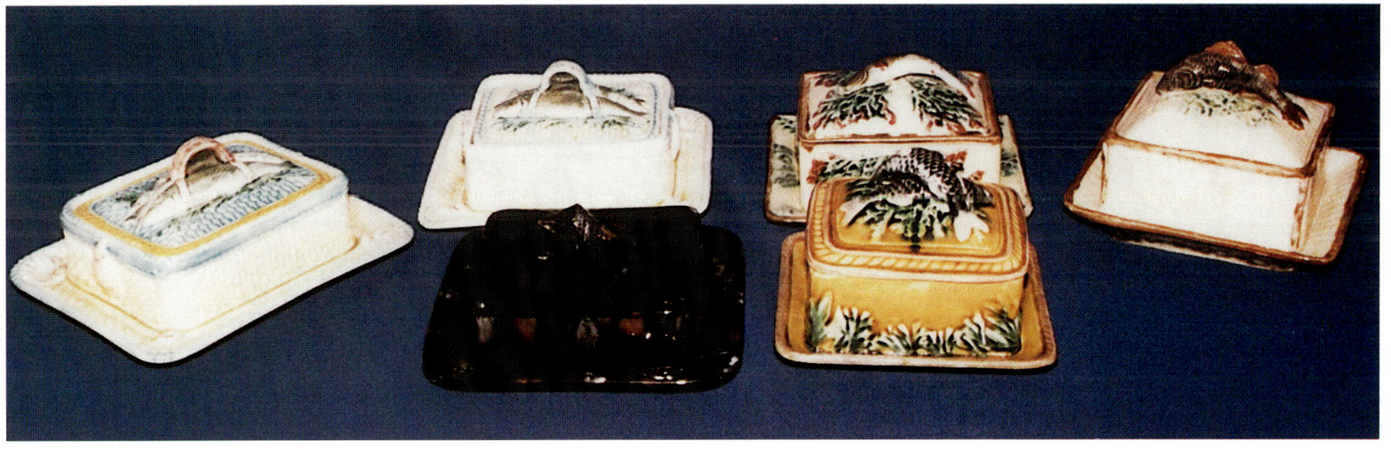

Front Row - Left to Right:
A purple mottled sardine box with fish handle on lid – **$200**

A basketweave sardine box – **$200**

Back Row – Left to Right:
Two basketweave and shell sardine boxes with ribbon handles –**$375**

Sardine box with green and red seaweed and a fish handle – **$275**

Sardine box with a fish handle – **$450**

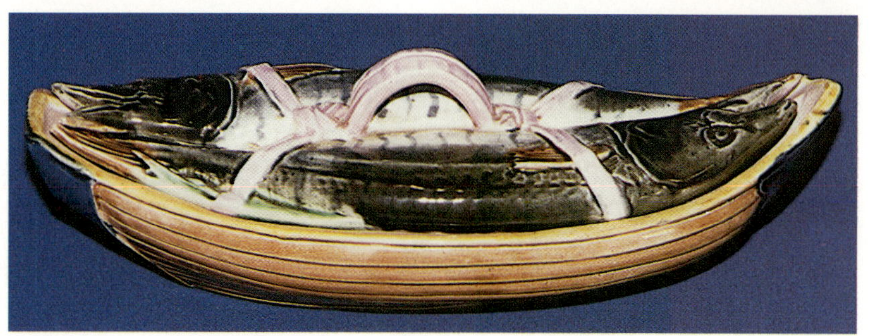

Sardine boat with a fish lid,
and a lavender bow handle, 12 1/2" long.
$1,300

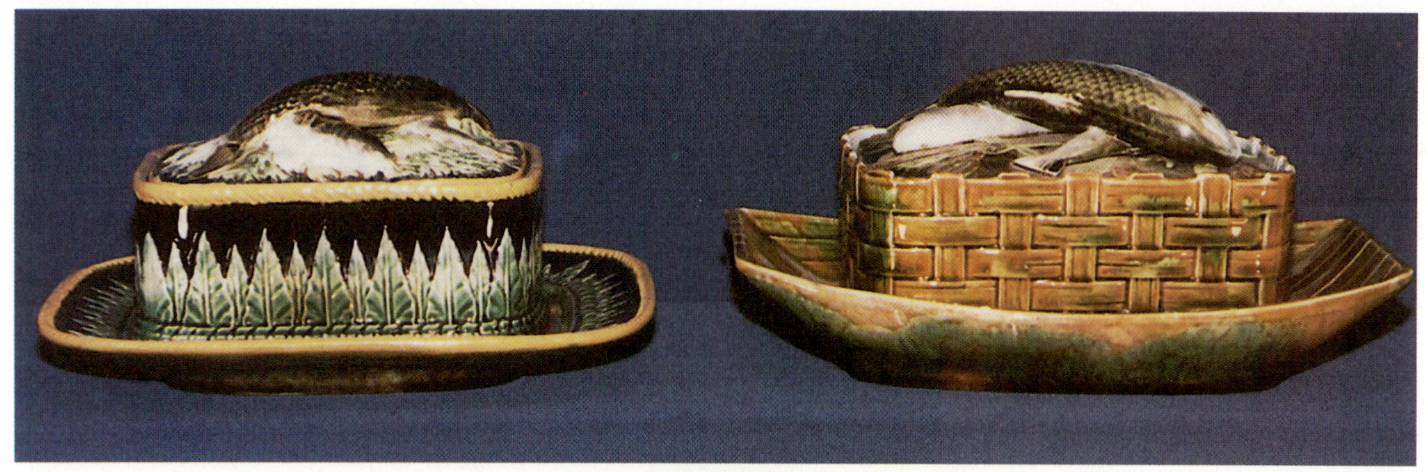

Left to Right:

George Jones cobalt and leaf sardine box with underplate.
$1,100

George Jones sardine basketweave box in a wooden boat, with turquoise interior.
$550

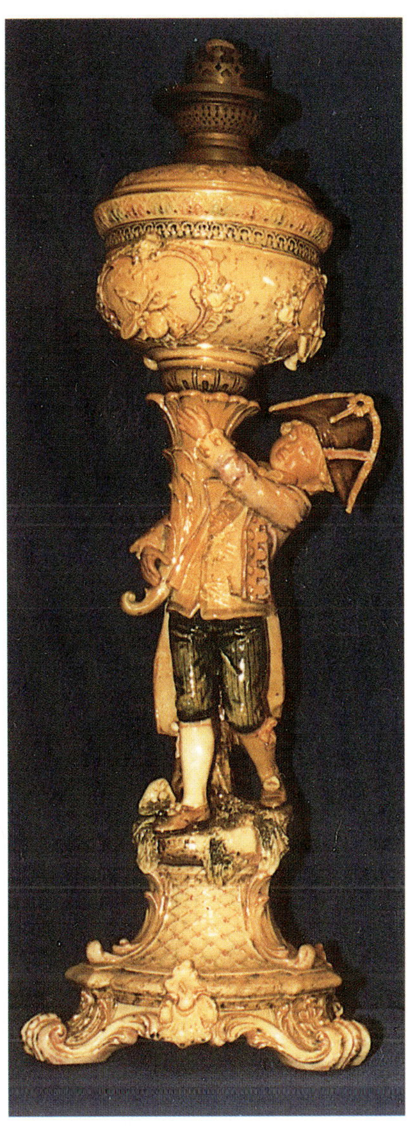

Victorian Majolica Banquet Lamp with boy supporting it, 26" tall.
$250

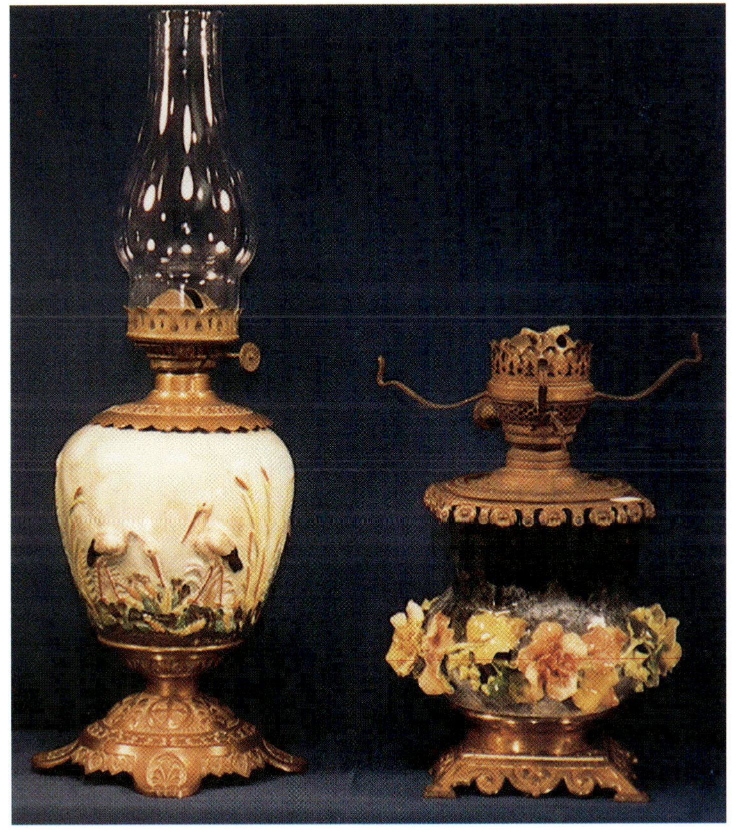

Left to Right:
Oil lamp with majolica base, with five herons in cattails, brass footed, 13" tall.
$500

French oil lamp, cobalt blue background with applied flowers in relief, 12" tall.
$200

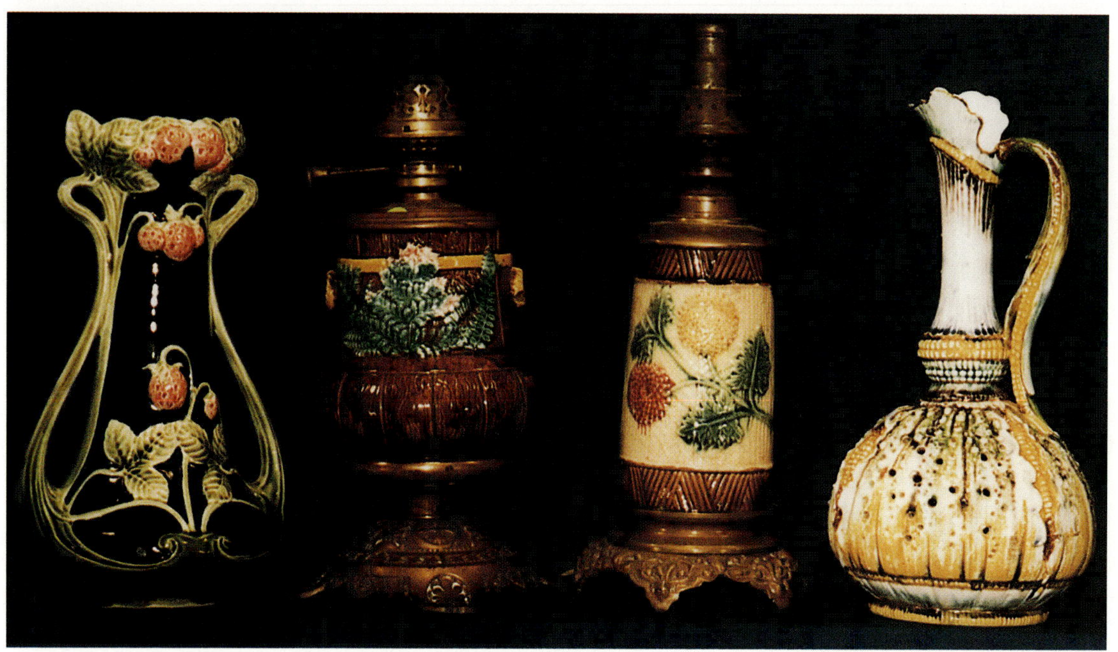

Left to Right:
Austrian strawberry vase with a black background, 12" tall – **$125**
Picket Fence and fern oil lamp – **$275**
Aster on a picket fence pitcher made into an oil lamp – **$125**
Continential Ewer with a corn base, 13" tall – **$125**

Left to Right:
Cobalt blue floral table lamps with red and white flowers, a cast iron base, 23" tall.
$200

Two french table lamps, 30" tall.
$150

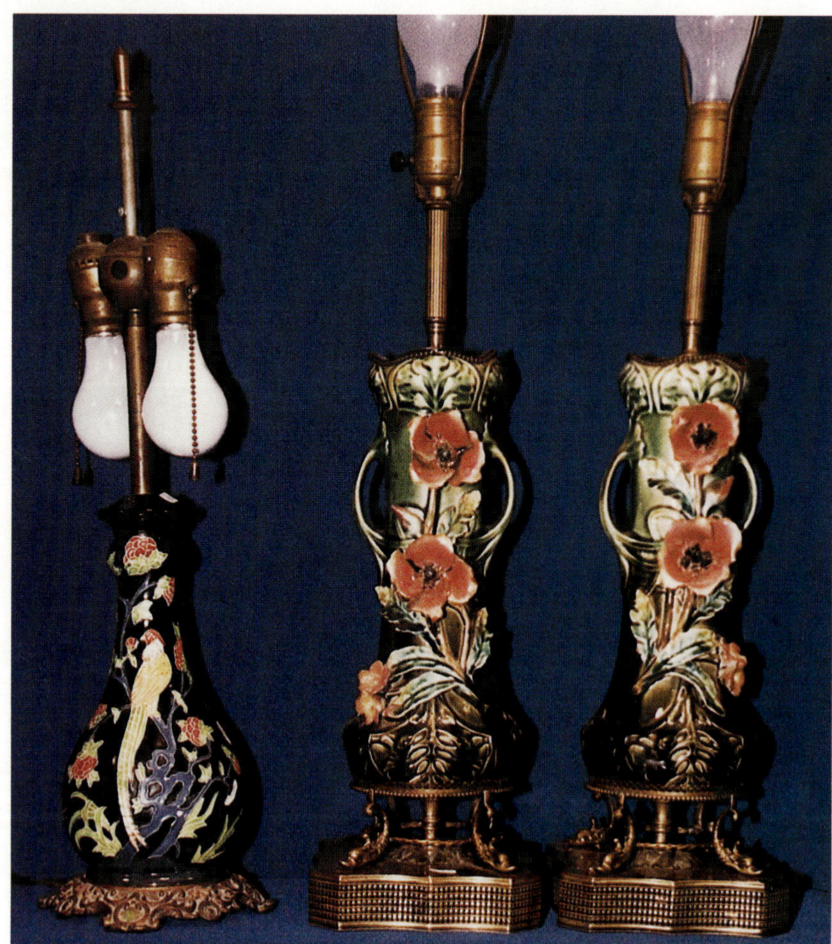

A pair of Table Lamp Bases by Wilhelm Schiller & Son. Cobalt blue with knights on horses in relief, 13" h.
$1350

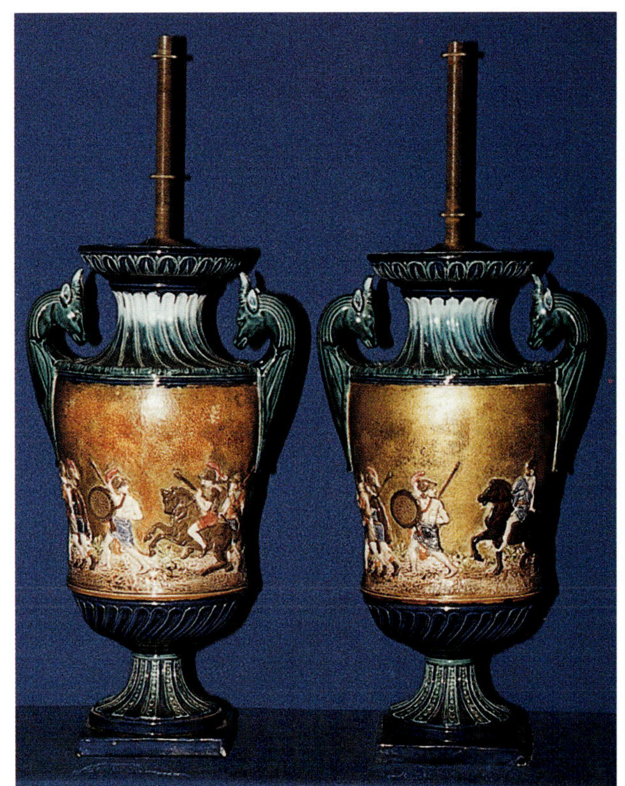

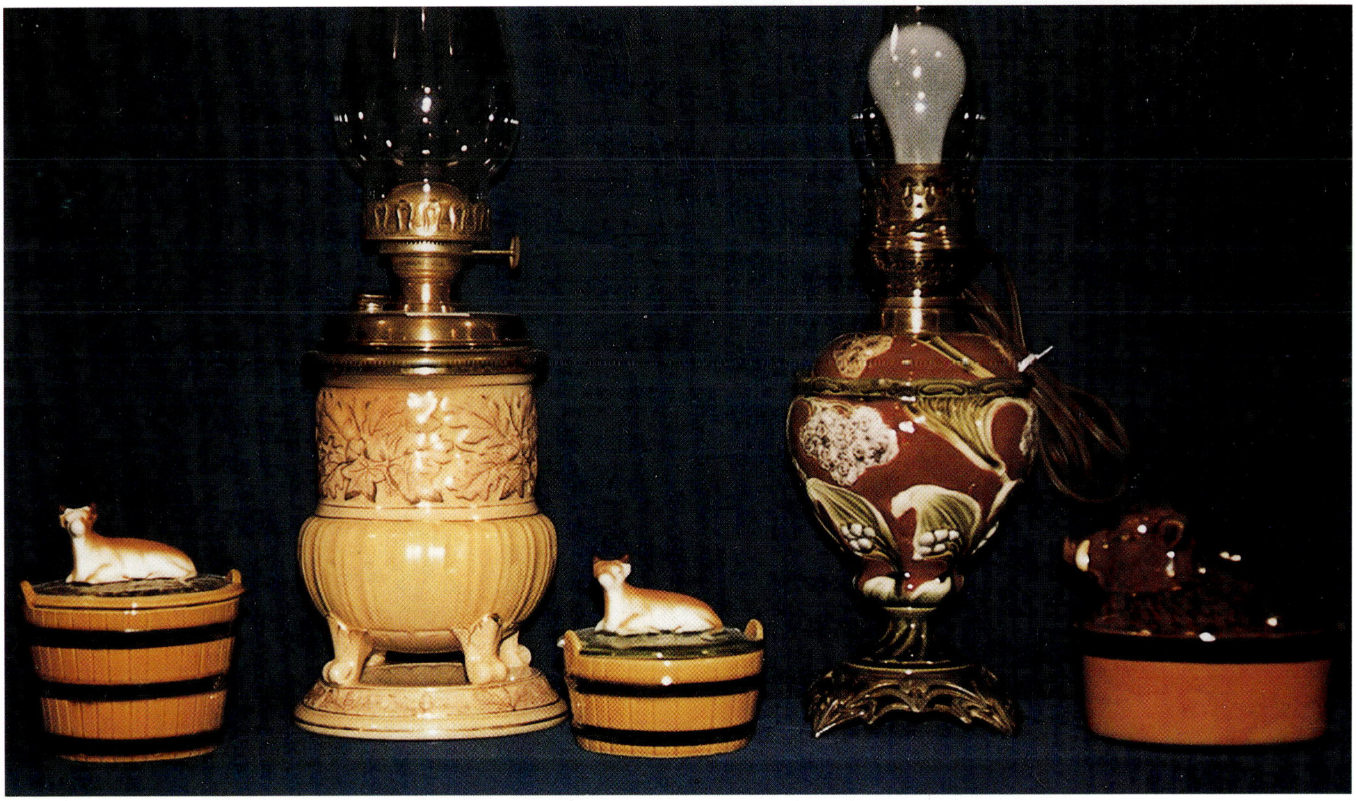

Left to Right:
Portugal cow covered butter tub – **$50**
Avalon oil lamp of oak leaves and acorns, 12 1/2" tall, (rare) – **$450**
Portugal cow covered butter tub – **$50**
Art Noveau lamp, red background with green, purple and white, 13" tall – **$225**
Boar covered butter tub – **$50**

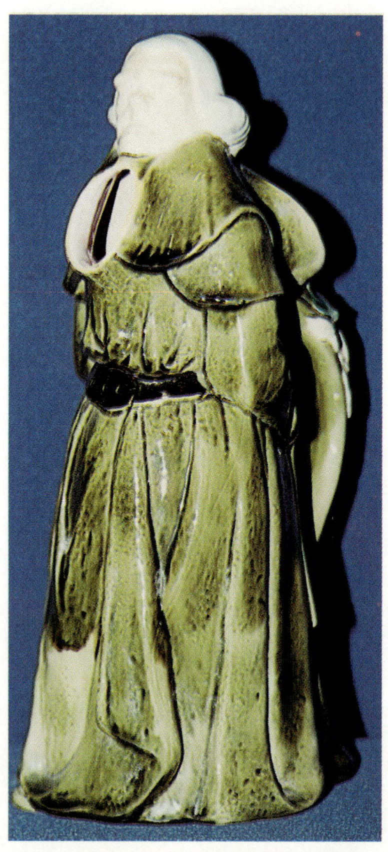

George Jones Monk figural pitcher in a green robe with white hair and a goat's head handle with lavender interior, #2729, 12" tall.

$550

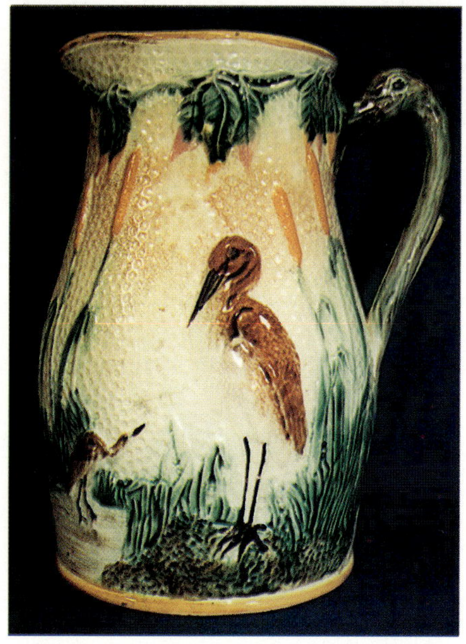

An eel handled pitcher with a stork in a marsh.

$350

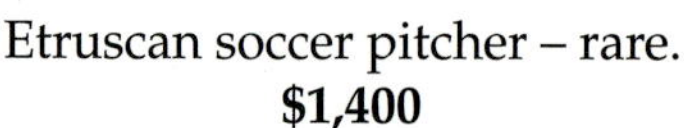

Etruscan soccer pitcher – rare.

$1,400

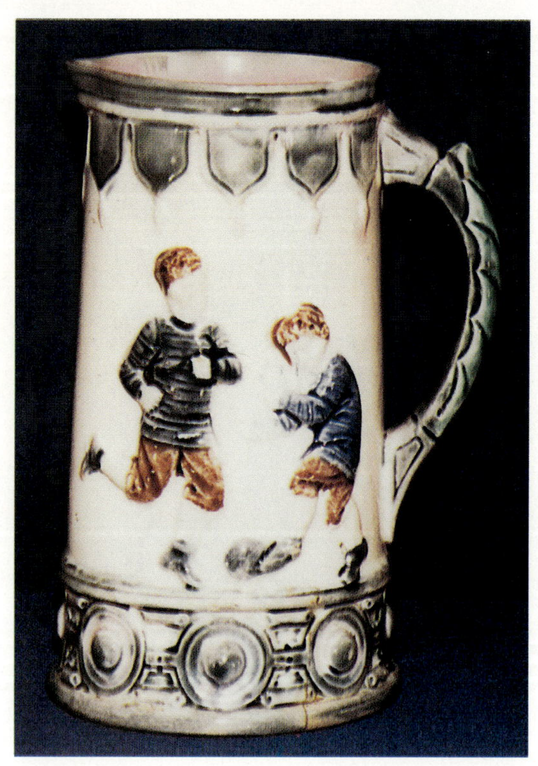

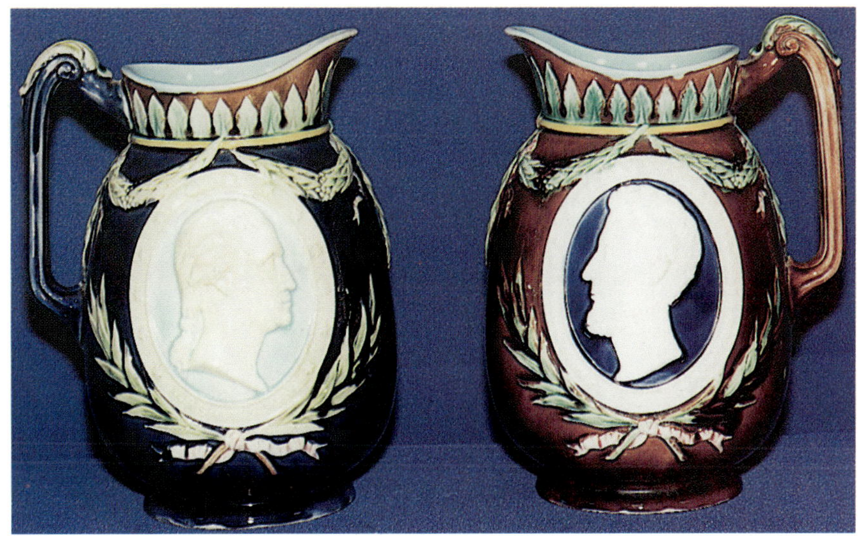

Two Wedgwood continental pitchers, one with Washington's silhouette, the other with Lincoln's.

For Reference Only

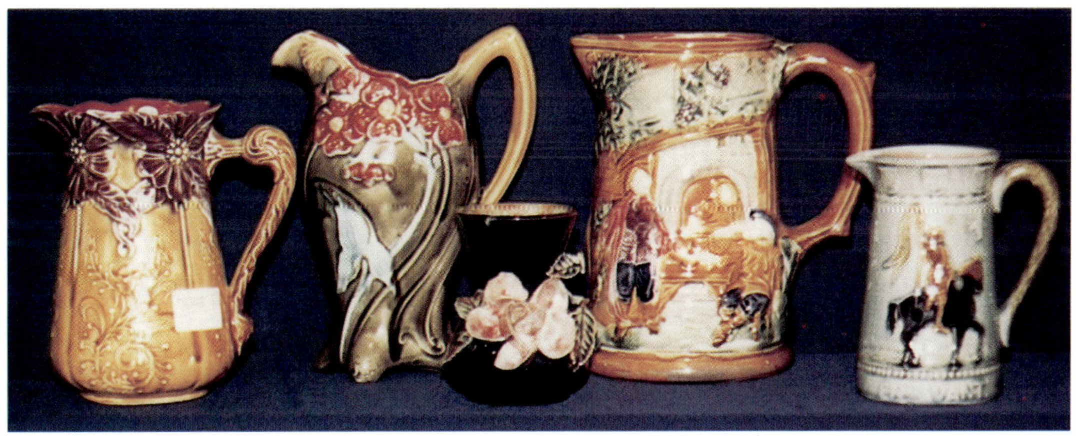

Front Row – Middle:
Cobalt vase with applied flowers, 4 1/2" tall – **$50**

Back Row – Left to Right:
French Onnaing floral pitcher, 7" tall – **$100**

French Onnaing floral pitcher, 9" tall – **$225**

French Onnaing pitcher with horses on one side and people on the other, 8 1/2" tall – **$200**

French "EN AVANTI" pitcher with man holding a flag on a horse in relief, 6" tall – **$200**

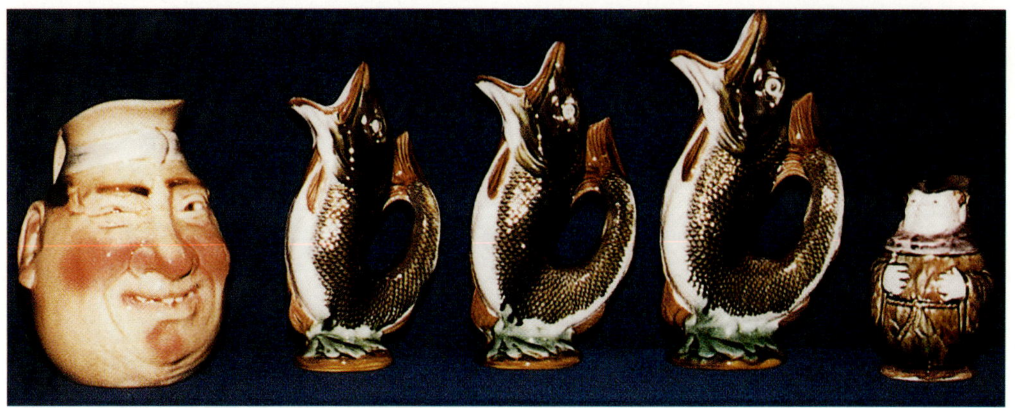

Left to Right:

Sarreguemines face pitcher with rosie cheeks, 81/4" tall – **$250**
Three graduated fish pitchers, a 9", 91/2", and 101/2" – **$225**
Toby figural pitcher with mottled coat and purple collar, 6" tall – **$175**

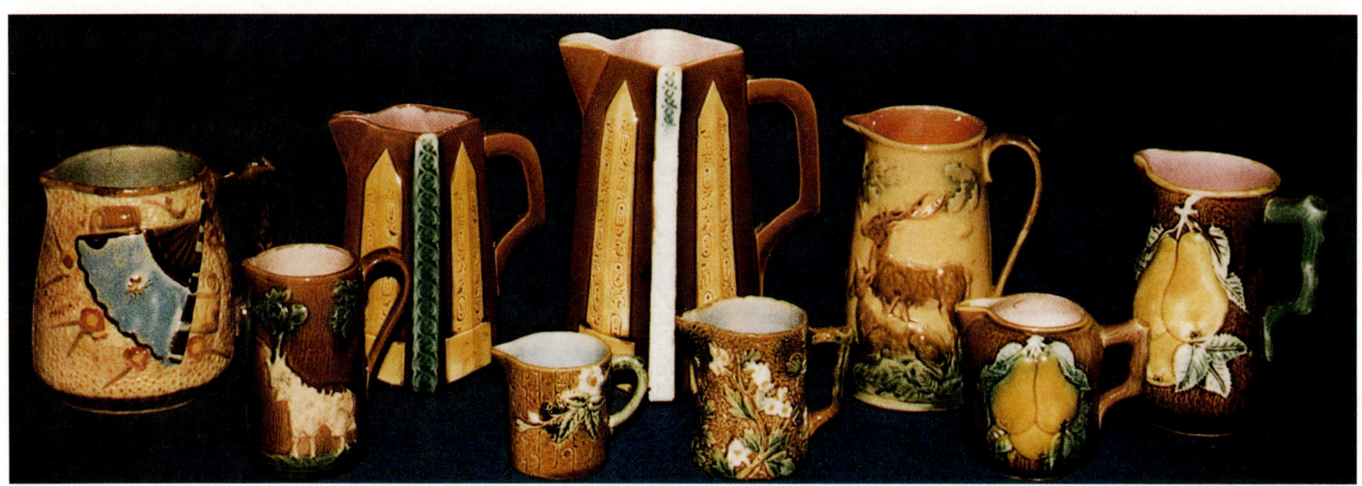

Front Row – Left ro Right:
Goat cream pitcher, 41/2" tall – **$150**
George Jones rustic creamer, 3" tall – **$225**
Holdcroft blackberry creamer, 21/2" tall – **$225**
Yellow apple and pear creamer, 31/4" tall – **$200**

Back Row – Left to Right
Fielding fan and scroll pitcher, 5" tall – **$50**
Two Egyptian four sided pitchers, 6" and 71/2" tall – **$50**
Reindeer pitcher, 6" tall – **$250**
Yellow apple and pear pitcher, 51/2" tall – **$200**

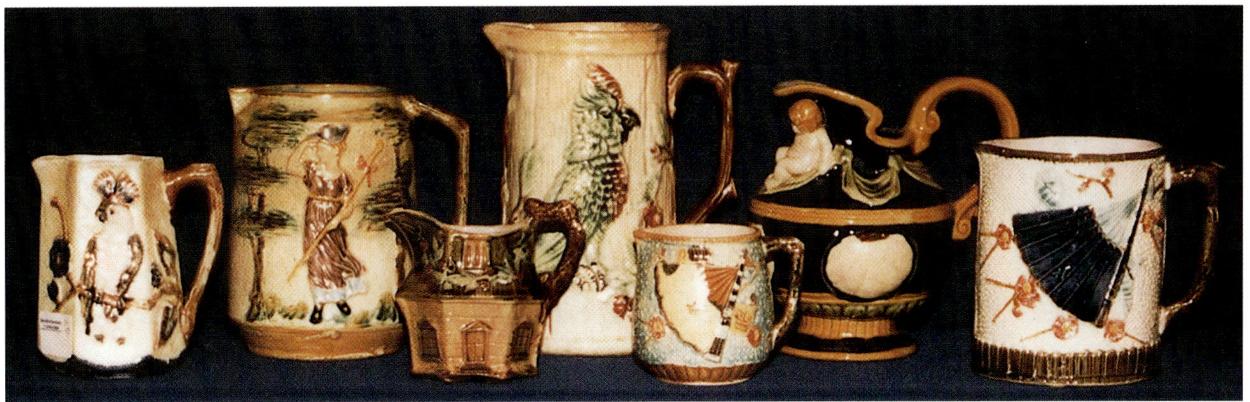

Front Row - Left to Right:
Cottage creamer, 3 1/2" tall, rare – **$150**
Fan and scroll creamer, 3 1/2" tall – **$175**

Back Row – Left to Right:
Fielding six sided parrot pitcher, cobalt blue accents, 5" tall – **$250**
Fielding lady in relief on the side of the pitcher, 6 1/4" tall – **$250**
Parrot on a branch pitcher, 7 1/2" tall – **$150**
Cobalt blue jug with a cherub on the spout, shells in relief, 6 1/4" tall – **$50**
Fielding fan and scroll design pitcher – **$200**

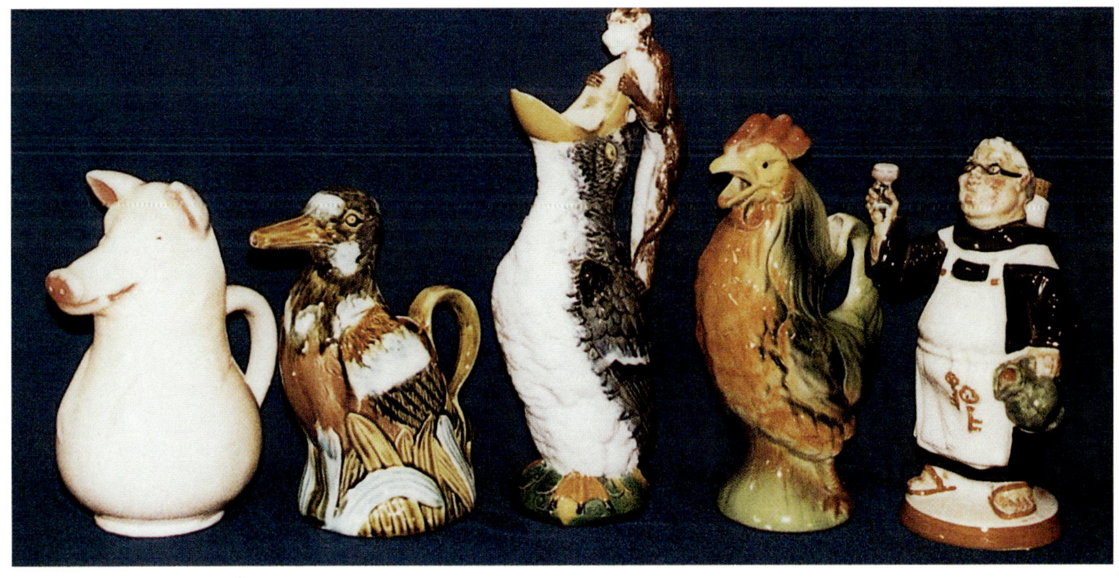

Left to Right:
Sarreguemines figural pig pitcher, 9 1/4" tall – **$225**
Frie Onnaing figural duck pitcher, 9 1/4" tall – **$200**
Brownfield duck pitcher with monkey handle, 14" tall – **$775**
St. Clement rooster pitcher, 11 1/4" tall – **$400**
Monk figural bottle holding a jug and glass, 10 1/2" tall – **$225**

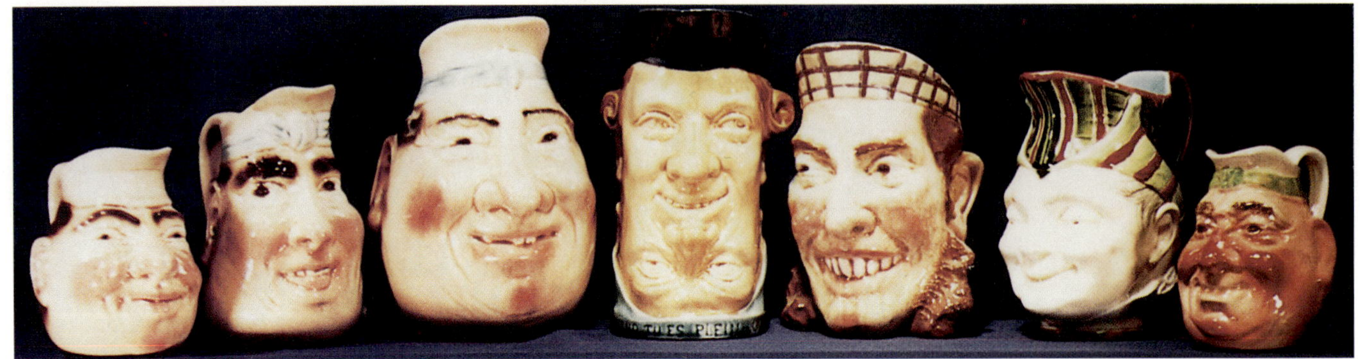

All of the pitchers in this photo are Sarreguemines, the sizes are listed from left to right.

5 1/4" tall – **$75**
6 1/2" tall – **$75**
8 1/2" tall – **$100**
double face, 8 1/2" tall – **$450**
#3181, 8 1/2" tall – **$75**
7 1/2" tall – **$225**
5" tall – **$100**

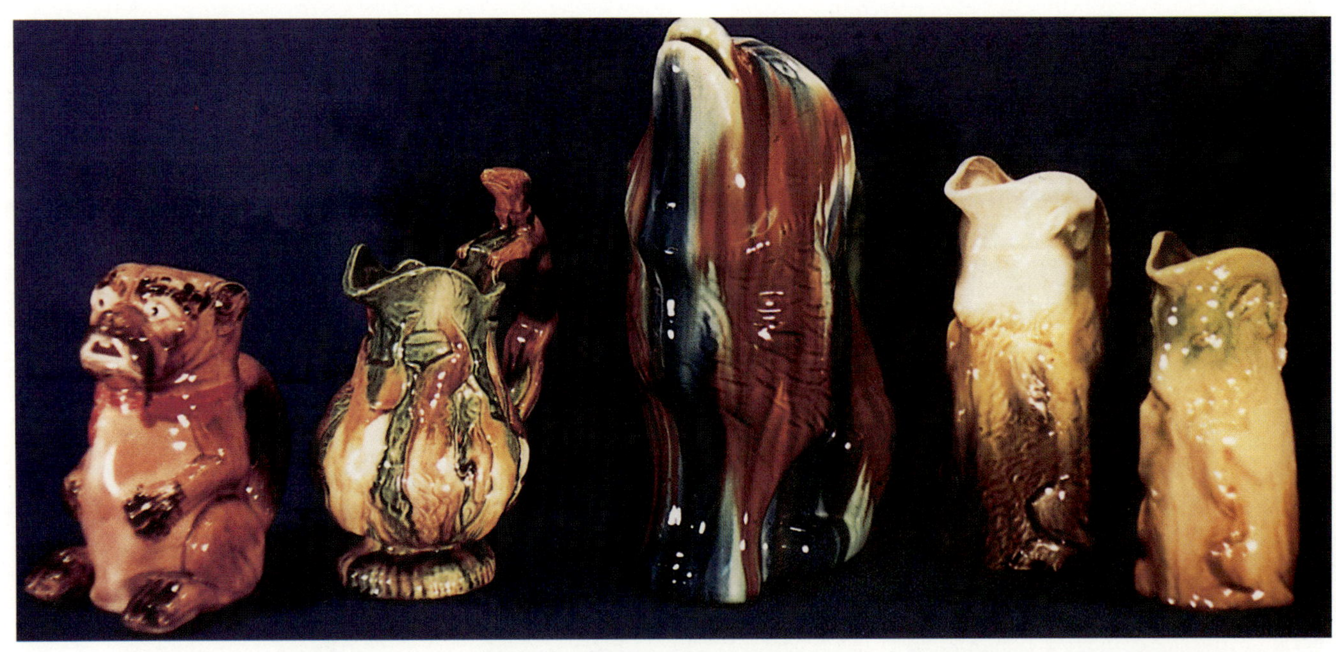

Left to Right:

Pug dog pitcher, 7 1/2" tall – **$250**

Portugal game pitcher, with a dog handle, mottled, 9 1/2" tall – **$275**

Mexican pig pitcher, 13 1/2" tall – **$25**

Ram pitcher, 9 1/2" tall – **$50**

Ram pitcher, 8 1/2" tall – **$100**

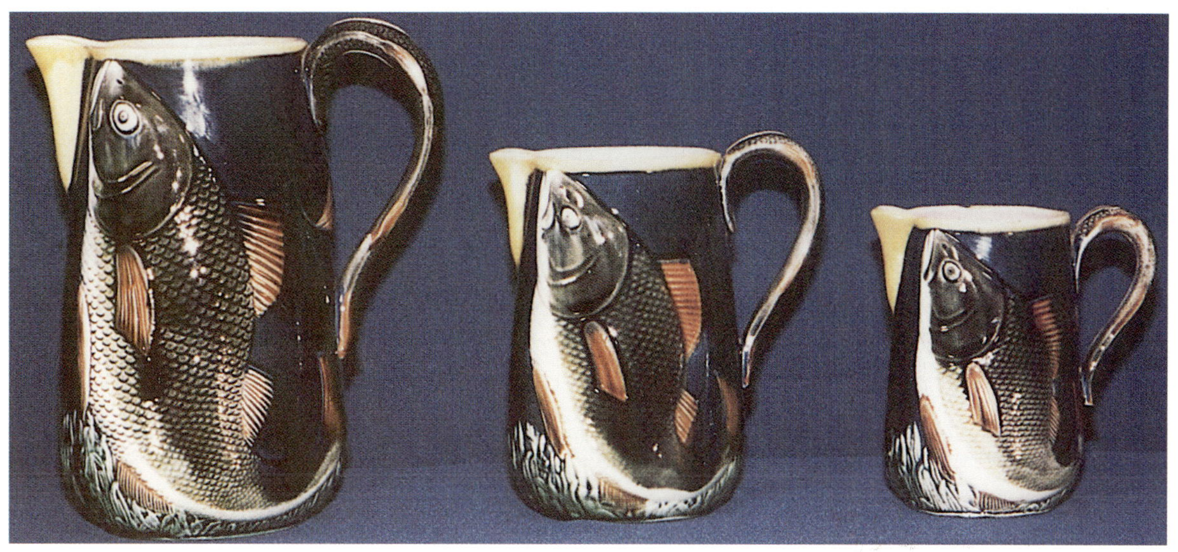

Three fish pitchers with fish handles, cobalt blue, 7 1/2", 6", and 4 1/2" tall.
$500

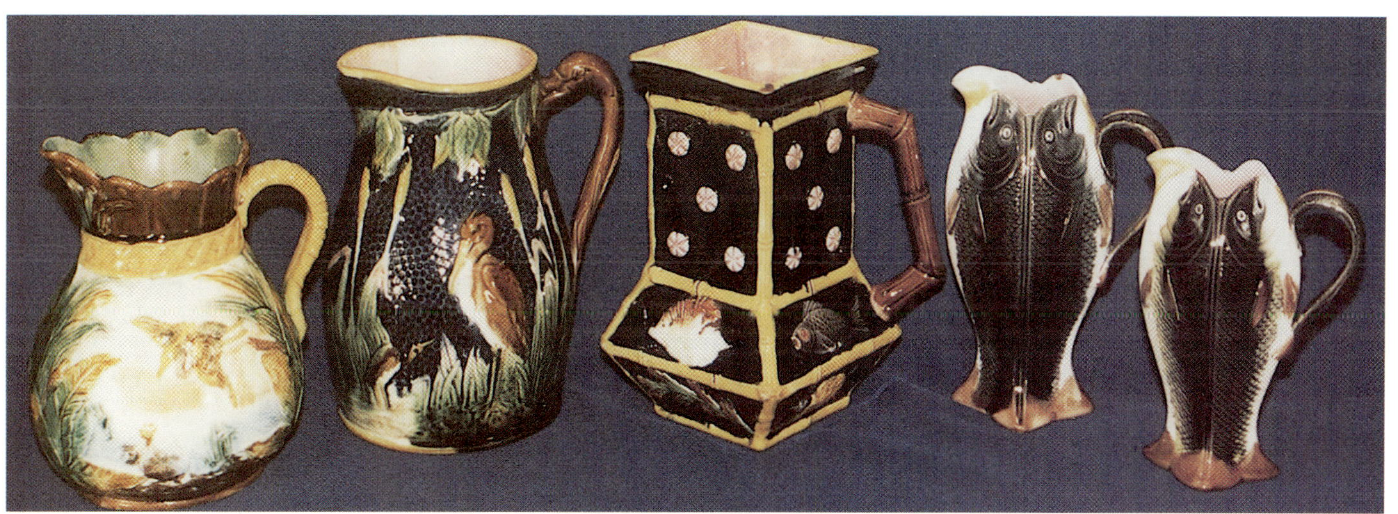

Left to Right:

Pitcher with a flying crane design on the side, 8 1/2" tall.
$250

Cobalt blue pitcher with a stork in a marsh and an eel handle, 9 1/2" tall. **$350**

A four sided cobalt blue pitcher with fish, turtles, shells and seaweed, 9 1/2" tall. **$450**

Two figural fish pitchers, four sided in two different sizes, one is 8 1/2" tall the other is 7 1/2" tall.
$350 each

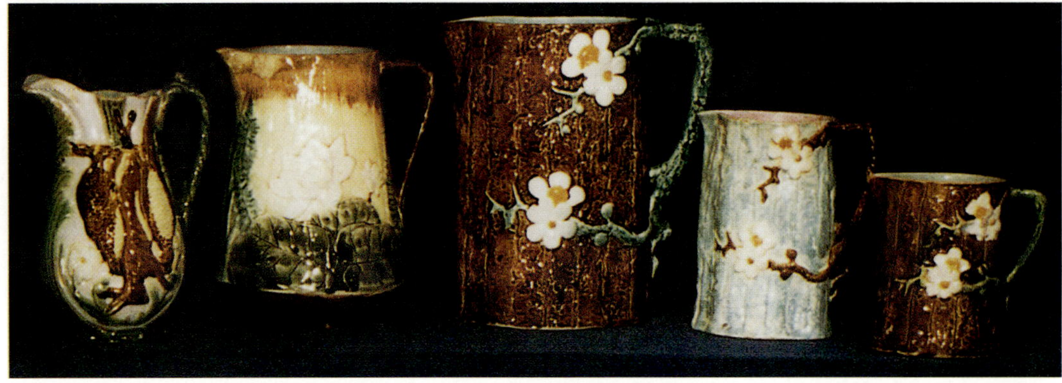

Left to Right:
Game pitcher by Holdcroft, 7" tall – **$275**
Lily pitcher by Holdcroft, 7 1/2" tall – **$100**
Dogwood pitcher by Holdcroft, 8 1/4" tall – **$225**
Dogwood pitcher by Holdcroft, 6" tall – **$75**
Dogwood pitcher by Holdcroft, 4 1/2" tall – **$75**

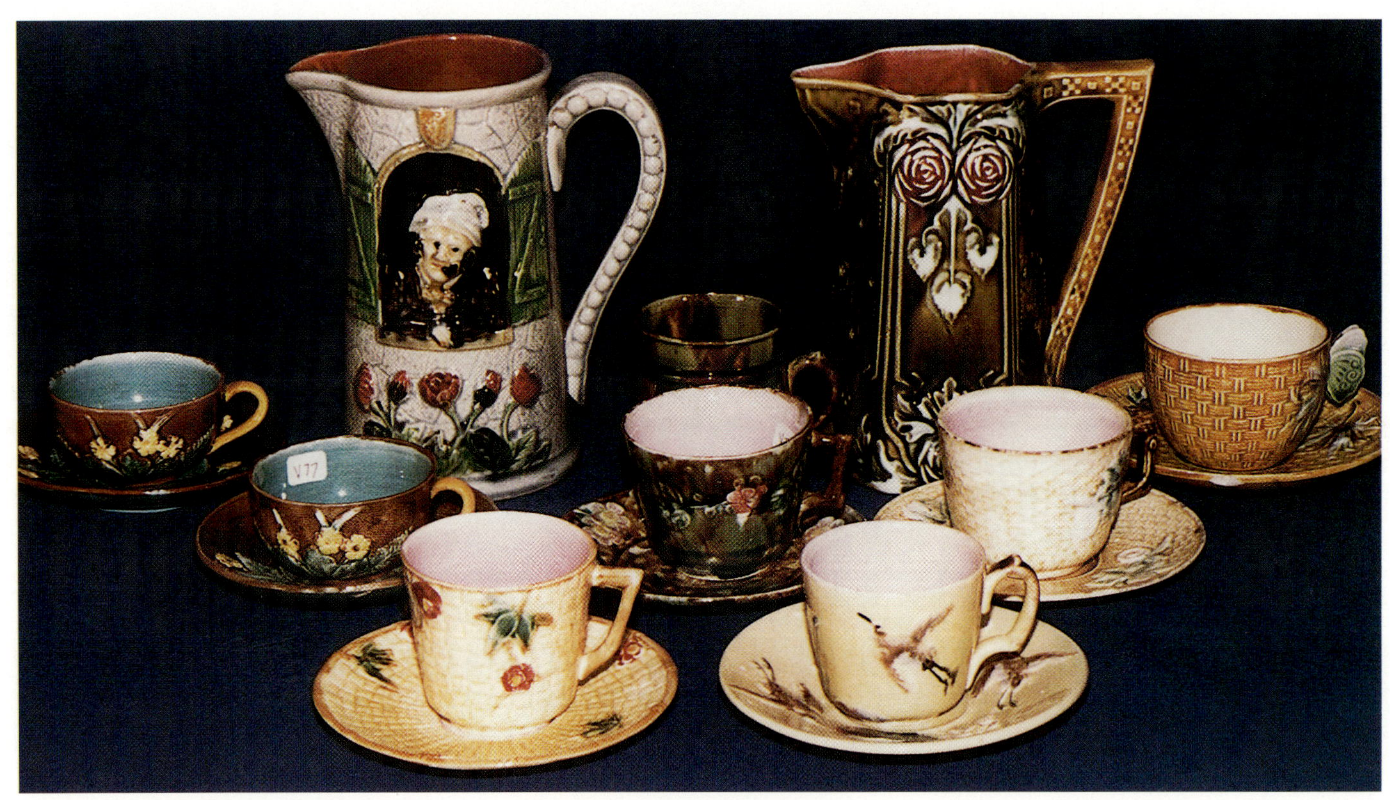

Front Row – Left to Right:
Basketweave and floral cup and saucer – **$50**
Yellow flying crane cup and saucer – **$50**
Second Row – Left to Right:
Brown cup and saucer with yellow flowers – **$175**
Dogwood on mottled ground cup and saucer – **$25**
Basketweave cup and saucer – **$50**
Back Row – Left to Right:
Brown cup and saucer with yellow flowers – **$175**
French pitcher one side a man the other a woman in a window, red interior, 7 1/2" tall – **$200**
Mottled green and brown mug, 3 1/4" tall – **$25**
Frie Onnaing six sided floral pitcher, 7 1/4" tall – **$125**
Basketweave cup and saucer with a butterfly handle – **$50**

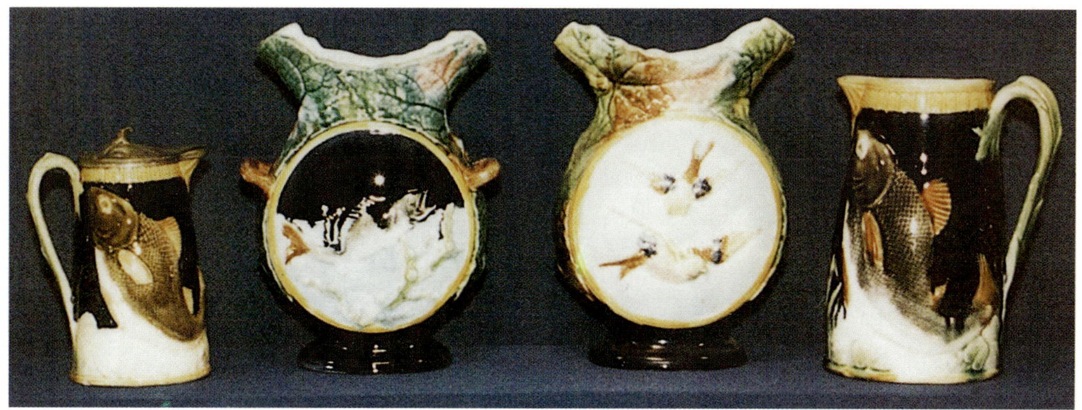

Left to Right:

Cobalt blue fish pitcher, 8" tall – **$375**

Two handled cobalt blue pitcher, $9\frac{1}{4}$" tall – **$325**

Two handled vase with birds, cobalt accents, $9\frac{1}{4}$" tall – **$325**

Cobalt blue fish vase, $9\frac{1}{2}$" tall – **$75**

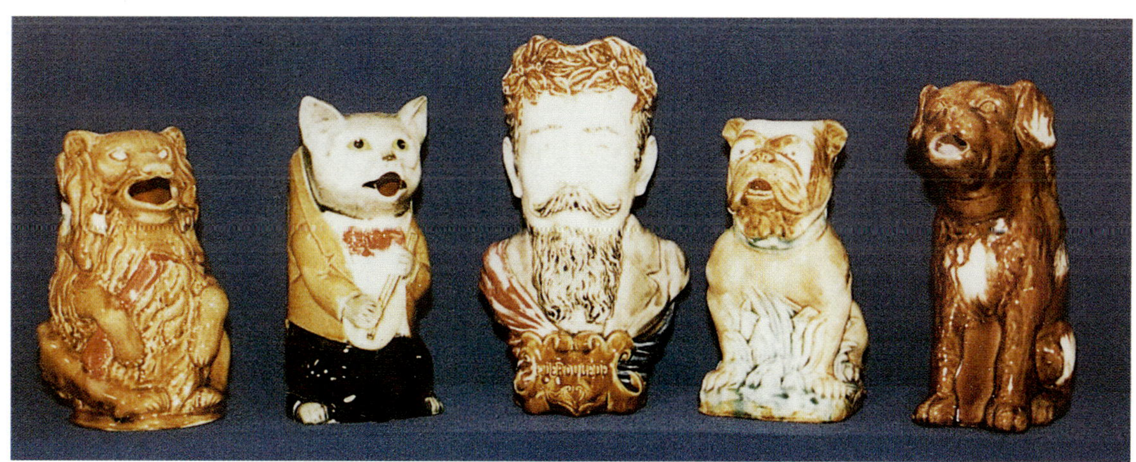

Left to Right:

Bear pitcher with red interior, $8\frac{1}{2}$" tall – **$400**

Figural pitcher of a cat playing the mandolin, 9" tall – **$775**

Frie Onnaing, P. Deroulede face pitcher, red interior, $10\frac{1}{2}$" tall – **$525**

Frie Onnaing bull dog pitcher, $8\frac{1}{2}$" tall – **$775**

Dog pitcher with lavender interior, $9\frac{1}{2}$" tall – **$600**

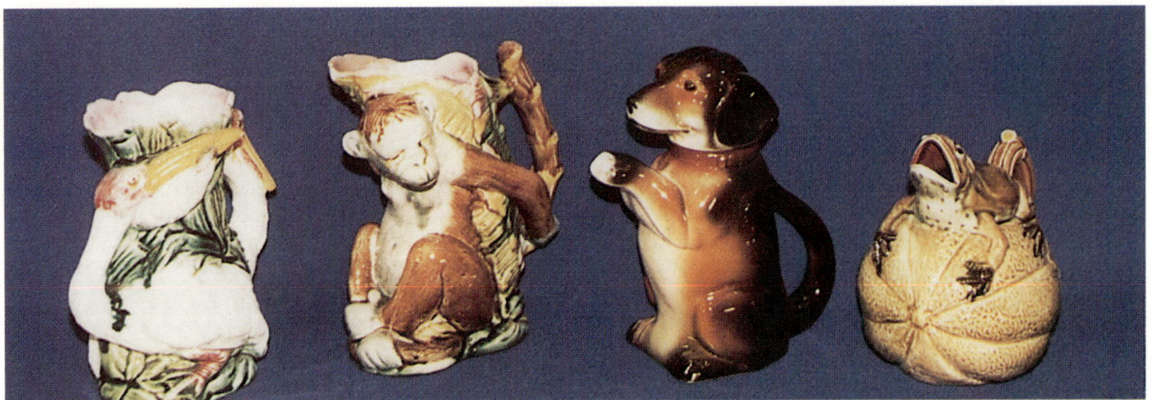

Left to Right:
Pelican pitcher, 7 1/2" tall – **$600**

Monkey pitcher with bamboo handle, 8" tall – **$375**

German Erphila hound coffee pot, 8 1/4" tall – **$125**

Frog on a melon pitcher, 6 1/2" tall – **$775**

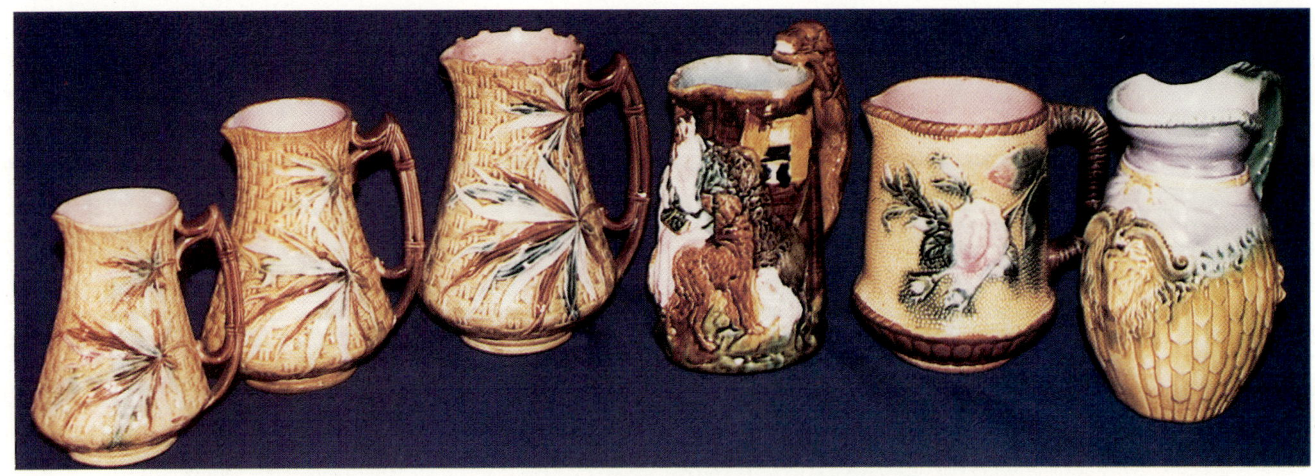

Left to Right:
The first three pitchers have English registry marks, and the design is basketweave and bamboo handles – **$50**

Hound handled pitcher with the picture of a woman feeding dogs, 8 1/2" tall – **$175**

Pink rose on yellow background pitcher, 7" tall – **$175**

English pitcher that has a green handle, lavender top, and a ram's head in relief on the side, and pink interior, 8" tall – **$250**

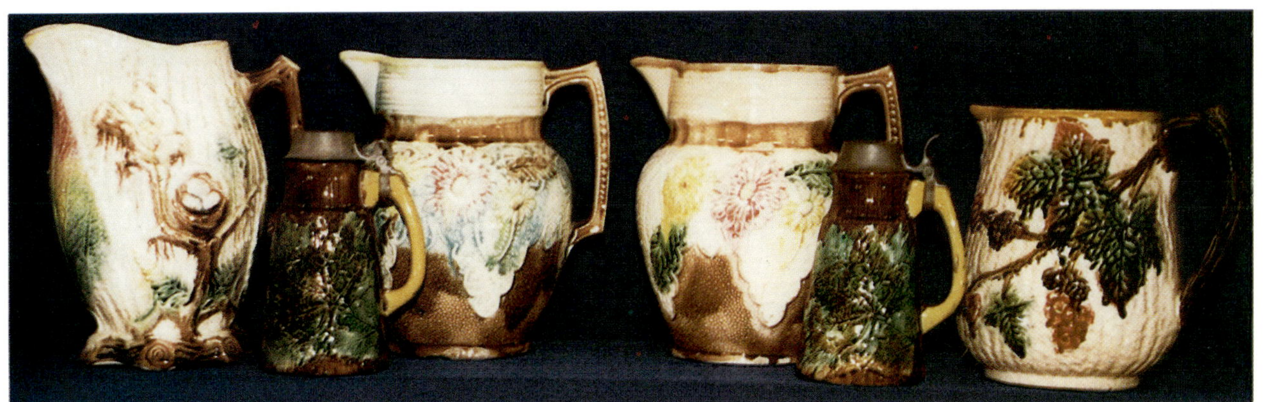

Left to Right:
Bird's nest pitcher, 9 1/2" tall – **$175**

Maple leaf on a picket fence pewter top syrup pitcher, 7" tall – **$250**

Two floral pitchers, 9" tall – **$75 each**

Maple leaf on a picket fence pewter top syrup pitcher, 7" tall – **$250**

Blackberry pitcher, 8" tall – **$75**

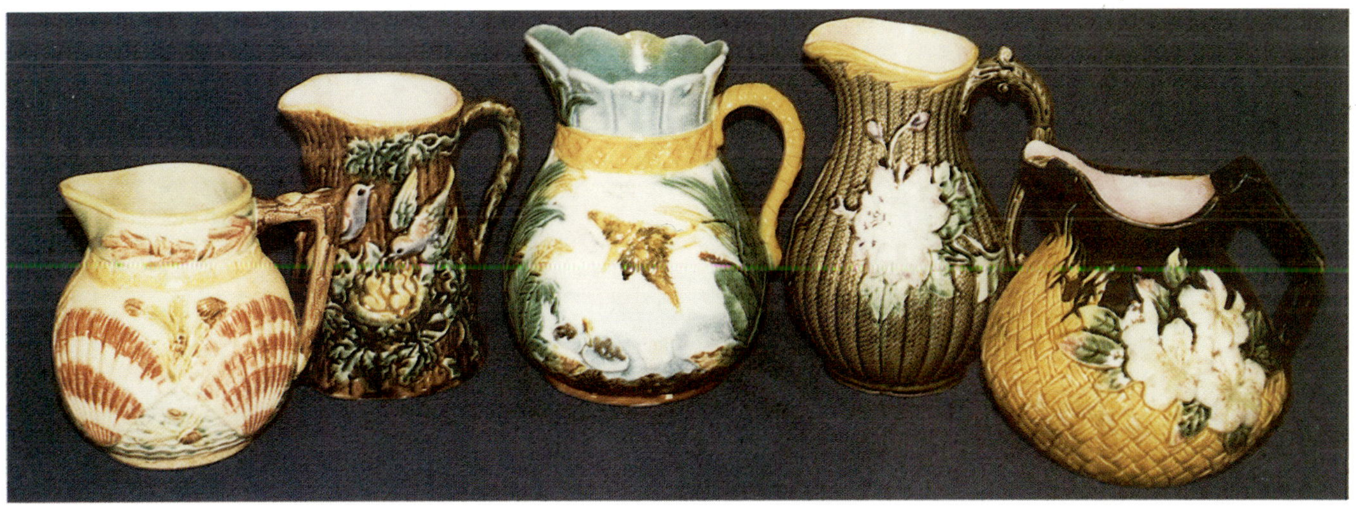

Left to Right:
Shell and seaweed pitcher, 6 1/2" tall – **$75**

Pitcher with birds feeding their young in the nest, 7 1/4" tall – **$75**

Turquoise pitcher with a flying crane pictured on the side – **$125**

English pitcher, gray background, floral design, 8 1/2" tall – **$225**

Cobalt blue, floral and basketweave pitcher, 7 1/4" tall – **$225**

PITCHERS, CUPS & SAUCERS, EWERS AND JUGS

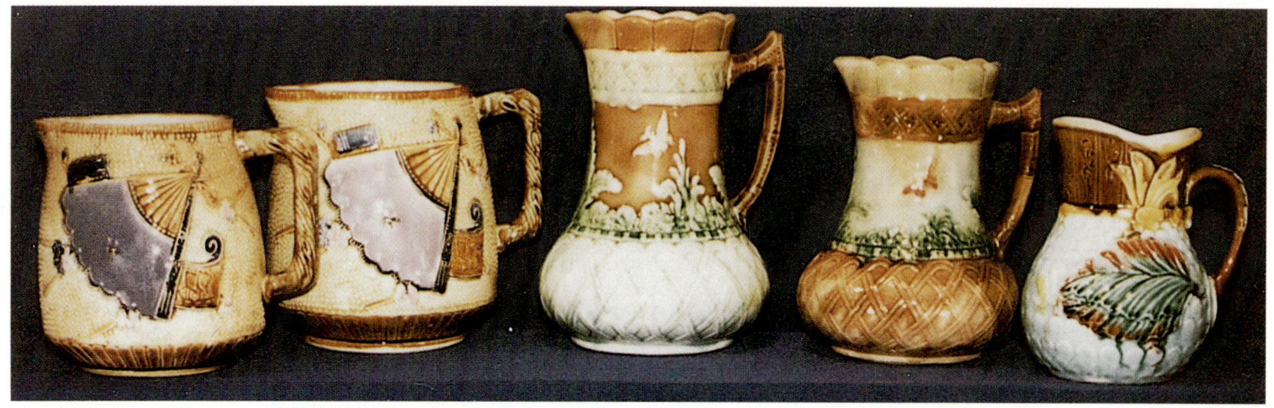

Left to Right:
Two fan and scroll pitchers, 6 1/2" tall and 7 1/4" tall – **$150 each**
Bird and basketweave pitcher, 9" tall – **$140**
Birds feeding their young pitcher – **$190**
Turquoise pitcher with brown picket fence top, 6 1/2" tall – **$140**

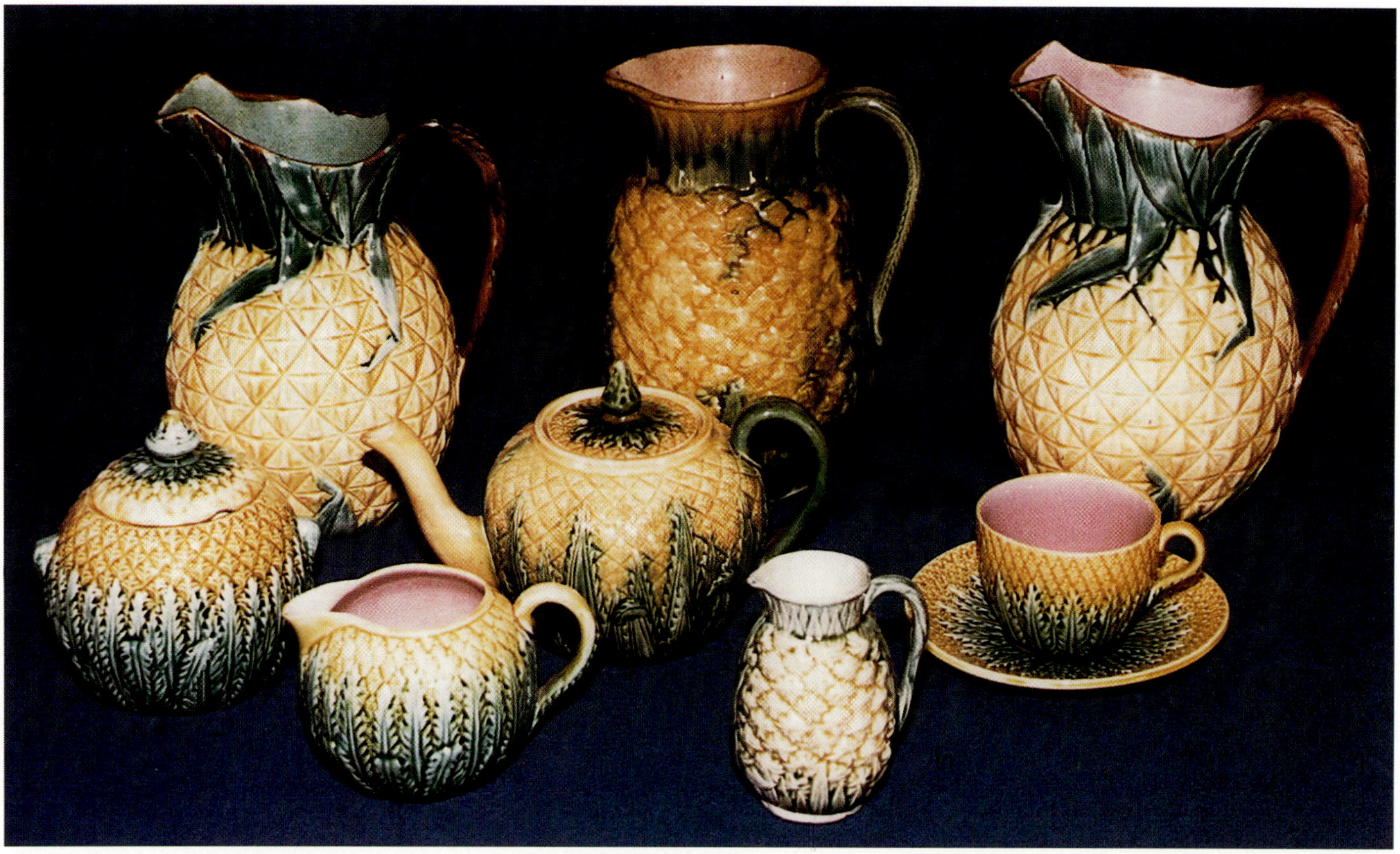

Front Row – Left to Right:
Pineapple creamer, 3" tall. This belongs with the sugar pictured on the middle row.

Miniature pineapple creamer, 4" tall – **$50**

Middle Row:
Pineapple tea set, sugar, teapot, cup and saucer (the creamer is pictured on the first row).
$250 set

Back Row – Left to Right:
Three pineapple pitchers, 8" tall – **$200** 8 1/2" tall – **$225** 9" tall – **$250**

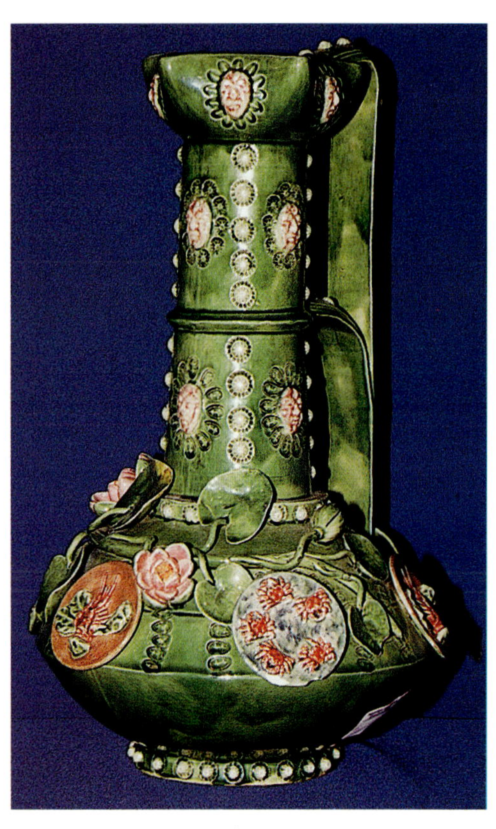

Portugal Palissy style ewer, 13 1/2" tall with applied medallions with faces, lobsters, crabs and water lily leaves applied.

$450

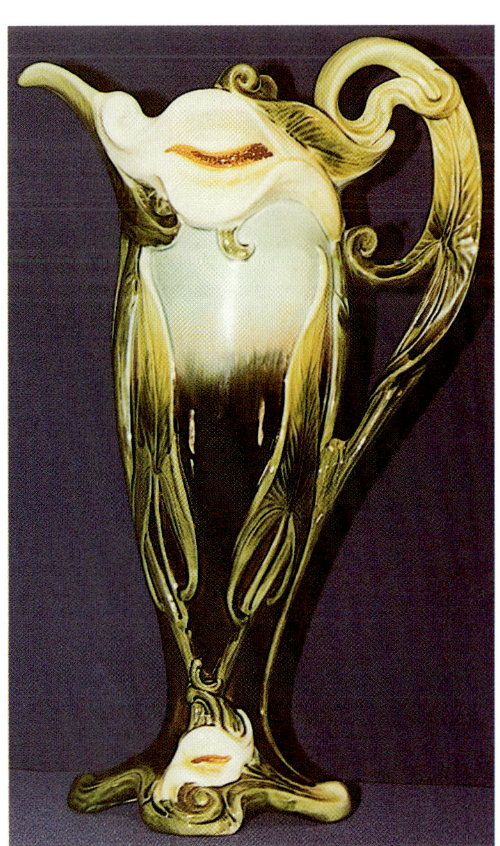

Austrian Ewer with a calla lily design, with a turquoise interior, 15" tall.

$775

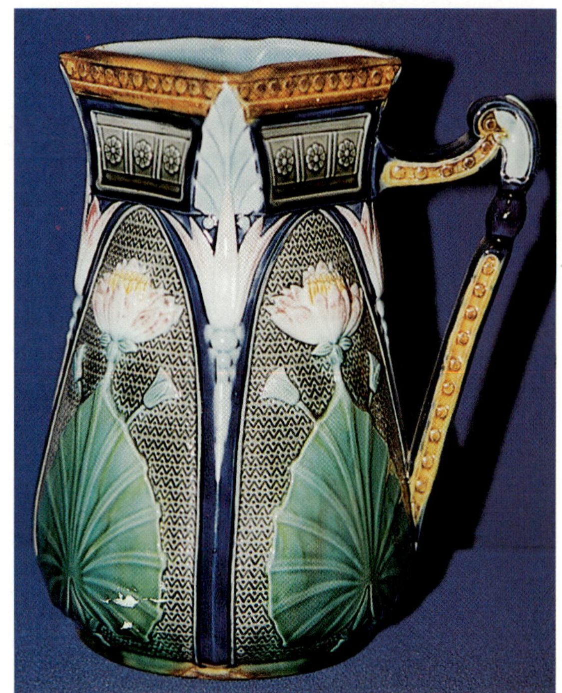

Copeland Lotus Jug, 7 1/2" tall.
$4500

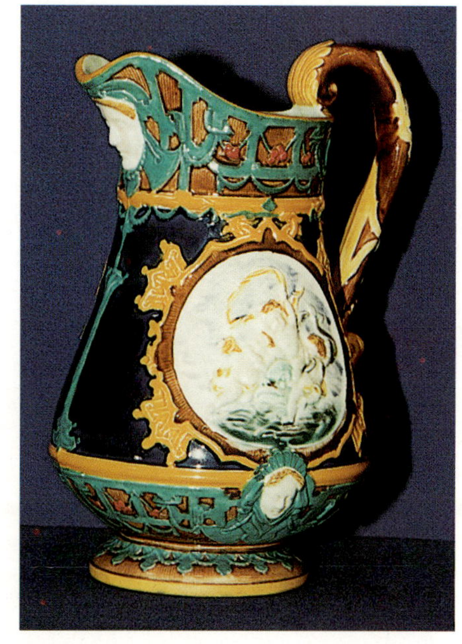

Wedgwood Elizabethan Jug, c. 1863, cobalt blue background with three cherubs on each side in relief, 8" tall.
$1100

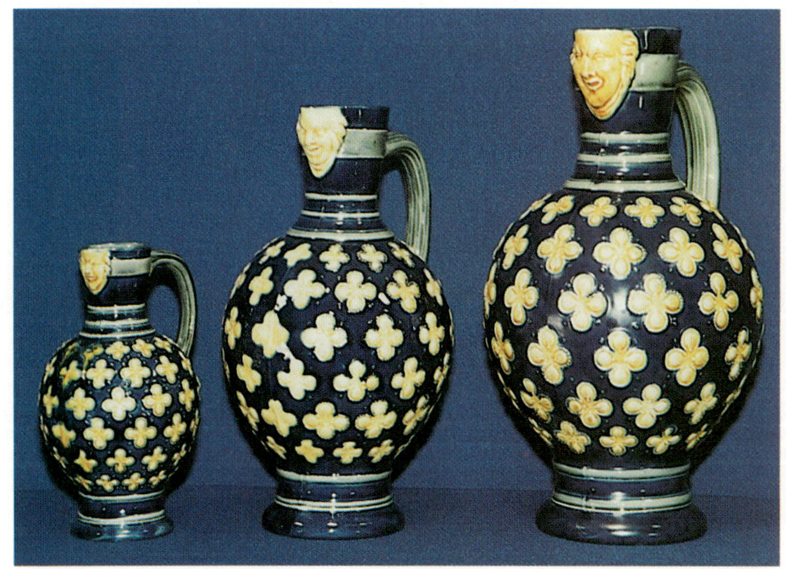

Set of three Minton graduated cobalt blue Verulam Jugs, with yellow faces on the spout. Sizes 6 1/2", 9 1/2" and 11 1/4" tall.
$325 each

Minton Protat Jug, with three cherubs in relief, 15" tall.
$1500

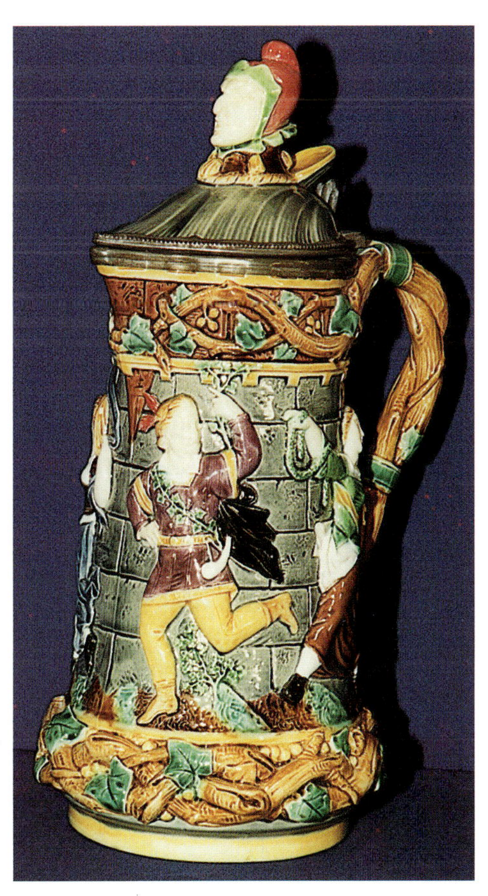

Minton tower jug with court jesters around the sides, 13" high.
$1400

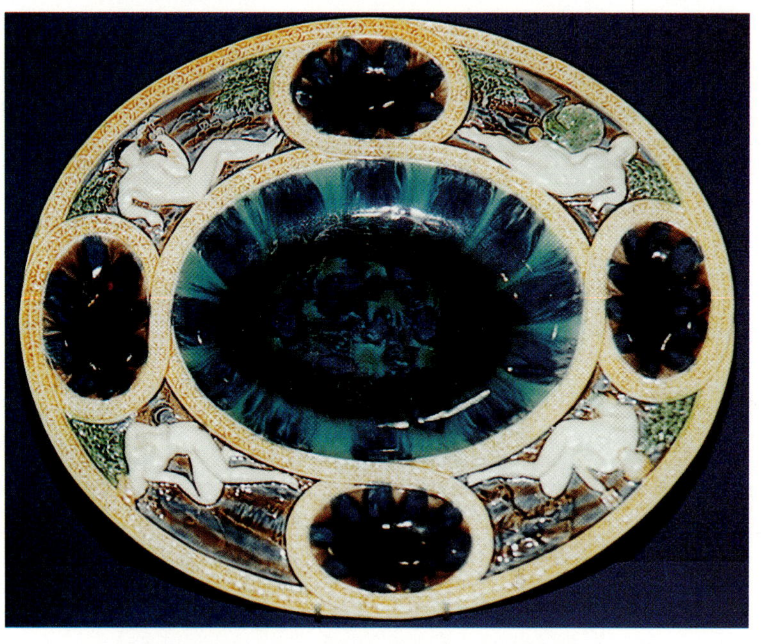

Ornamental platter, Minton, modelled after Palissy's classic style of work, 12 1/4" x 14 1/2".
$500

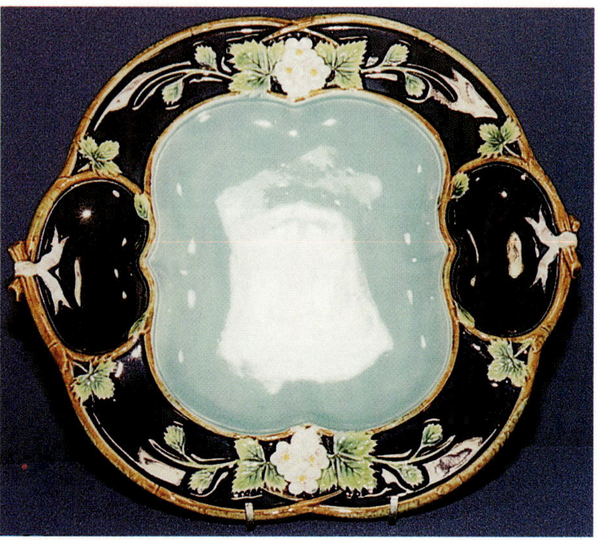

George Jones cobalt strawberry plates, turquoise center with dipping wells on each side, 8 1/2" x 9 1/2".
$1300

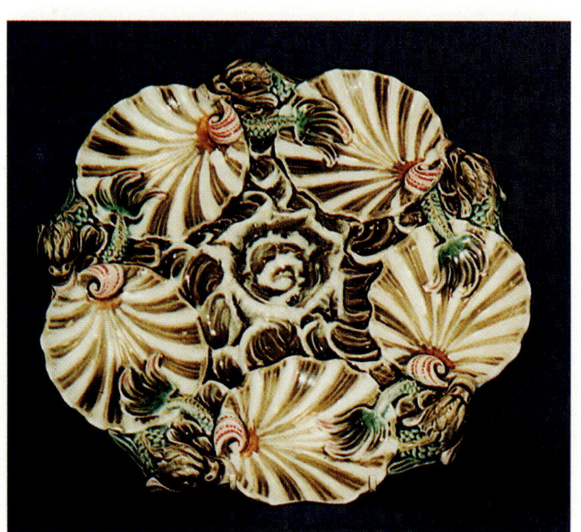

Wedgwood dolphin oyster plate, 9 1/4" diameter.
$900

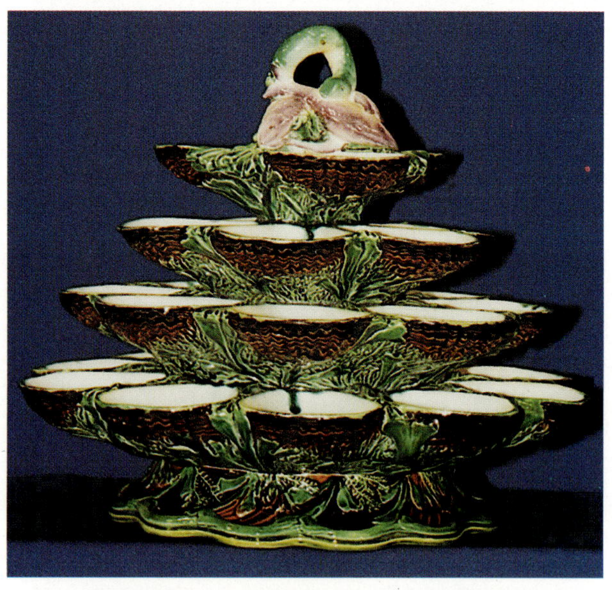

Minton four tiered oyster server, 10" tall.
$3900

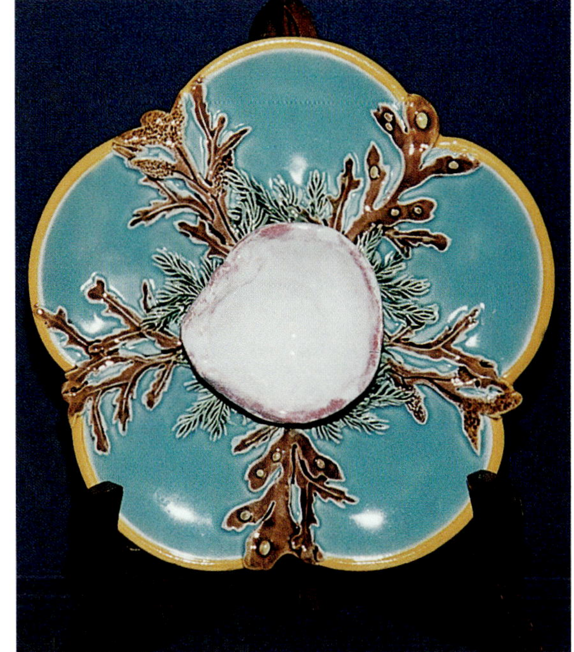

George Jones Oyster Plate, turquoise with white raised center shell, 7".
$900

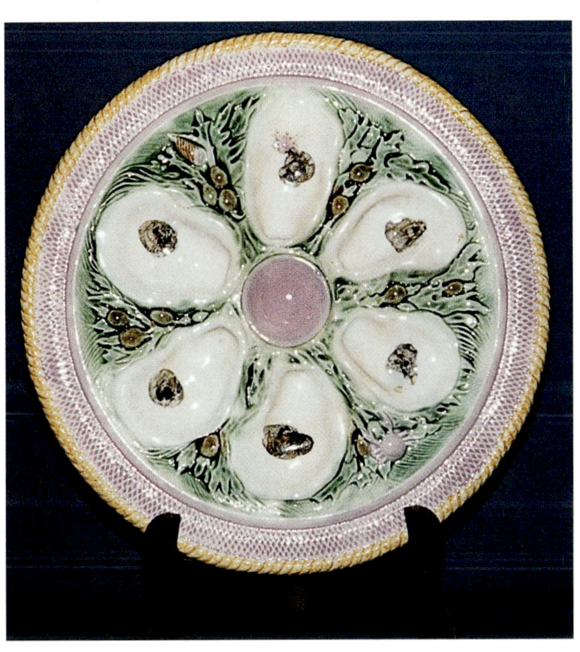

Etruscan Oyster Plate with lavender border, 10". *(This piece is probably the rarest of all Etruscan pieces.)*
$3500

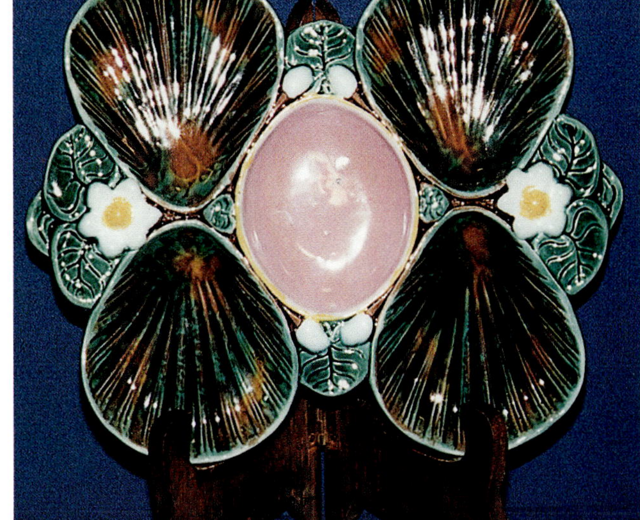

Minton Water Lily Oyster Plate, five part, 9" x 7 1/2".
$900

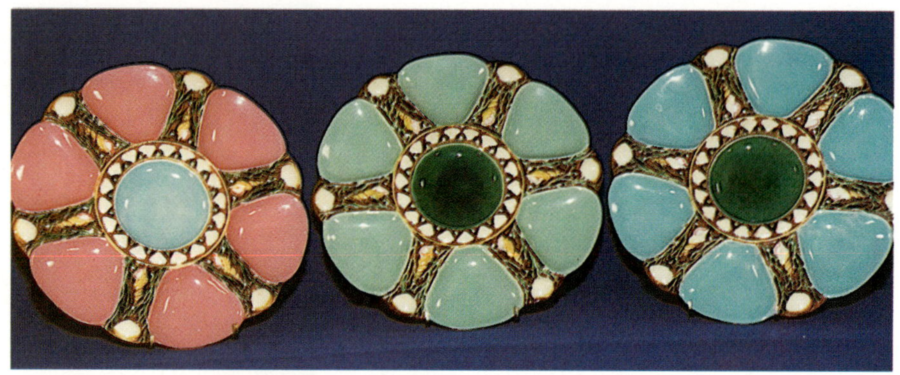

Three oyster plates, different colors.
$600 each

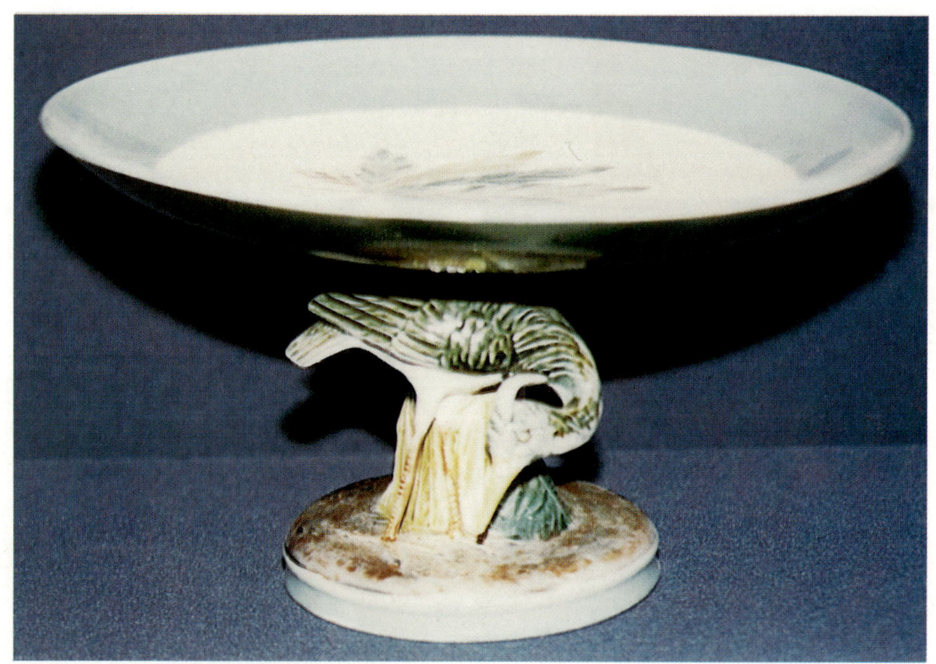

Holdcroft stork footed fern plate with turquoise border, 5 1/2" h x 10" d.
$400

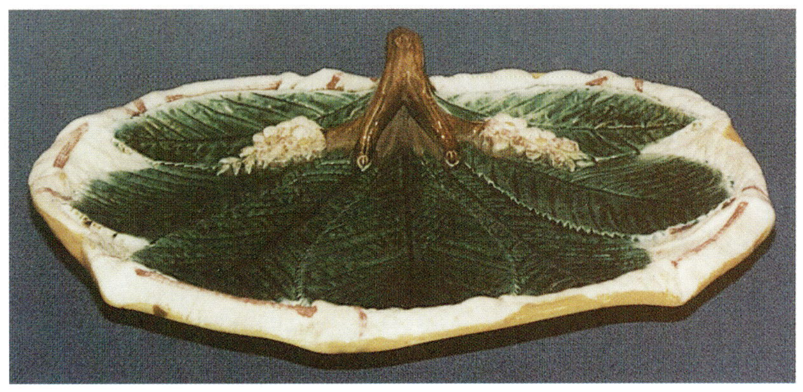

George Jones handled leaf napkin tray, 11 x 11 1/2".
$325

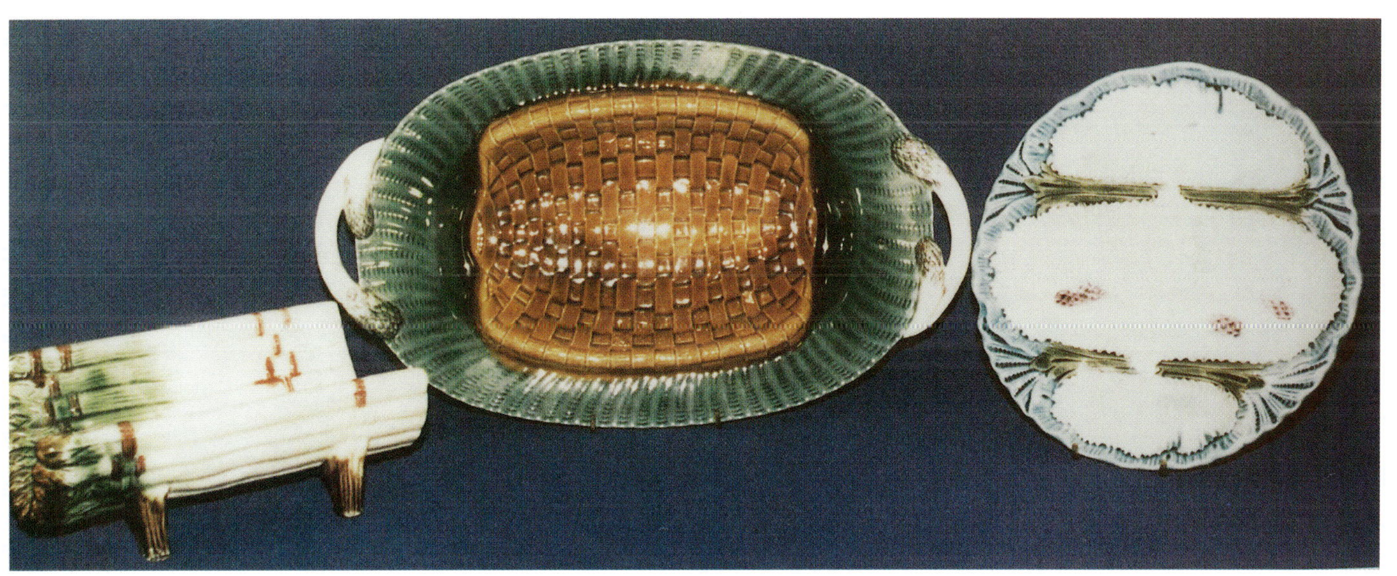

Left to Right:

Asparagus cradle, 9" l – **$150**

Asparagus platter with basketweave center, 10" x 16 1/2" – **$125**

French asparagus plate, 9 1/2" – **$200**

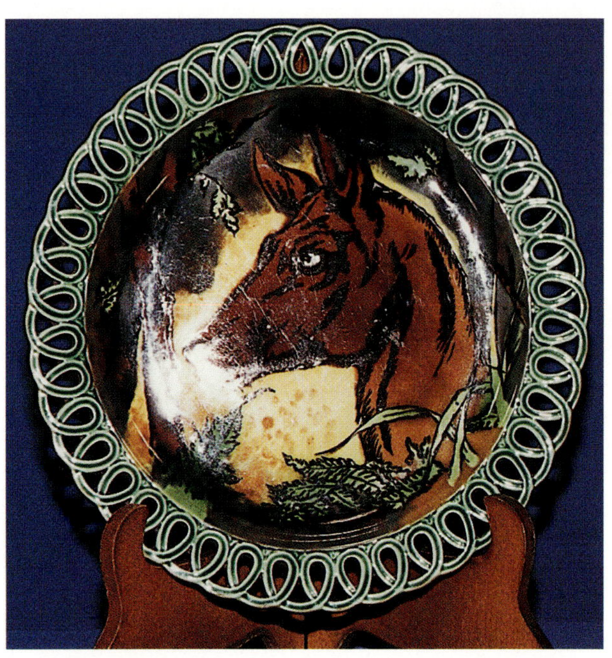

Wedgwood horse plate with open lattice border, 9 1/4" tall.

$1200

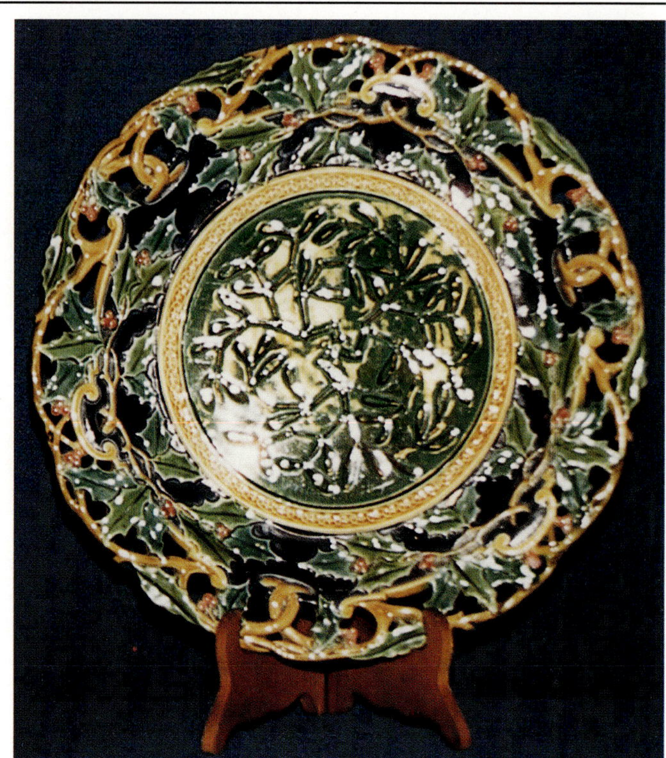

Minton Christmas holly and berry charger, cobalt blue with red , green, yellow and brown, mold #726, 15" tall.

$1100

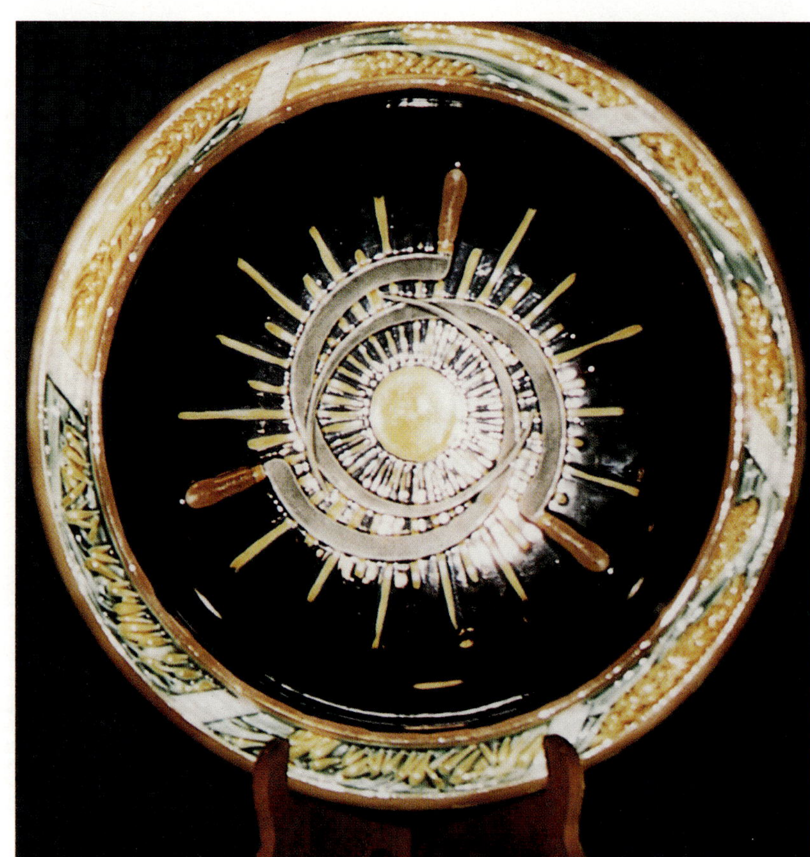

Wedgwood cobalt round wheat platter, 3-hand corn scythes in center, 2" h x 13 1/4" d.

$875

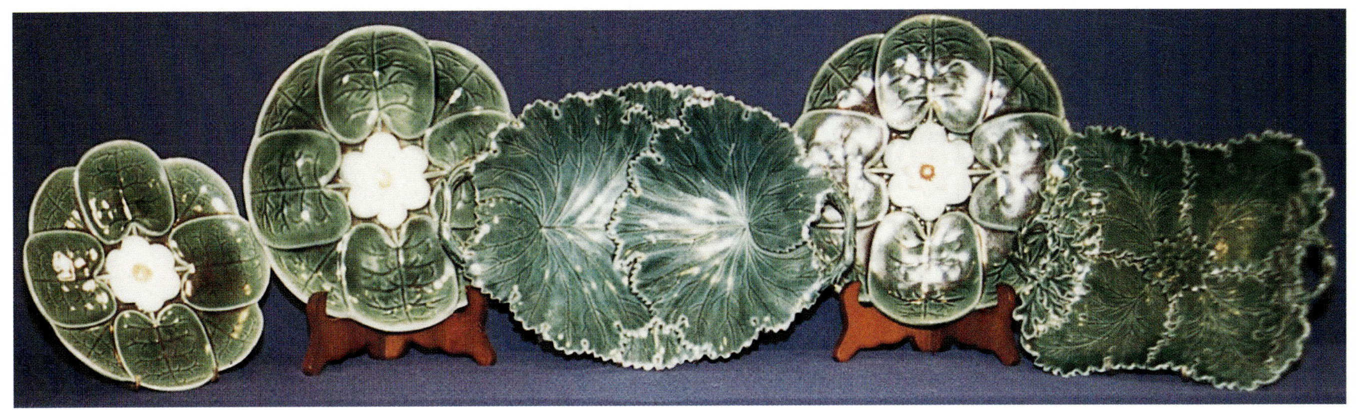

Left to Right:

Pond lily plate, 8" dia. – **$175**
Water lily plate, 9 1/4" dia. – **$150**
Copeland oval deep bowl – **$75**
Pond lily plate, 9 1/2" – **$150**
Two handled platter, 7" h x 10", oak leaf and acorn in relief – **$150**

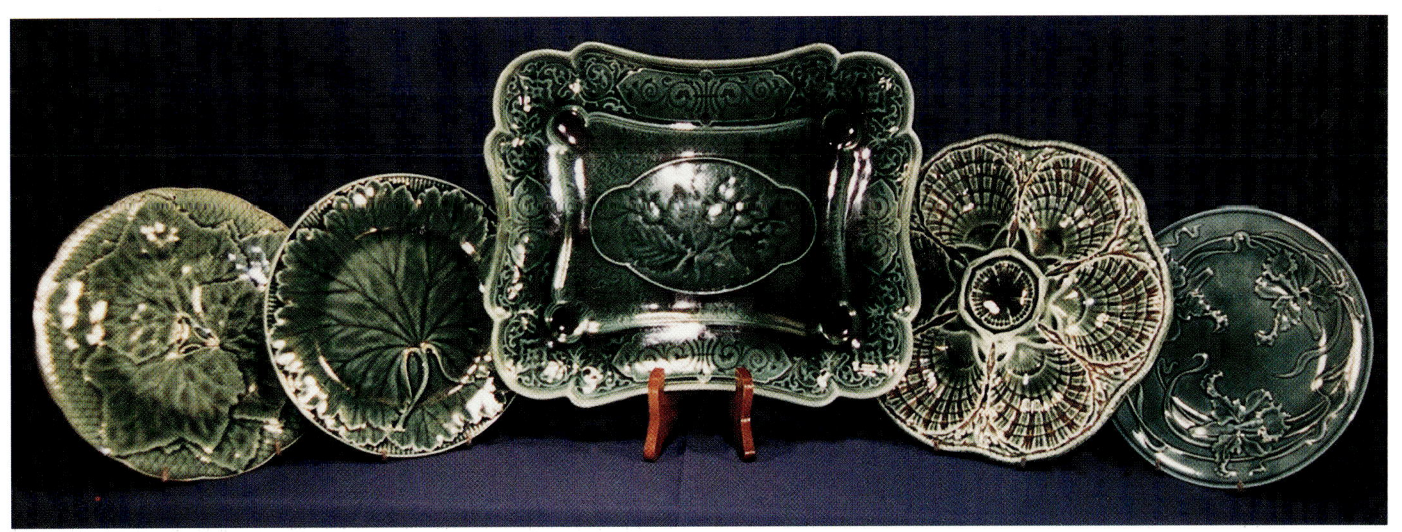

Left to Right:

Wedgwood maple leaf plate, 8" tall – **$75**
Three leaf on basket plate – **$75**
Sarreguemines platter, 10" x 12 1/2" – **$200**
Sarreguemines oyster plate, 10" – **$150**
Morning glory plate, 8" – **$75**

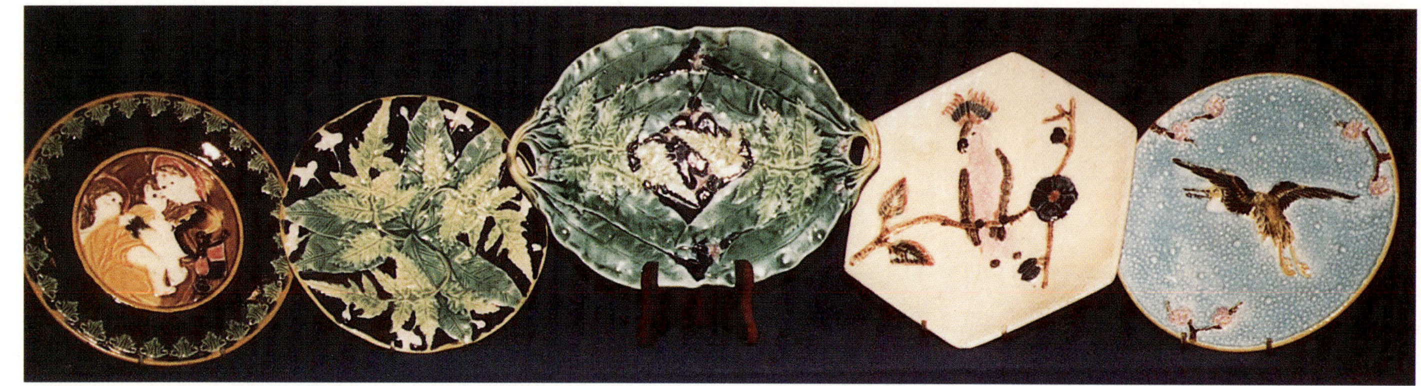

Left to Right:

Father, mother and child plate with cobalt border, 81/2" –.**$100**

Cobalt blue plate covered with fern and floral pattern – **$300**

Cobalt blue platter covered with leaves and ferns – **$250**

Hexagon parrot plate with an English registry mark, 91/2" – **$75**

Holdcroft bird in flight plate, 81/4" – **$150**

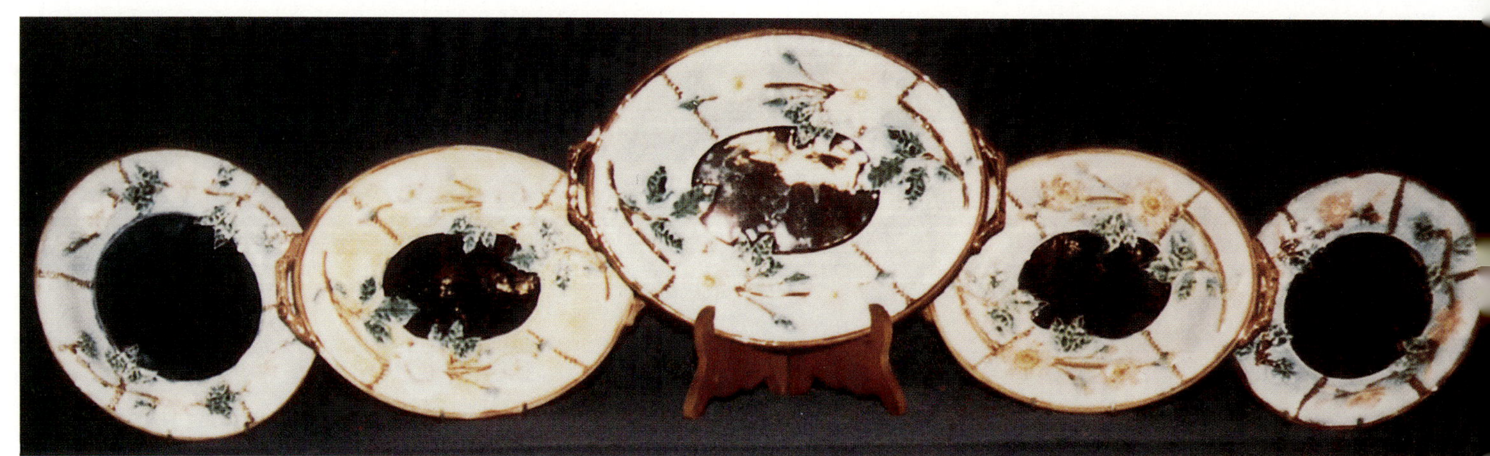

Left to Right:

Wild rose plate with cobalt blue center, 81/2", turquoise – **$225**

Wild rose platter, cobalt blue center, 111/2", yellow – **$350**

Wild rose on basket platter with cobalt blue center – **$325**

Wild rose with cobalt blue center platter, 111/4" – **$150**

Wild rose plate with cobalt center, 71/2" – **$100**

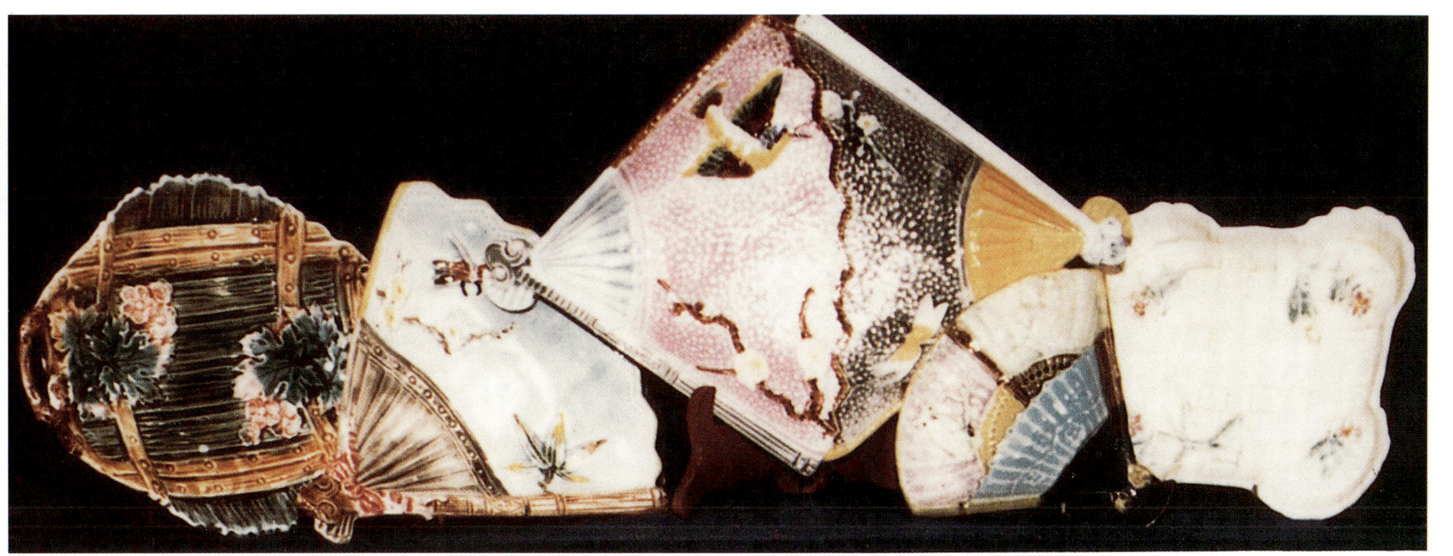

Left to Right:
Barrel style and floral platter – **$75**
Dragonfly and fan shape dish, 10 1/2" – **$225**
Eureka bird and fan platter, 11" x 16 1/2" – **$300**
Fan shape dish with owl – **$100**
Basketweave and floral tray – **$75**

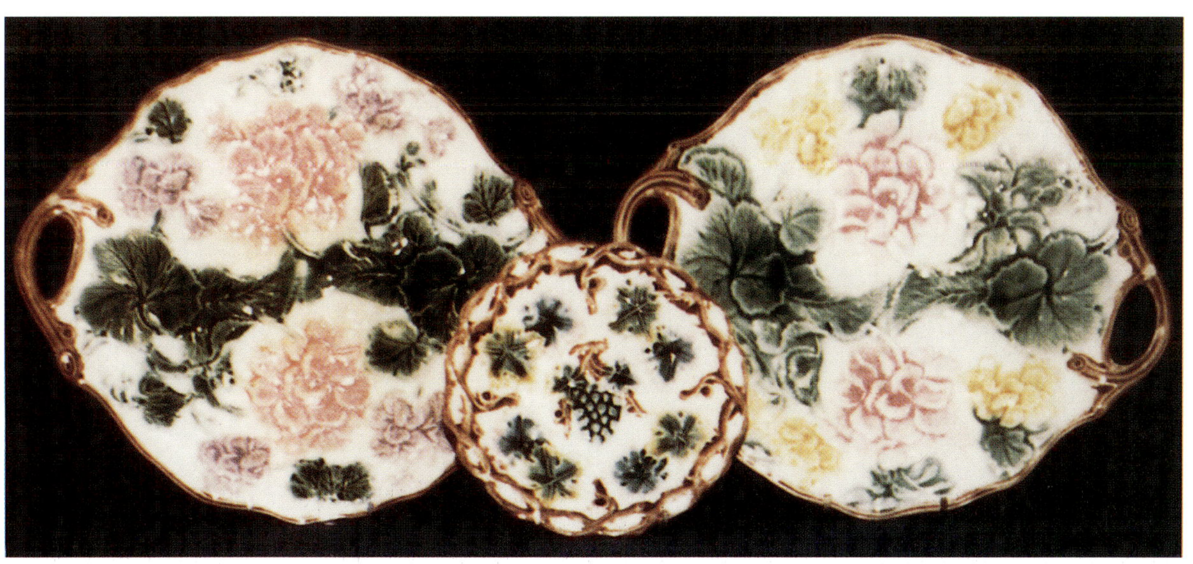

Left to Right:
Etruscan geranium platter – **$300**
Etruscan grape plate, 6 1/4" – **$50**
Etruscan geranium platter – **$250**

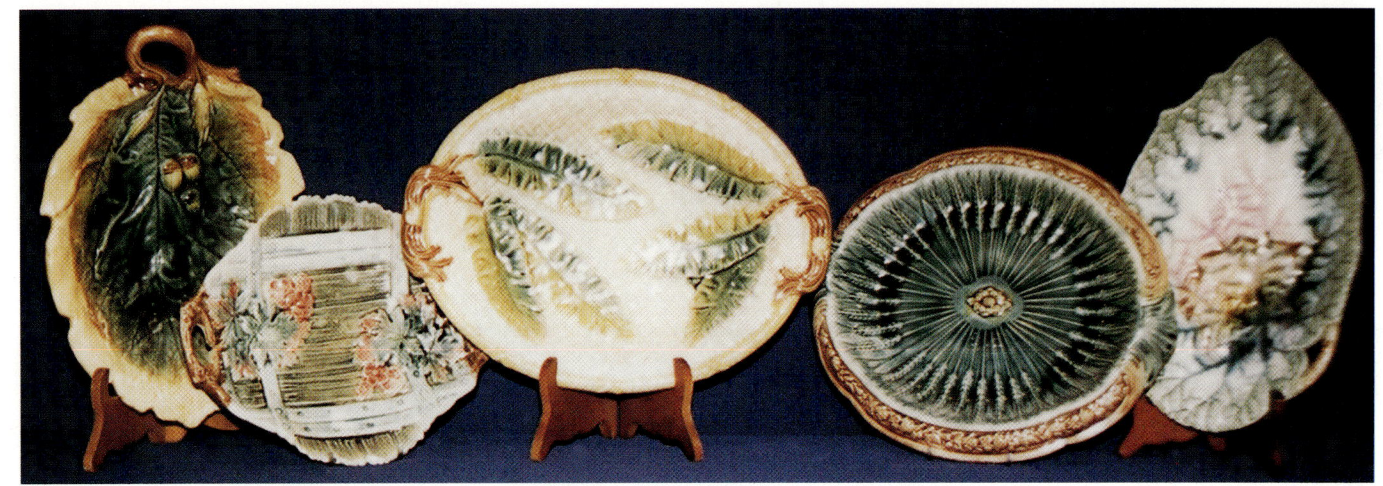

Left to Right:

Oak leaf with acorn tray, 12 1/2" – **$200**

Barrel and staves platter – **$50**

Oval banana leaf platter, 14" – **$125**

Brown and green wheat bread tray, 12 1/2" – **$150**

Begonia leaf with handle, 12" – **$175**

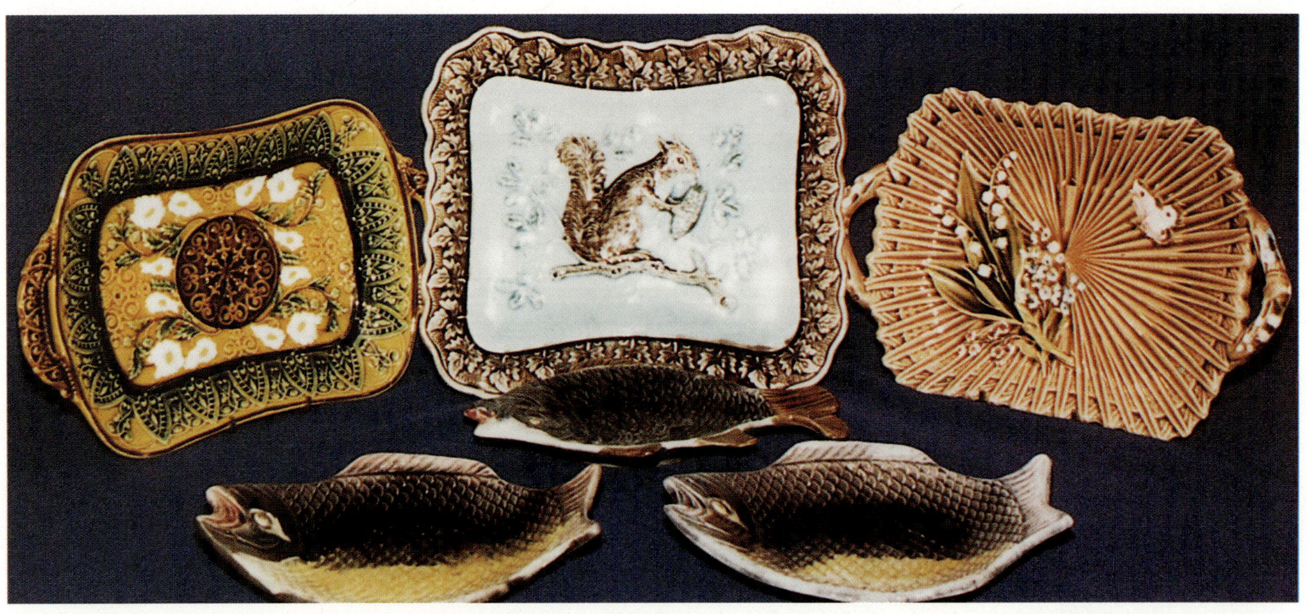

Front:

Three fish dishes – **$125 each**

Back Row:

VBS yellow daisy platter with handles, 12 1/4" – **$75**

Squirrel with ear of corn platter, 10" x 12" – **$325**

VBS tray, butterfly and lily of the valley design, 13" – **$50**

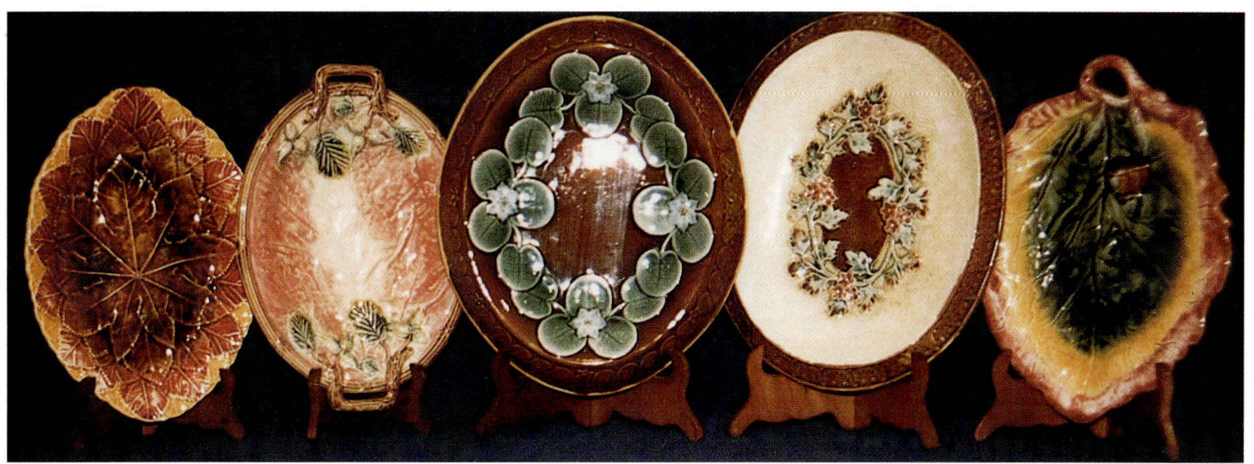

Left to Right:

Leaf bread platter, 11 1/4" – **$150**

Bread platter with leaves and blossoms in relief, 12" – **$325**

Pond lily bread tray, 13" – **$325**

Bread Platter with floral center, 13 1/4" – **$150**

Oak leaf bread tray with acorns – **$200**

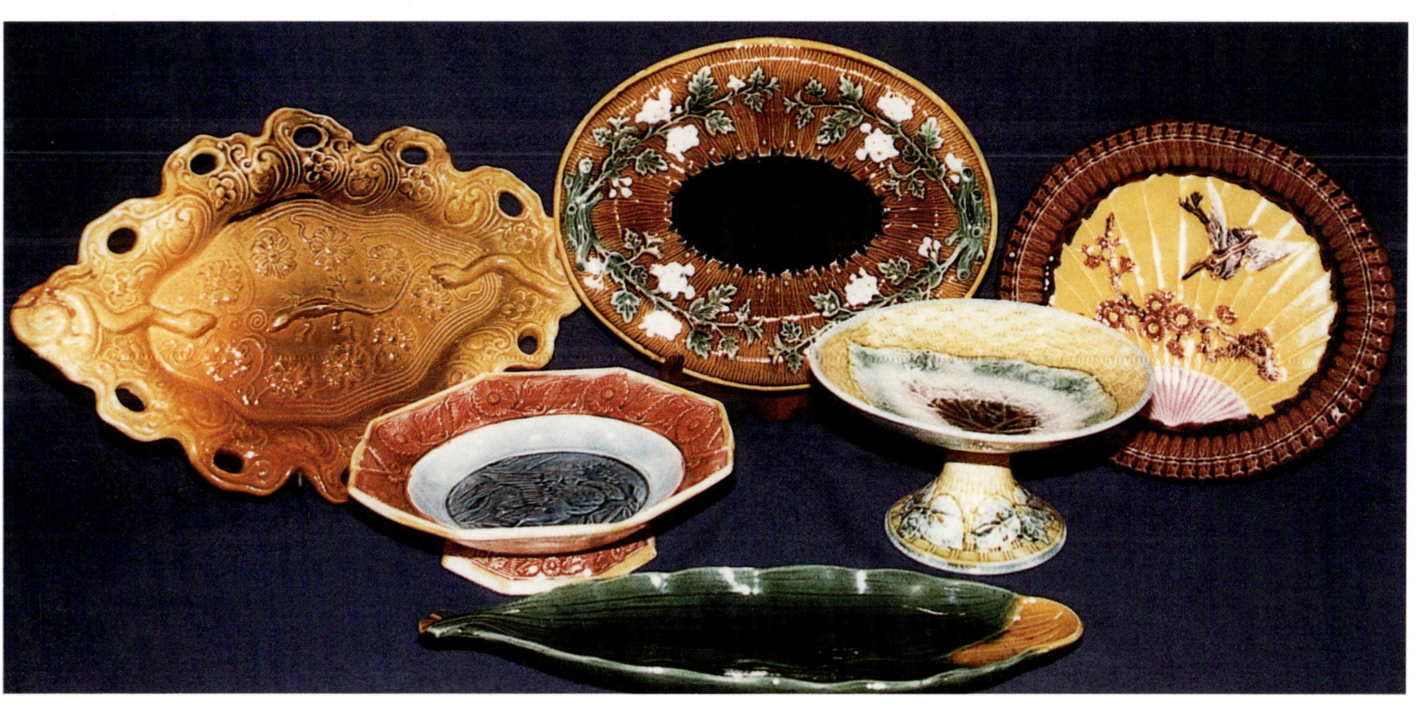

Front Row:

Corn leaf tray, 15 1/2" – **$75**

Middle Row:

Footed bowl in red and turquoise, 10" – **$50**

Begonia leaf on basket compote – **$250**

Back Row:

Palissy styled platter with snake handles and lizard center, 11 1/2" x 17" – **$50**

Platter, designed like a picket fence with cobalt center, 13" – **$300**

Bird and fan oval platter with brown bamboo border, yellow center – **$275**

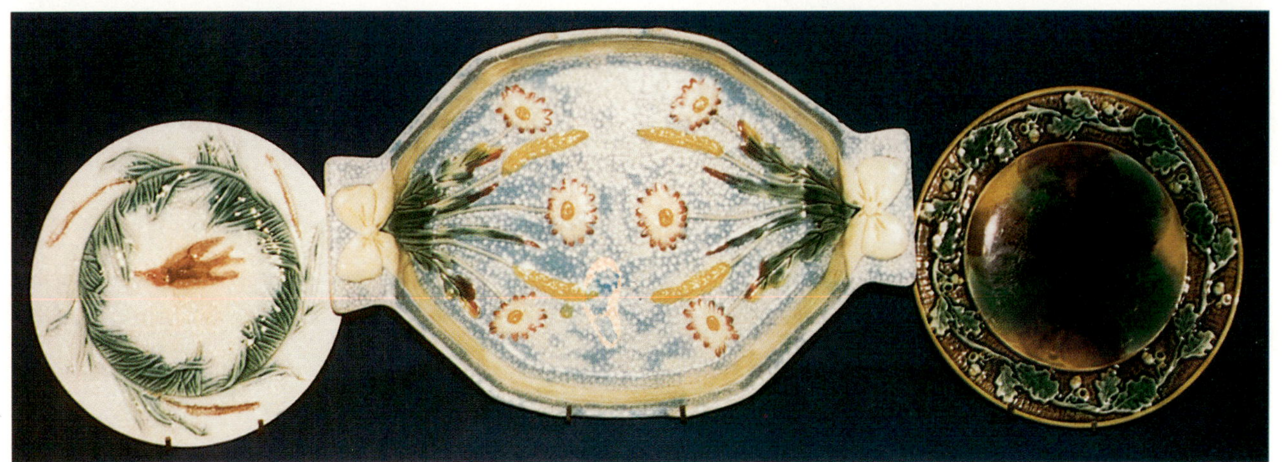

Left to Right:

Bird in flight with cattails circling the plate, 8 1/2" – **$50**

Fielding daisy and ribbon platter, 16 1/4" – **$500**

Mottled plate, oak leaves and acorns on border – **$175**

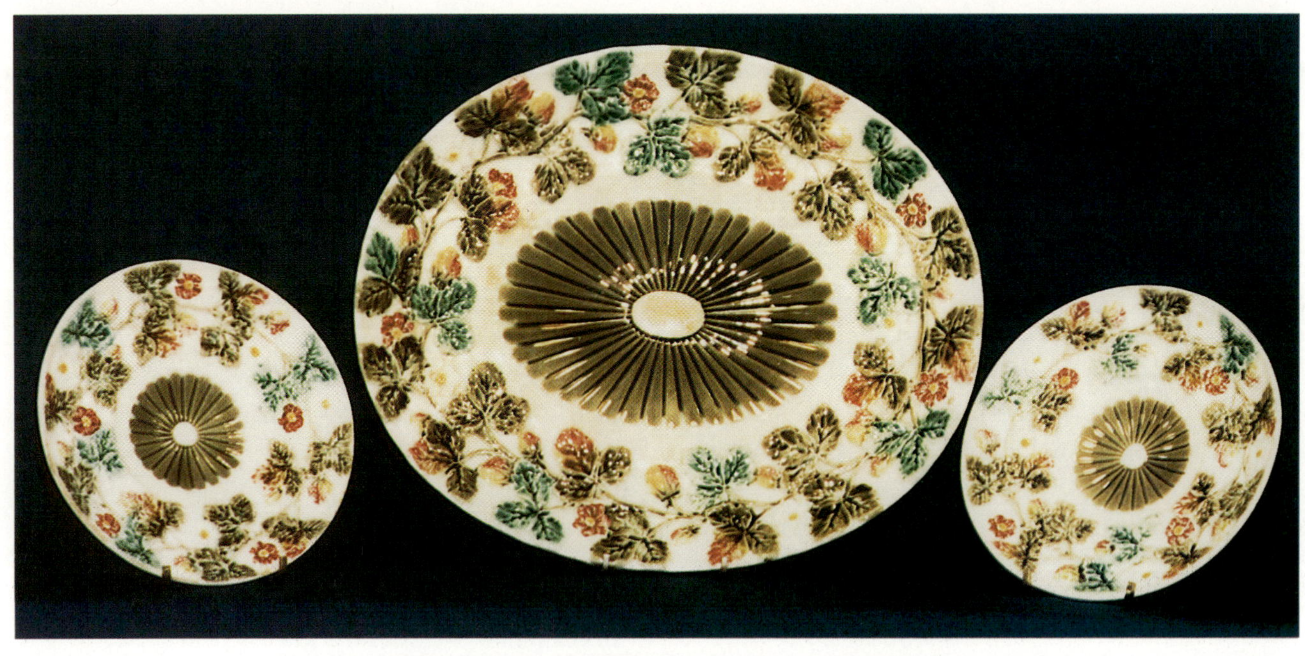

Wedgwood strawberry platter and plates. The plates are 7", and the platter measures 10 1/2" x 13".
$825/set

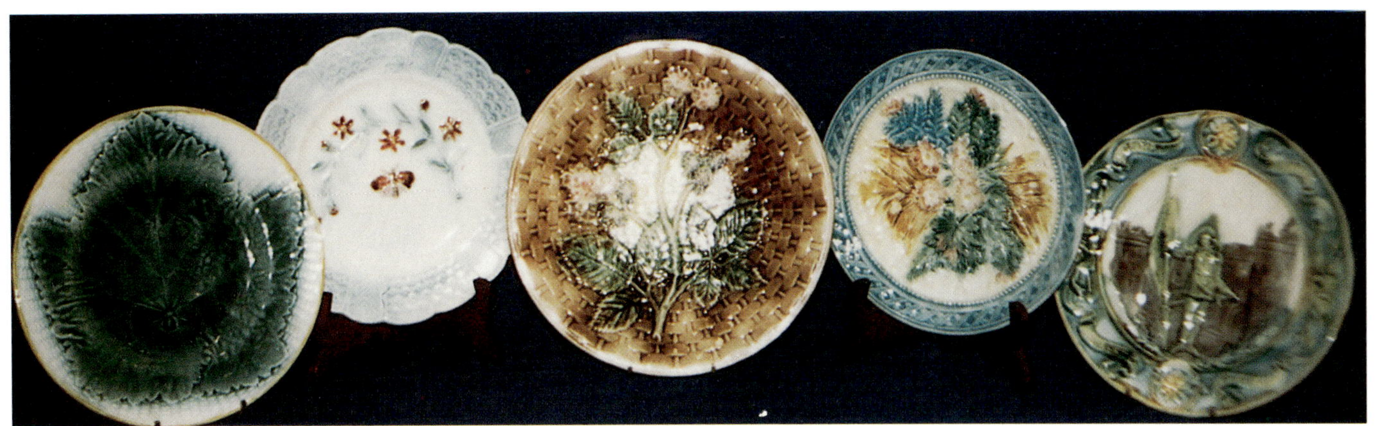

Left to Right:
Maple leaf on basket plate, 9" – **$100**

Turquoise floral plates with butterfly in center, 9" – **$50**

Brown basketweave plate with blackberries, 10" – **$125**

Floral basketweave plate, turquoise border, 8 1/2" – **$100**

Joan of Arc plate, 8 1/2" – **$225**

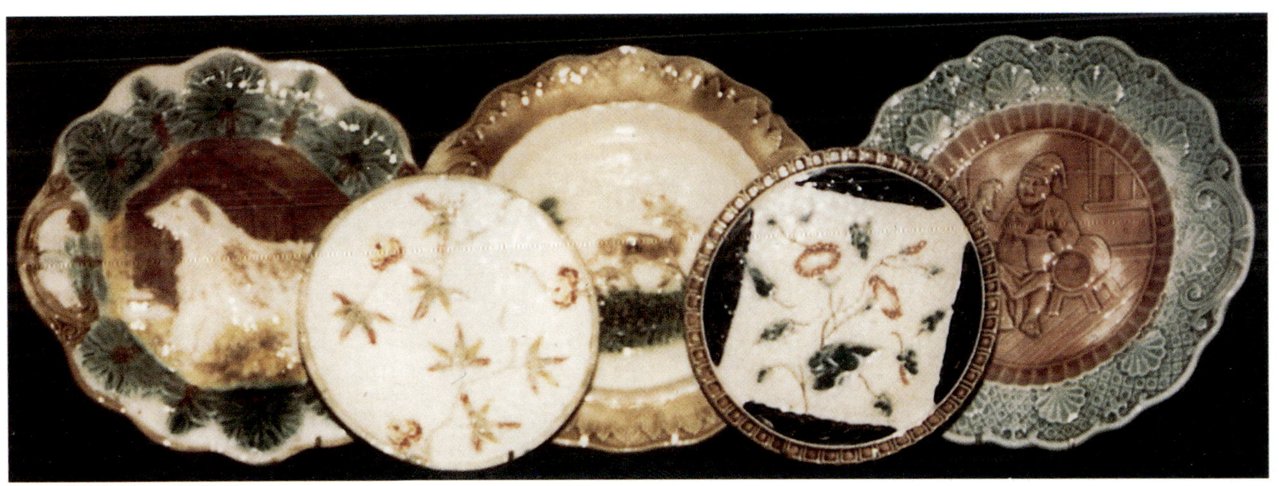

Front Row – Left to Right:
White basketweave plate, oriental flowers, 7 1/2" – **$75**

Cobalt plate with a white napkin in the center designed with morning glories, 8" – **$125**

Back Row – Left to Right:
Dog and dog house platter – **$175**

Deer and dog platter, 11" – **$175**

Toby platter, 11" – **$50**

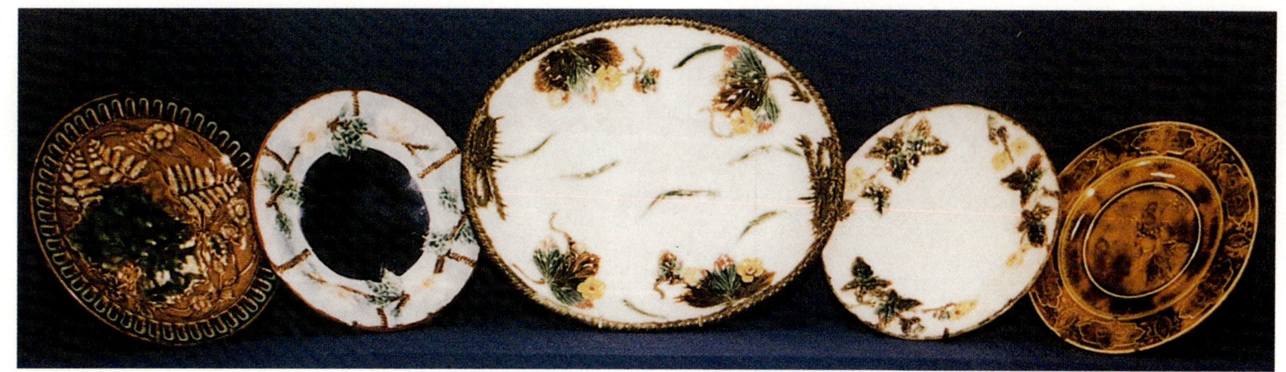

Left to Right:
Leaf and fern plate with lattice border, 8" – **$25**

Wild rose and rope plate with cobalt blue center, and a turquoise border – **$75**

Clifton strawberry platter – **$125**

Clifton blackberry plate, 7 1/2" – **$100**

Sarreguemines mottled strawberry plate, 7 1/2" – **$100**

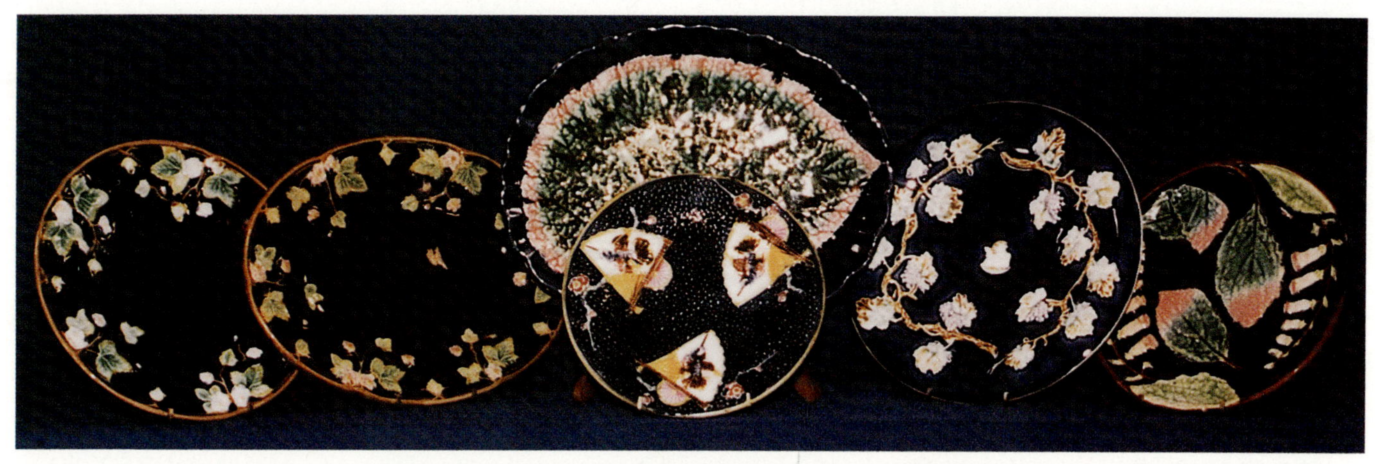

Front:
Cobalt blue Boulton bird and fan plate, 7 1/2" – **$125**

Back Row – Left to Right:
Two cobalt strawberry leaf and blossom plates, 8 1/4". **$175 each**

Begonia leaf platter, pink border on cobalt blue, 12" . **$375**

Grapevine plate with angel in center – **$125**

Cobalt blue bellflower plate, 8" – **$250**

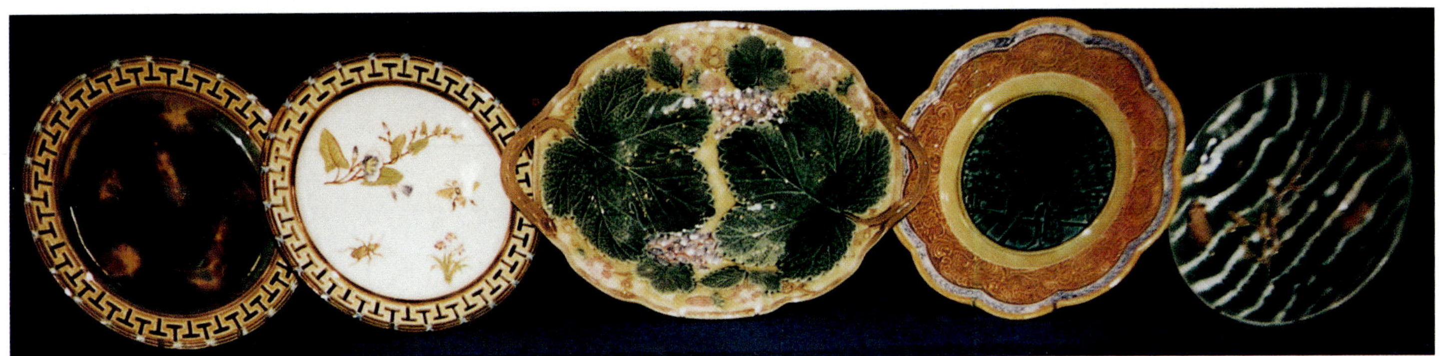

Left to Right:
Wedgwood reticulated border plate, 8 3/4" – **$150**

Wedgwood reticulated border plate, 8 1/2" – **$150**

Wedgwood strawberry platter – **$325**

Wedgwood scalloped edge plate with a Victorian scene in the middle – **$150**

Wedgwood swimming seal plate, 7 1/4" – **$225**

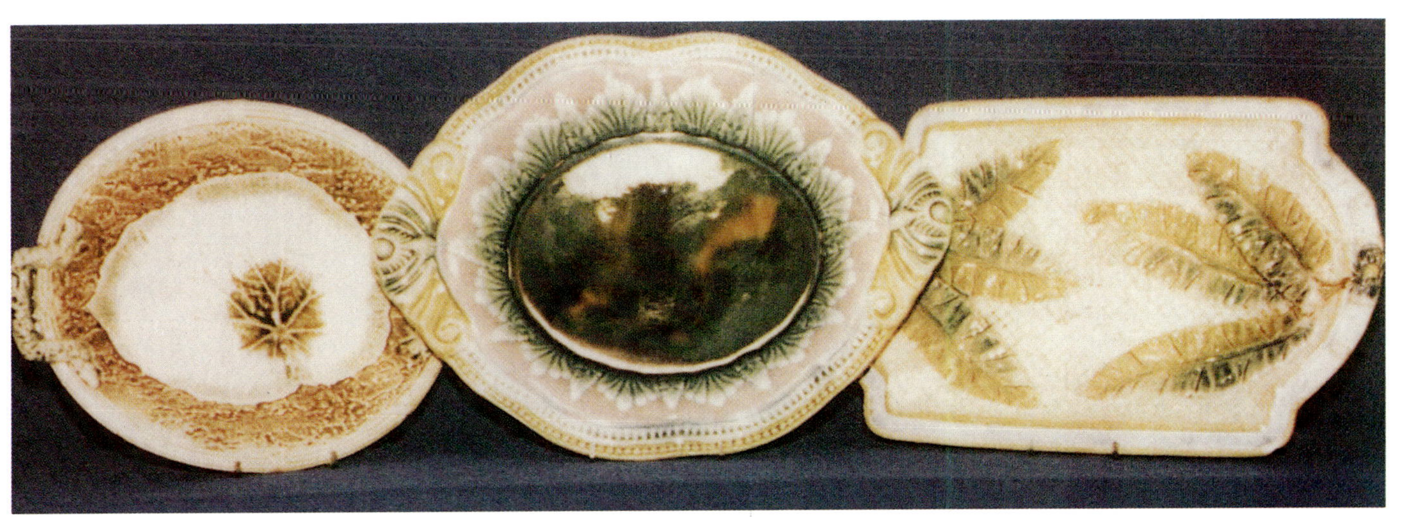

Left to Right:
Begonia leaf on bark platter – **$125**

Mottled center oval bread tray, pink border – **$375**

Banana leaf and bow platter – **$50**

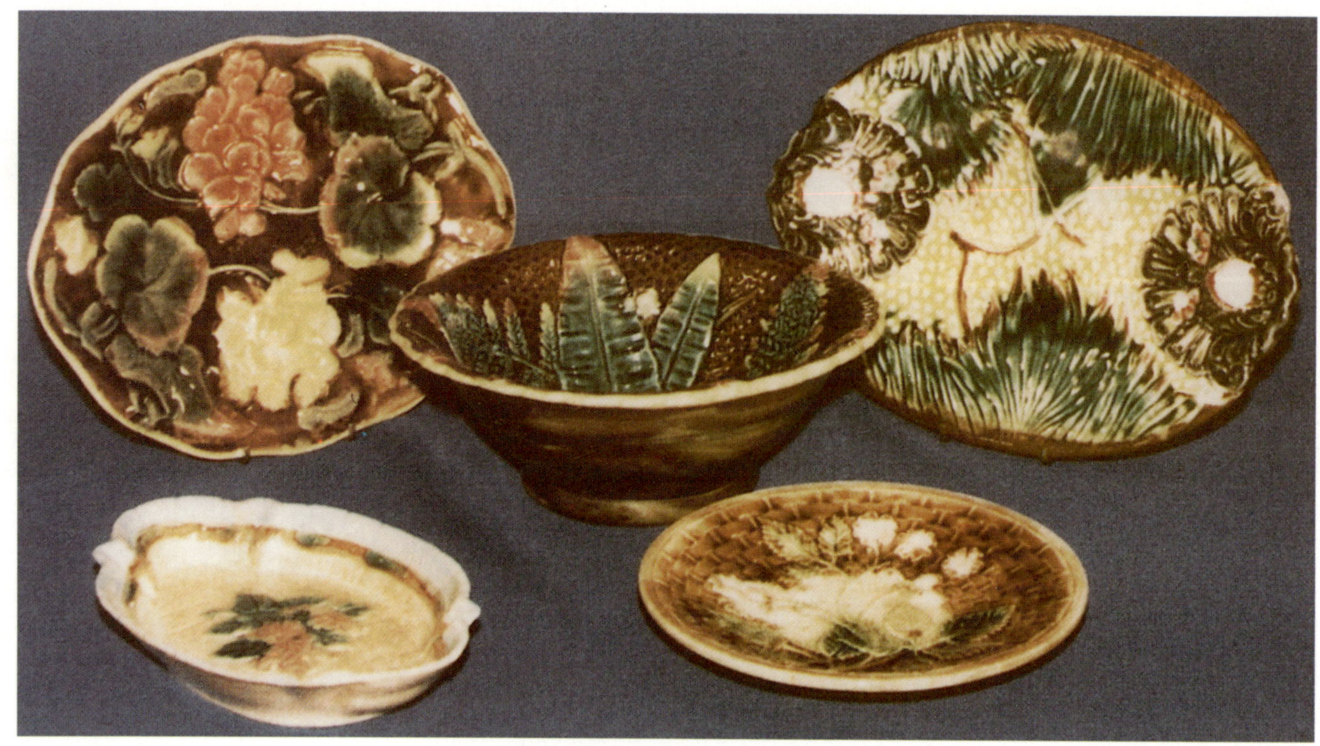

Front Row – Left to Right:
Oval picket fence and floral tray, 6" x 9 1/4" – **$25**

Blackberry and floral basket plate – **$50**

Back Row – Left to Right:
Geranium platter, 11 1/2" – **$100**

Leaf and fern deep bowl – **$150**

Cameo platter, 12 1/2" – **$100**

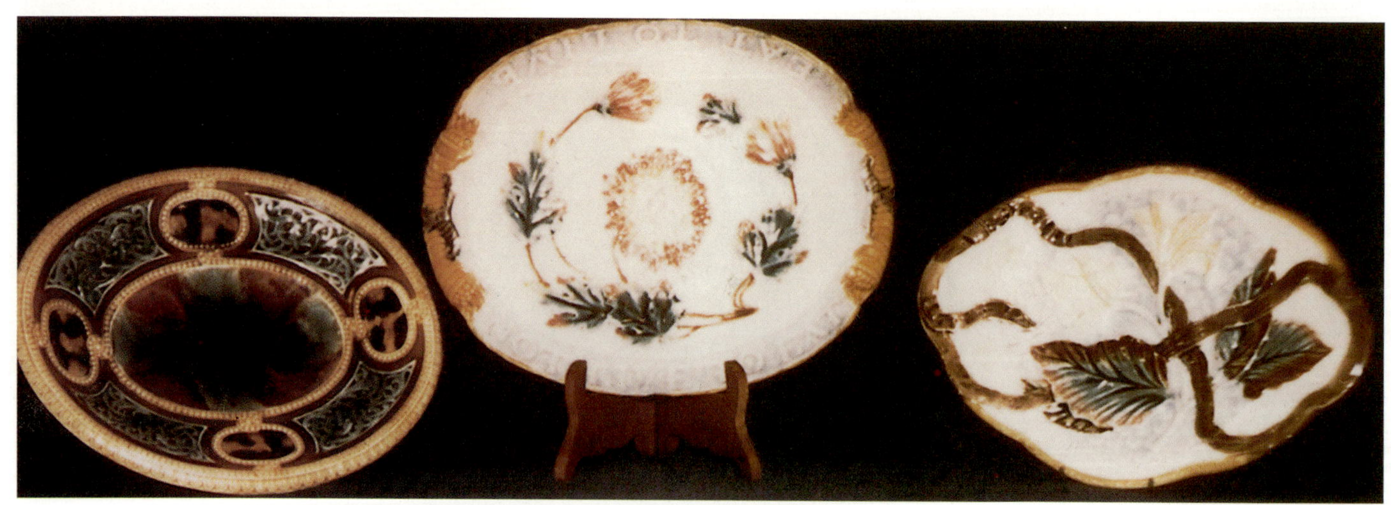

Left to Right:
Footed platter, 12", mottled green and brown center with cobalt blue accents – **$325**

Aster bread platter reads "Eat to Live Not Live to Eat" – **$275**

English belt buckle and floral platter, 12 1/2" – **$150**

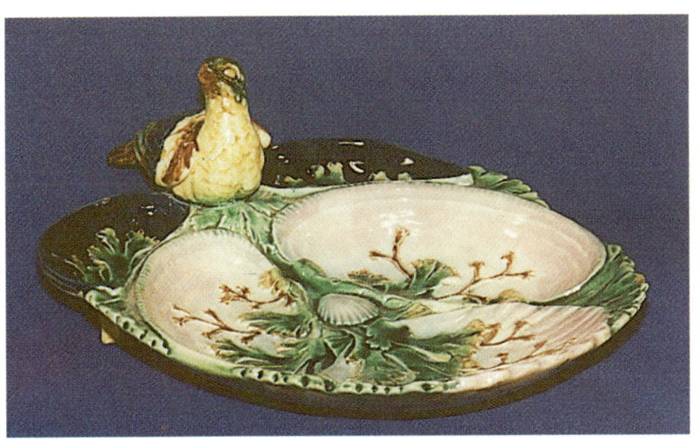

Shell serving dish with a bird sitting on the edge, cobalt blue, green and brown, 13 1/2" long.
$450

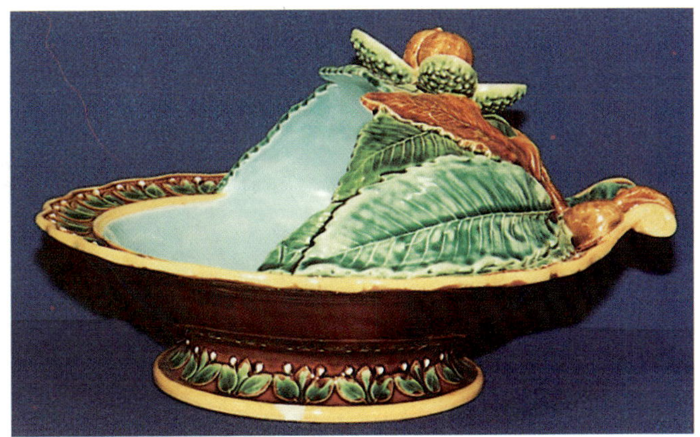

Minton chestnut dish with turquoise interior – **$1,100**

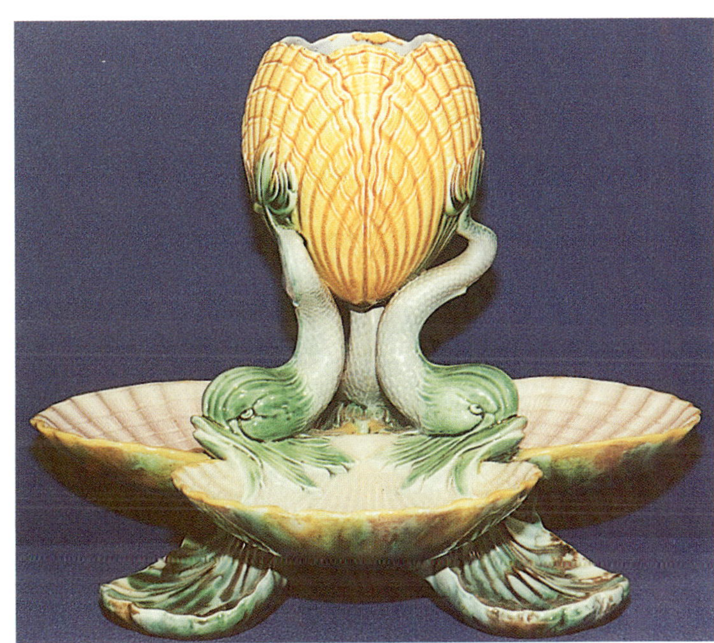

A shell condiment dish with a yellow shell supported up in the middle by three dolphins, 9 x 11 1/2".
$1200

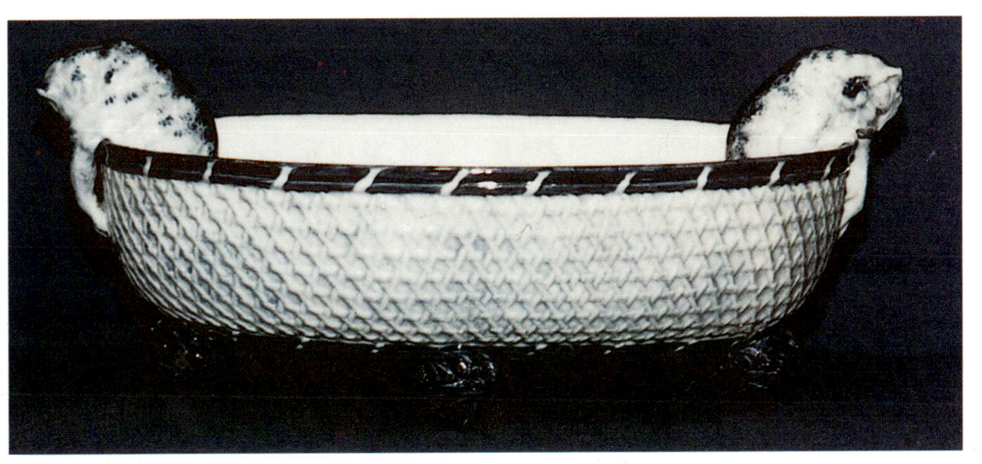

Minton blue and white cat dish with cats reaching over on both ends, 5" h x 7 1/2" w x 12" l.
$850

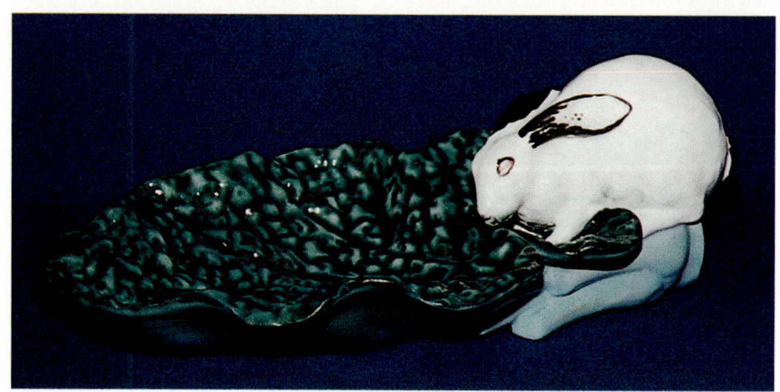

Minton Cabbage Leaf Dish with white rabbit on it, 9 1/2" l.
$3000

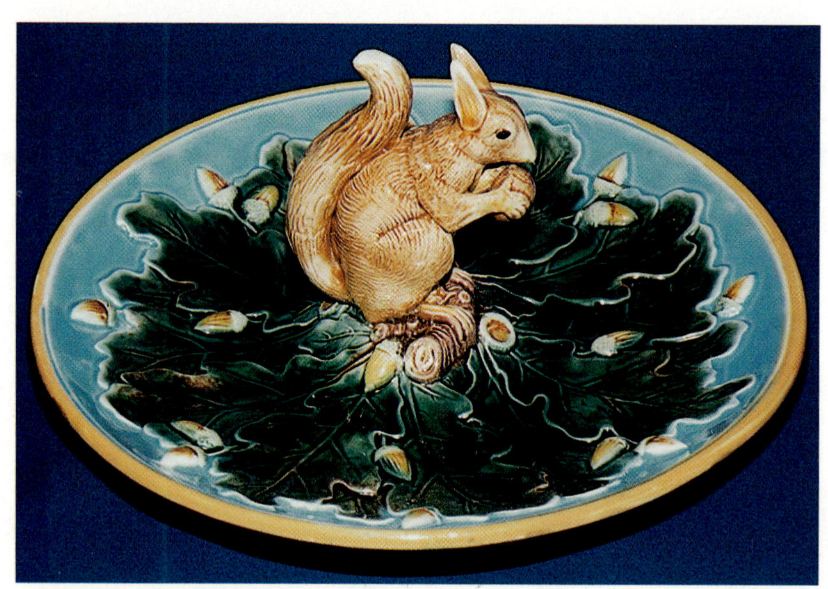

George Jones squirrel nut dish.
$1400

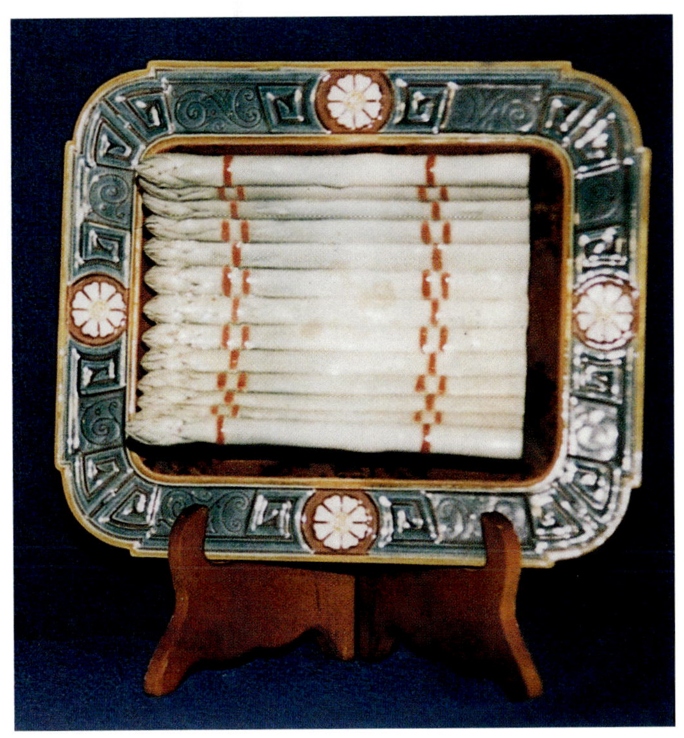

Minton asparagus server.
$600

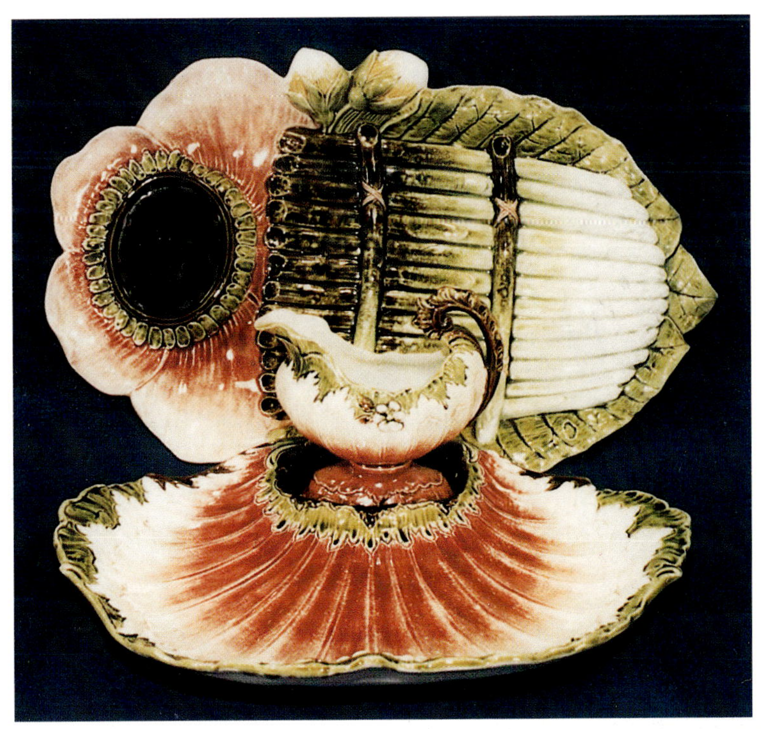

Austria asparagus server with creamer, 10" x 13".
$375

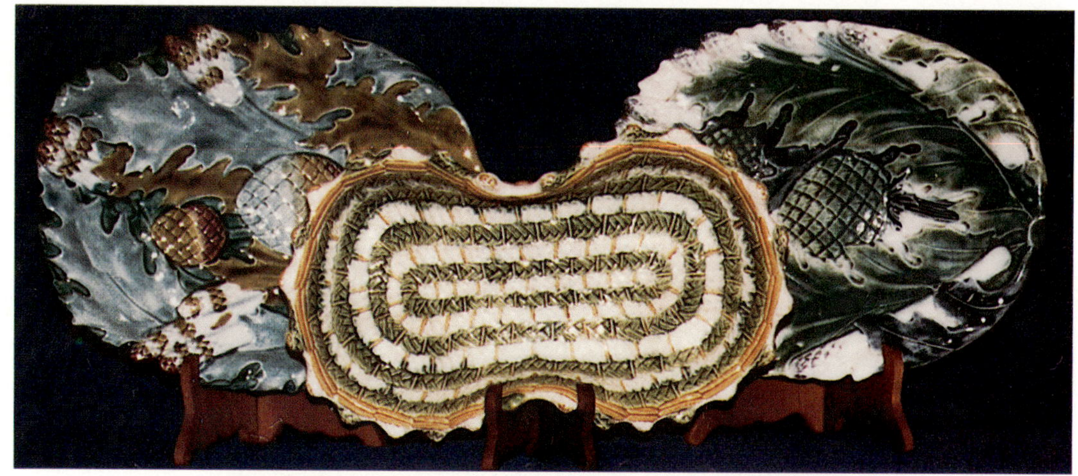

Front Row:
Basketweave asparagus platter, 8 1/2" x 15" – **$275**

Back Row:
Asparagus platter, turquoise, green and purple, 11" x 14" – **$350**

French asparagus platter, 14" – **$225**

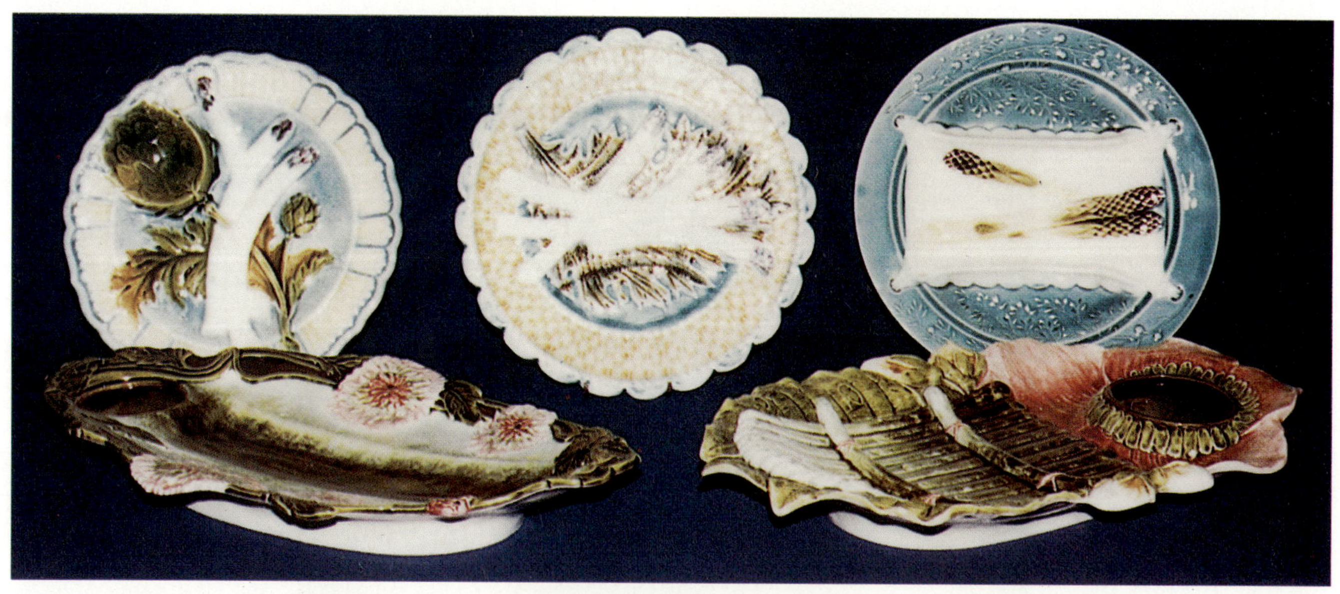

Front Row:
Two Julius Dressler asparagus platters
Left: 10" x 17" l Right: 11" x 16" l.
$275 each

Back Row:
Three French asparagus plates one is 9 1/2" the other two are 10" – **$250 each**

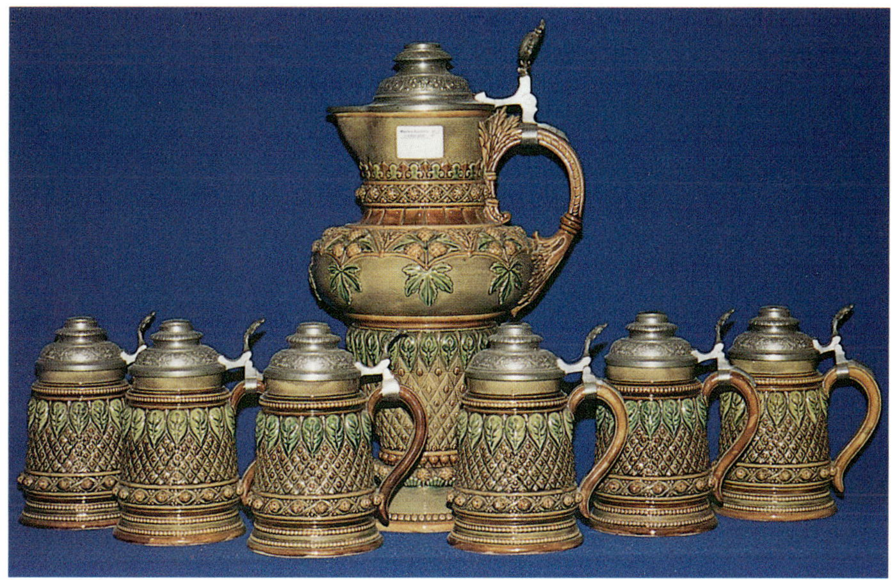

Wilhelm Schiller & Son large tankard (15"), with pewter top and six matching steins (61/2") that have pewter tops also. The tankard is marked Patent 52, steins are marked 54. Pineapple design in relief.

$1300/set

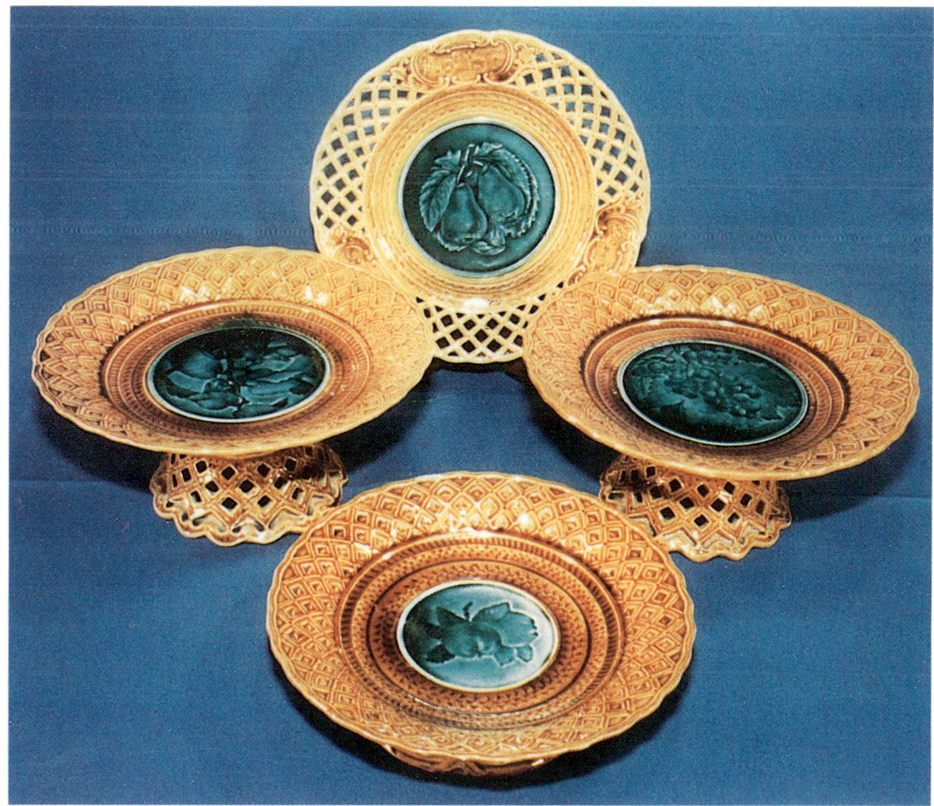

Rubelles S & M set which includes three compotes, and a plate, with a green scenic center of fruit or flowers.

$40-60 each

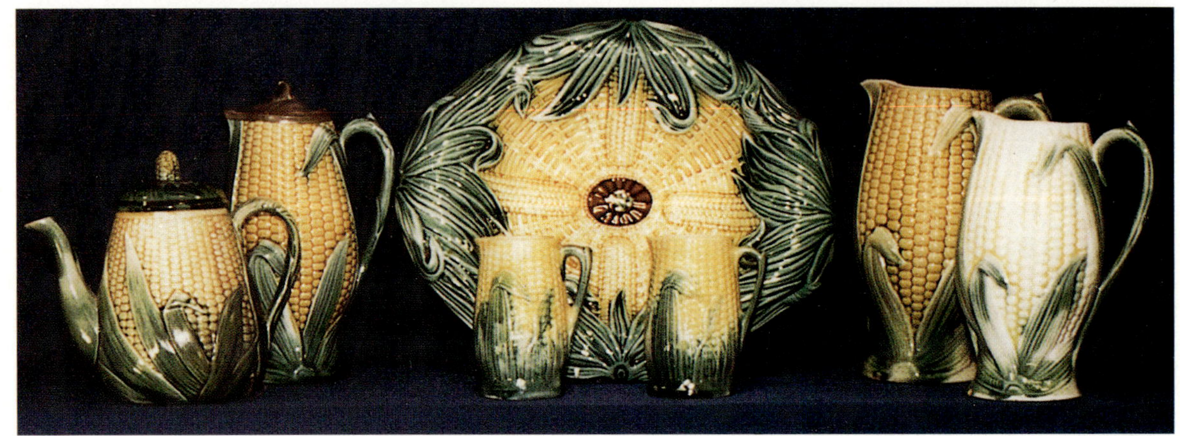

Left to Right:
Corn teapot, 7" – **$110**

Corn pitcher – **$375**

Corn bread platter, 13 1/2" – **$475**

2 corn creamers in front of the platter, 4 1/2" – **$50 ea.**

2 corn pitchers, one is 8 1/2" the other 8" – **$175 ea.**

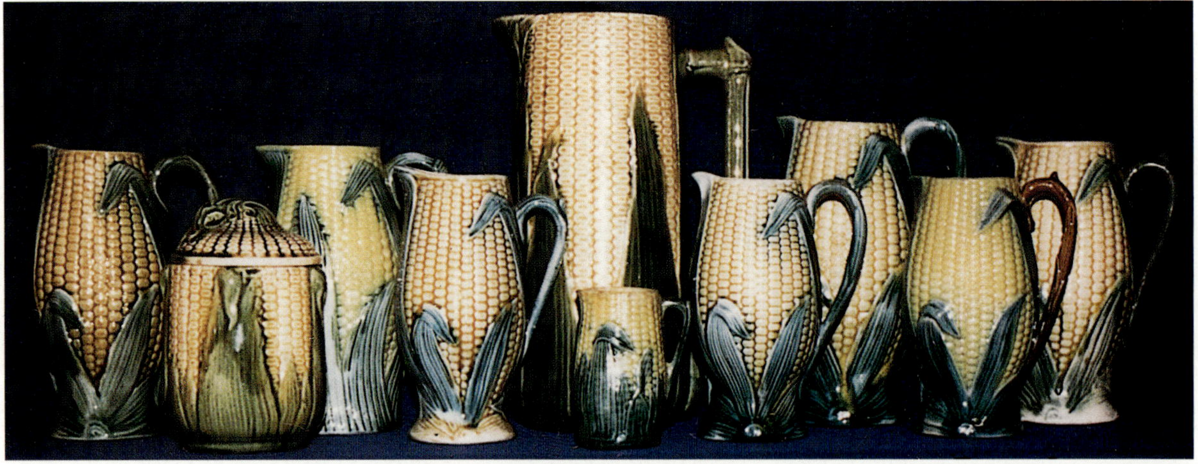

Corn style collection of pitchers and a covered jar, ranging in size (from left to right:) 8 1/2" , 8", 12 1/4", 7 1/2", 4 1/2", 9" and the jar is 7" tall.
$75-175 each

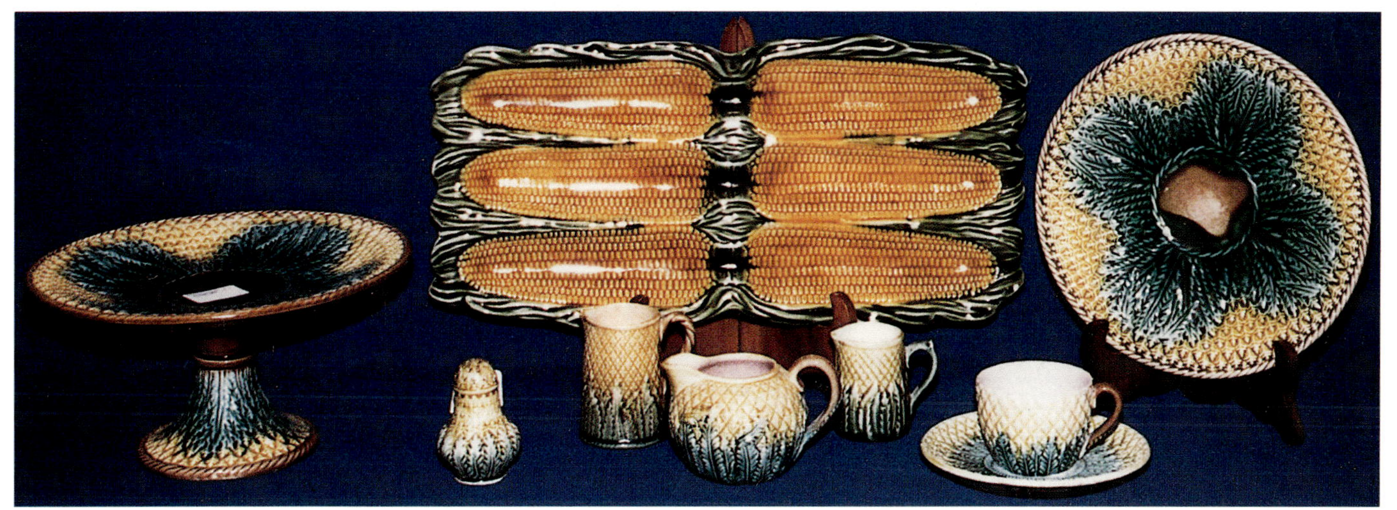

Back Row – Left to Right
Pineapple cake stand, 5 1/4" h x 10" d – **$250**

Portugal corn tray for six ears of corn, (not part of the set), 7 1/2" x 16 1/2" – **$100**

Pineapple plate, 9" – **$225**

Front Row – Left to Right
Pineapple shaker, 3" – **$100**

Three pineapple creamers – **$75-100 each**

Pineapple cup and saucer – **$200**

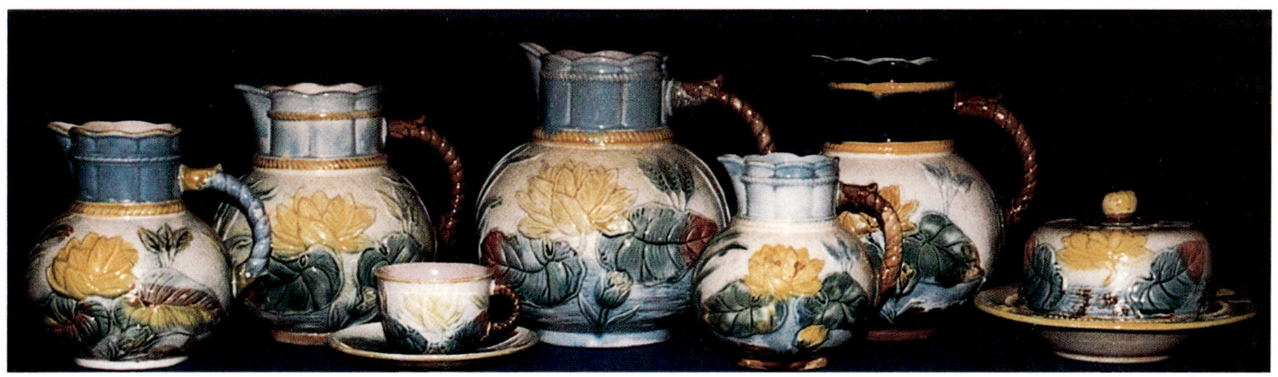

Several pieces of a Samuel Lear water lily collection, including five different sized pitchers 6 1/2", 7 1/2", 8 1/2", 8" has a cobalt blue top, and a 5 1/2". The set also includes a cup and saucer and a butter dish.

Pitchers – **$150-225**
Pitcher with cobalt rim – **$275**
Cup and saucer – **$175**
Covered butter dish – **$400**

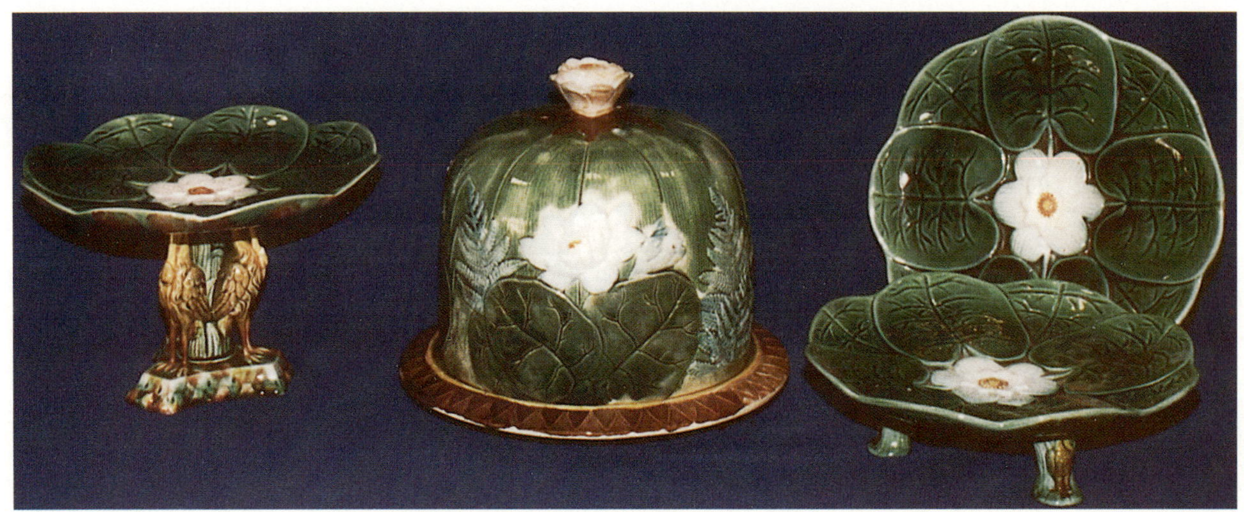

Left to Right:
Pond lily cake stand with three storks holding the plate up, 6" h x 9 1/4" d – **$275**

Holdcroft water lily cheese bell, 8 1/2"h – **$825**

Pond lily plate, 9 1/4" – **$125**

Pond lily three footed plate with storks on feet, 9"d x 3" h – **$175**

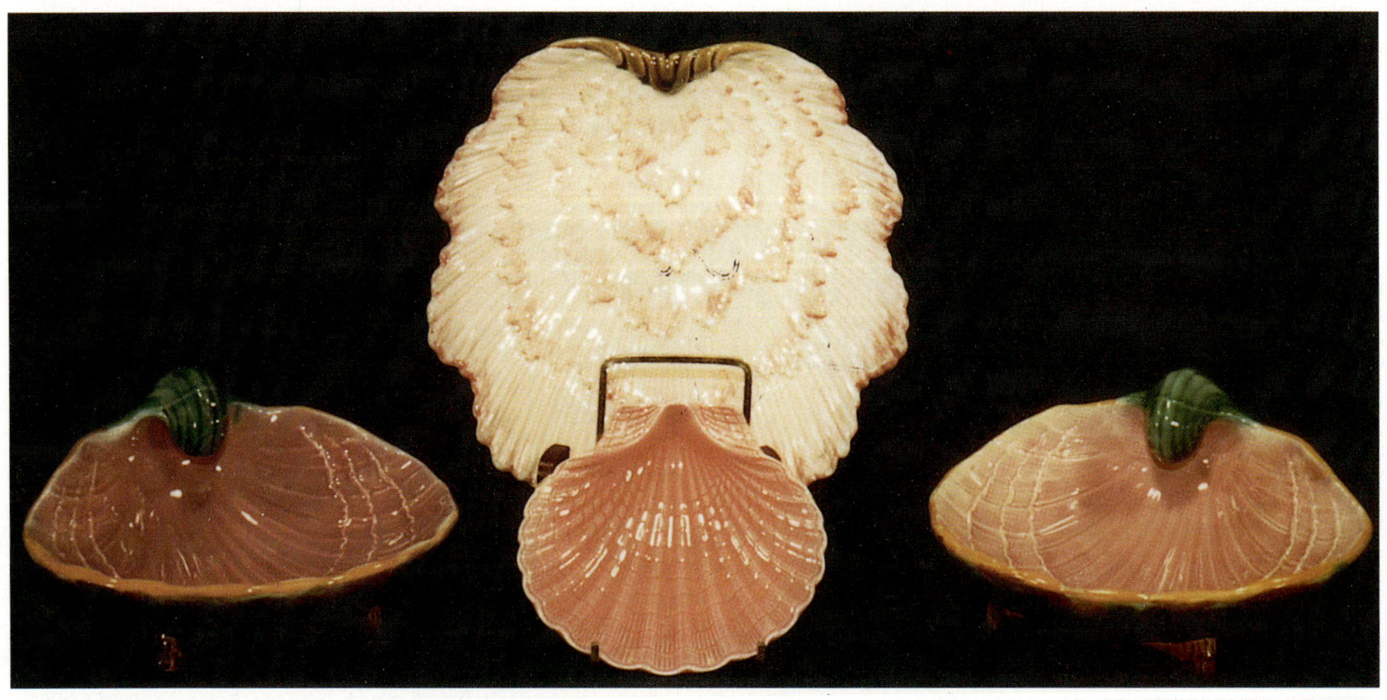

Set of George Jones designed lavender shell dishes.

On the far left and right are two bowls with feet – **$250**
In the middle is a condiment tray – **$300**
And the big plate in the back – **$325**

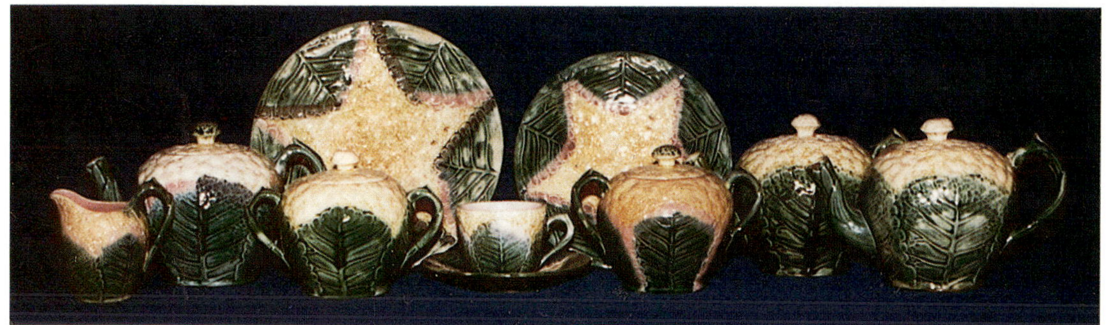

Etruscan cauliflower set that includes a 9" plate, 8" plate, 3 piece tea set, cup and saucer, two sugars, and a teapot.

9" plates – **$100-200**
8" plate – **$200-225**
Creamer – **$200**
Teapot – **$300**
Sugar – **$200**
Cup and saucer – **$225**
2 Sugars – **$200 each**
Teapot – **$300**

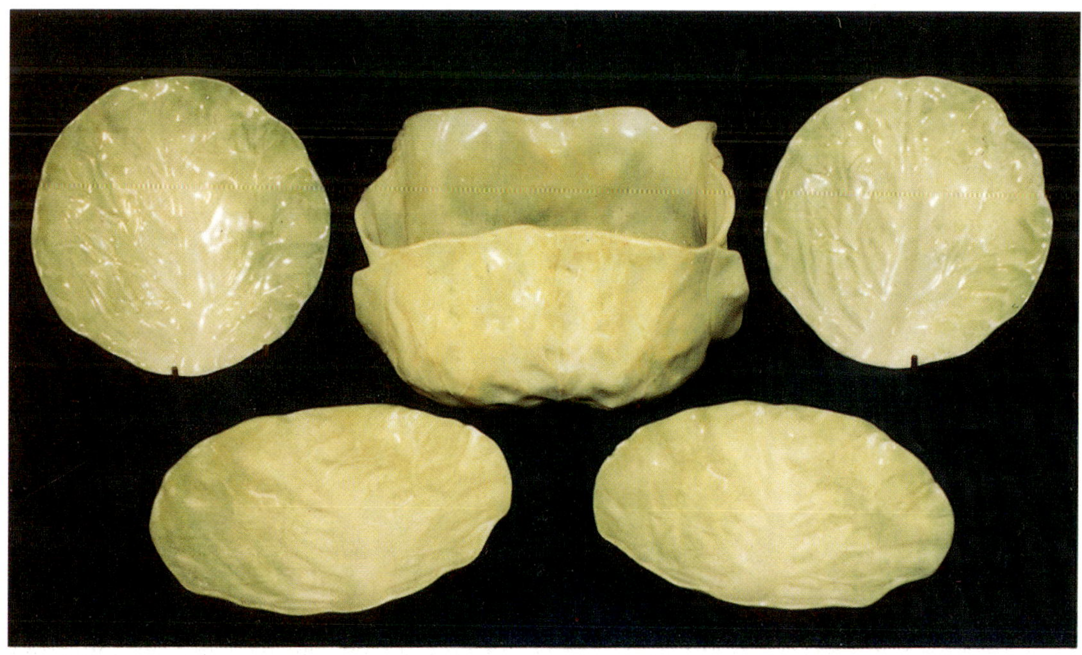

Lettuce leaf salad bowl and four of the six plates that go to the set. The bowl is 9" sq. x 5" h. The plates are 7 1/2" d – **$150 each piece**

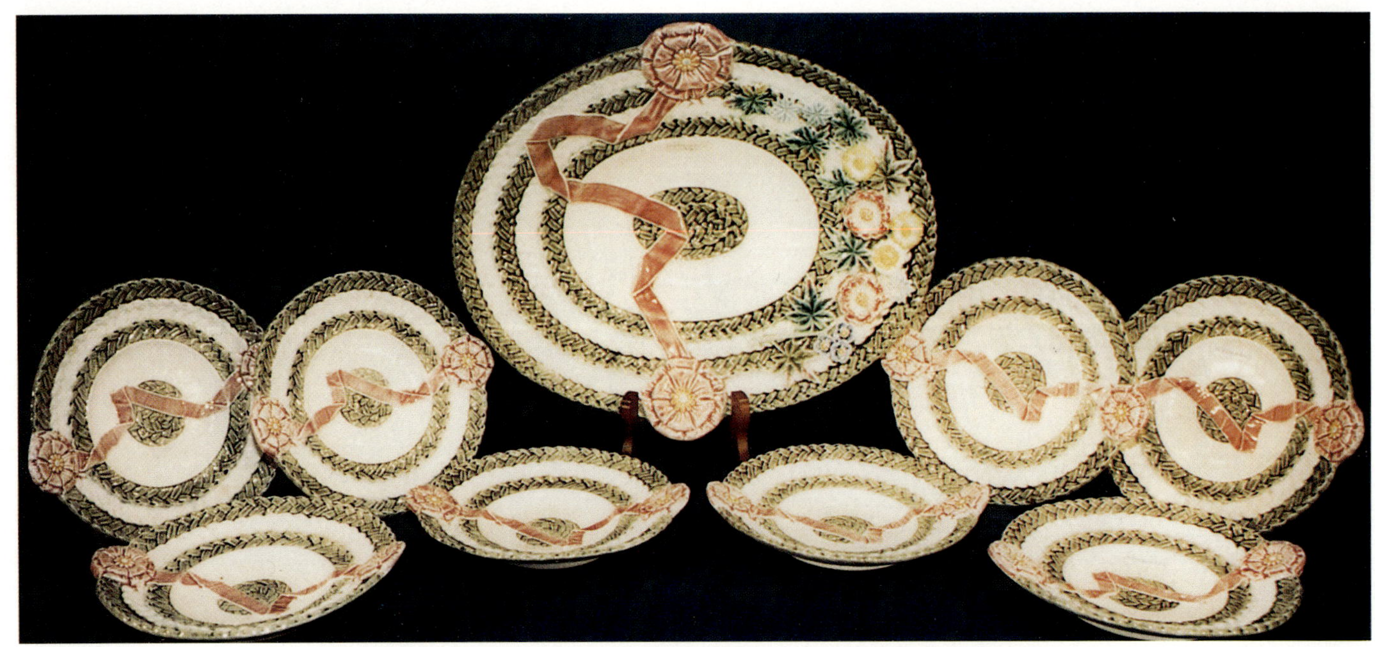

Wedgwood ribbon and bow platter and eight matching dishes, 11" x 13" and the dishes are 71/2" – **$1550 a set**

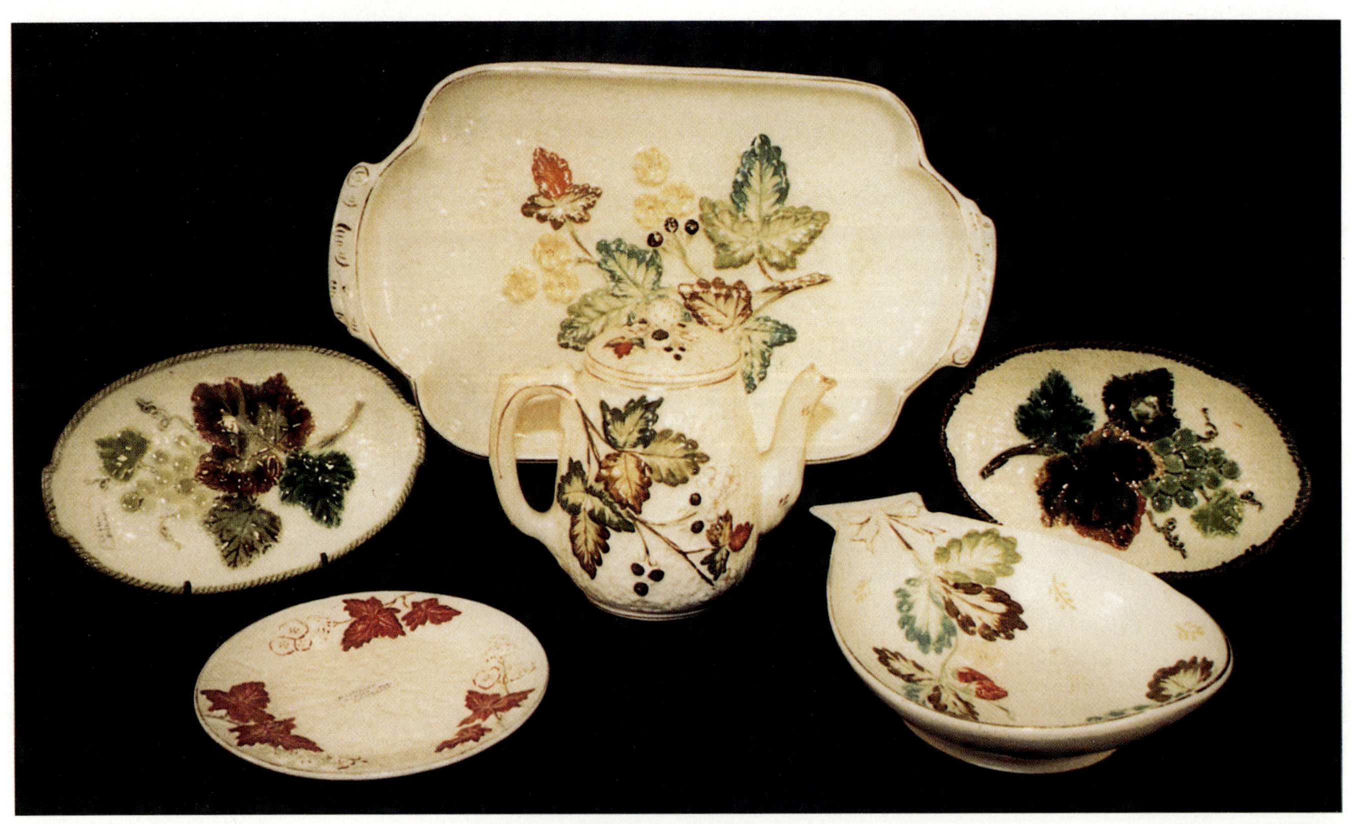

Front Row – Left to Right

Avalon plate, 7" – **$22** & Avalon strawberry bowl, 71/2" x 91/2" – **$75**

Back Row – Left to Right

Two Clifton oval grape pattern relish dishes found at the far left and right. They are both 51/2" x 9" – **$75 ea.**

Avalon Coffee Pot – **$25** Platter, 91/2" x 161/2" – **$100**

Left to Right:
Palissy Plaque with two lizards, four frogs, one turtle, 12", Portuguese – **$1350**

Palissy Urn with serpent handles and faces with drapes of vines and berries, 10"h x 11" w – **$1000**

Palissy Plaque with lizards and snakes on the grass, 9" d – **$1000**

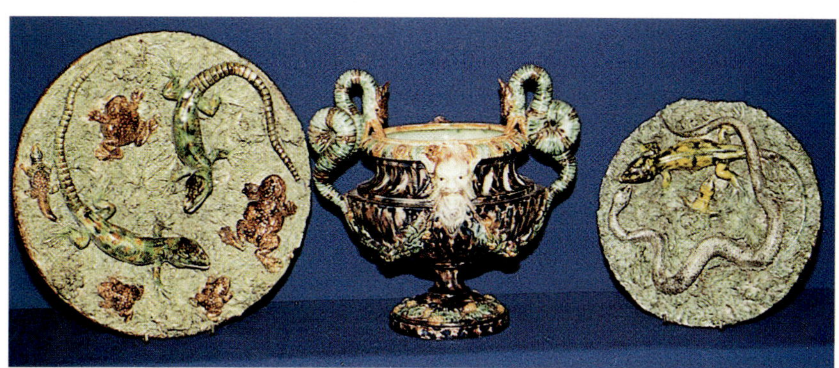

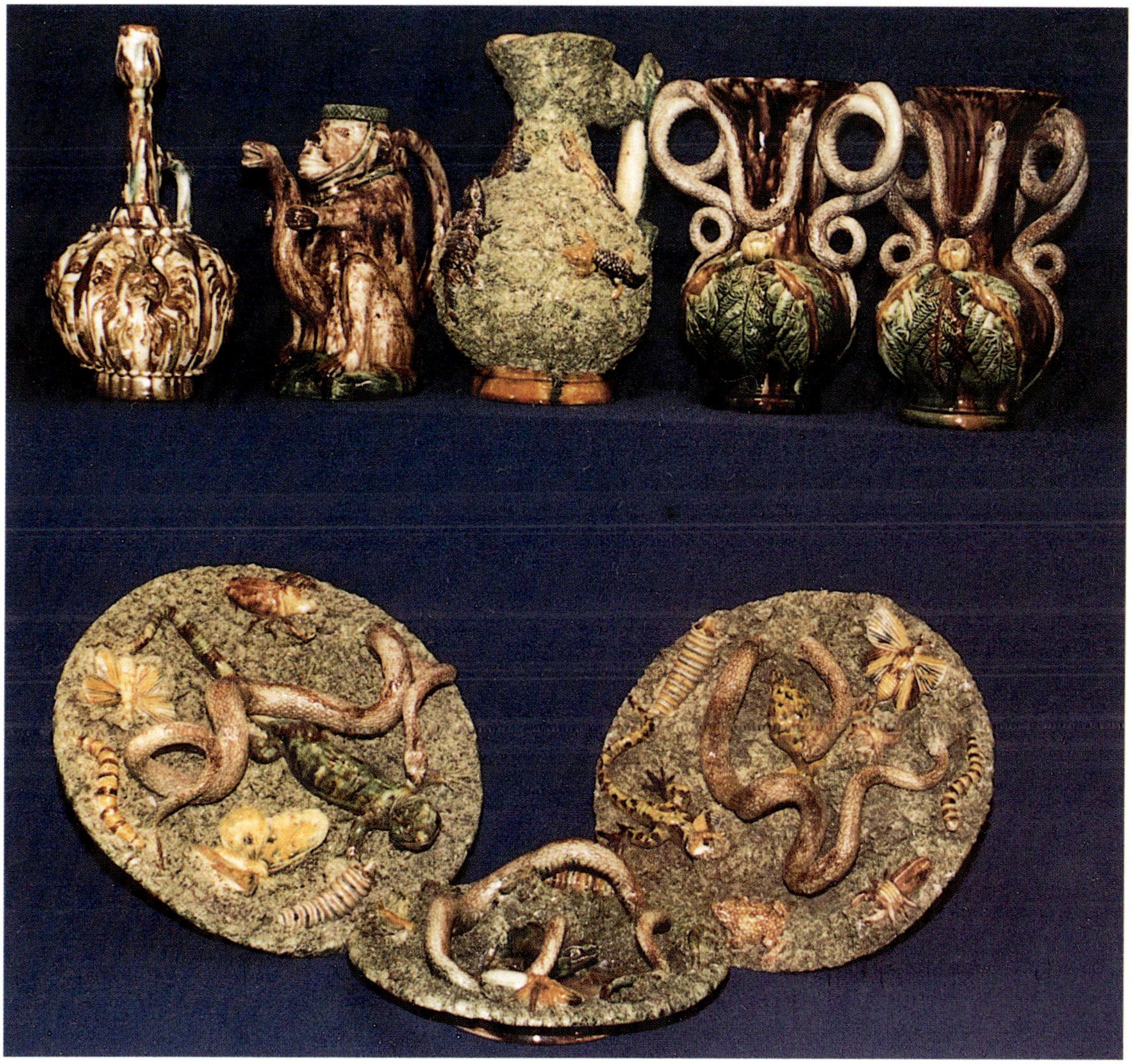

This collection is all done in the Palissy style by Jose A. Cunha, Caldas Rainha, Portugal.

Top Row
Ewer – **$50**
Figural Monkey Pitcher, 9" – **$600**
Ewer, 11" high – **$325**
Pair of Vases, 10" tall – **$550 ea.**

Bottom Row
Plaques – **$1000 each**

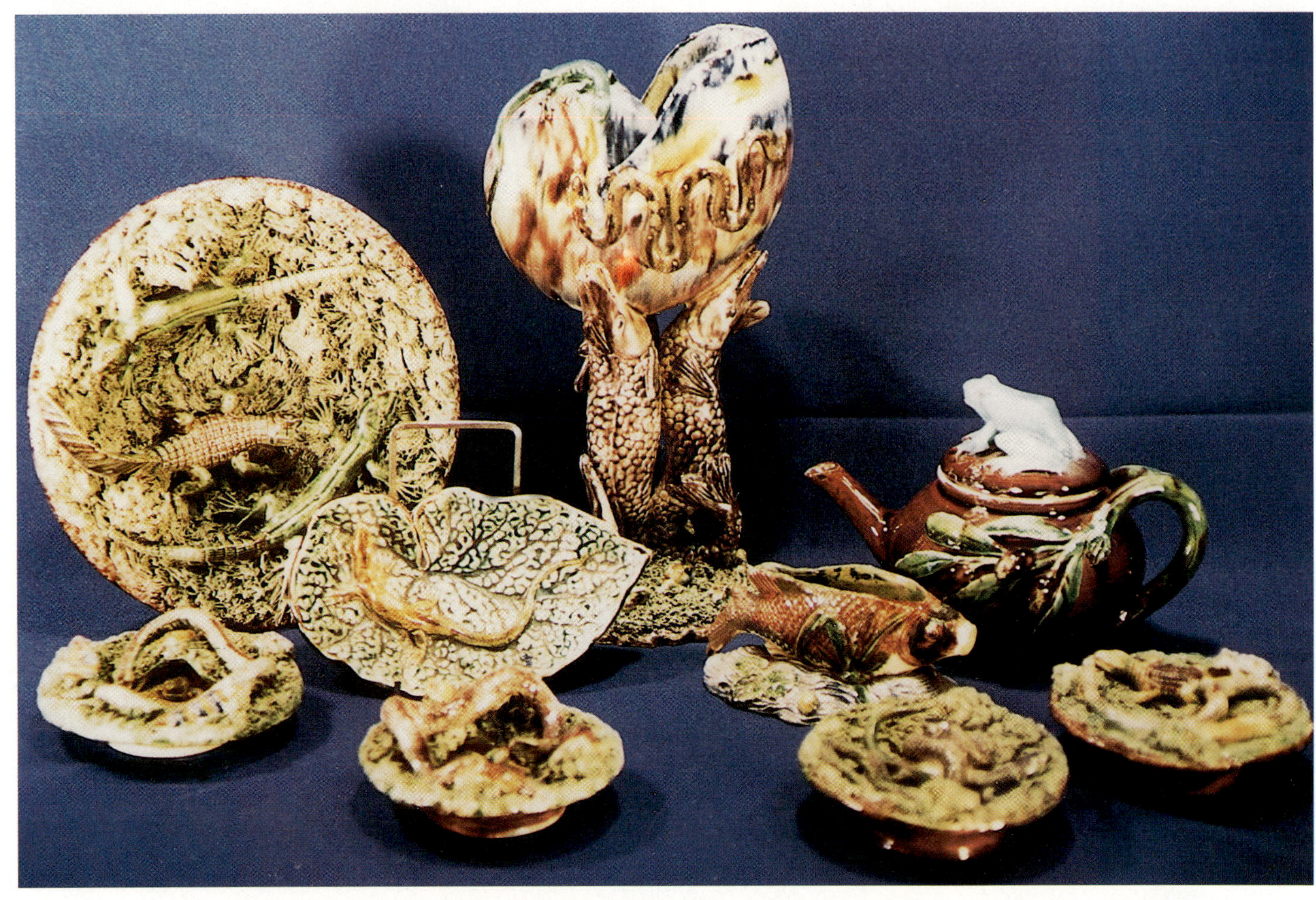

All these pieces done in the style of Palissy.

Front Row – Left to Right:
Four mafra small plaques, 41/2" d – **$300 each**

Middle Row – Left to Right:
Begonia leaf with lizard, 61/2" l – **$300**

Fish calling card holder, 21/2" x 51/4" – **$125**

Back Row - Left to Right:
Plaque with two lizards and an alligator, 81/2" – **$550**

A shell with three alligators supporting it, and a lizard and snake on shell, 11" – **$500**

Teapot with frog on the lid – **$775**

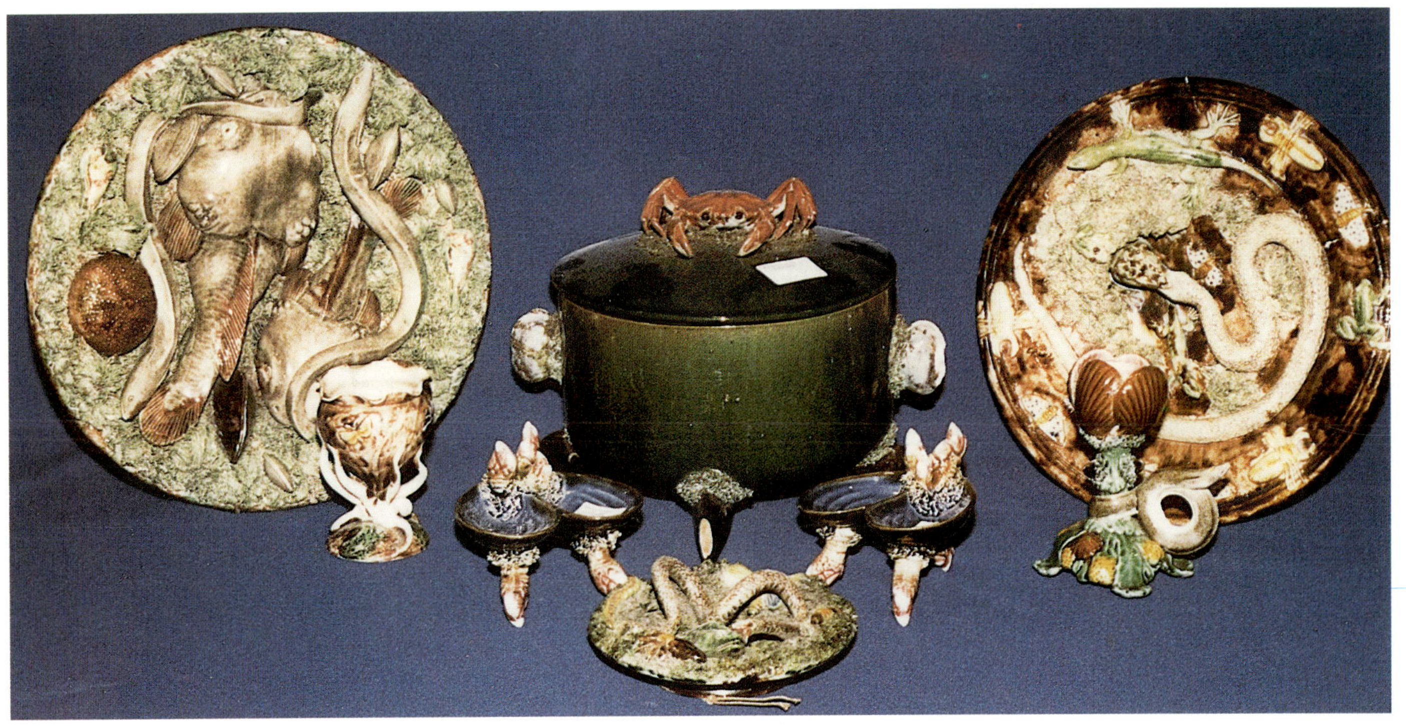

Front:
Cunha Palissy plate with a snake, frog, beetle and butterfly on it – **$ 550**

Middle – Left to Right:
Palissy vase with four butterflies in relief, signed "T.S.", 4" – **$175**

Two Palissy style shells with coral feet – **$50**

Palissy finger candle stick, snake handle, 5" – **$125**

Back – Left to Right:
Mafra Caldus Palissy charger, with two large fish, two snakes and shells, 12" – **$925**

Portugal green covered pot with a red crab on the lid, shell feet and handles, 8" h – **$75**

Palissy charger, with a snake, lizard in a cave, frogs, beetles and butterflies, 10 1/2" – **$550**

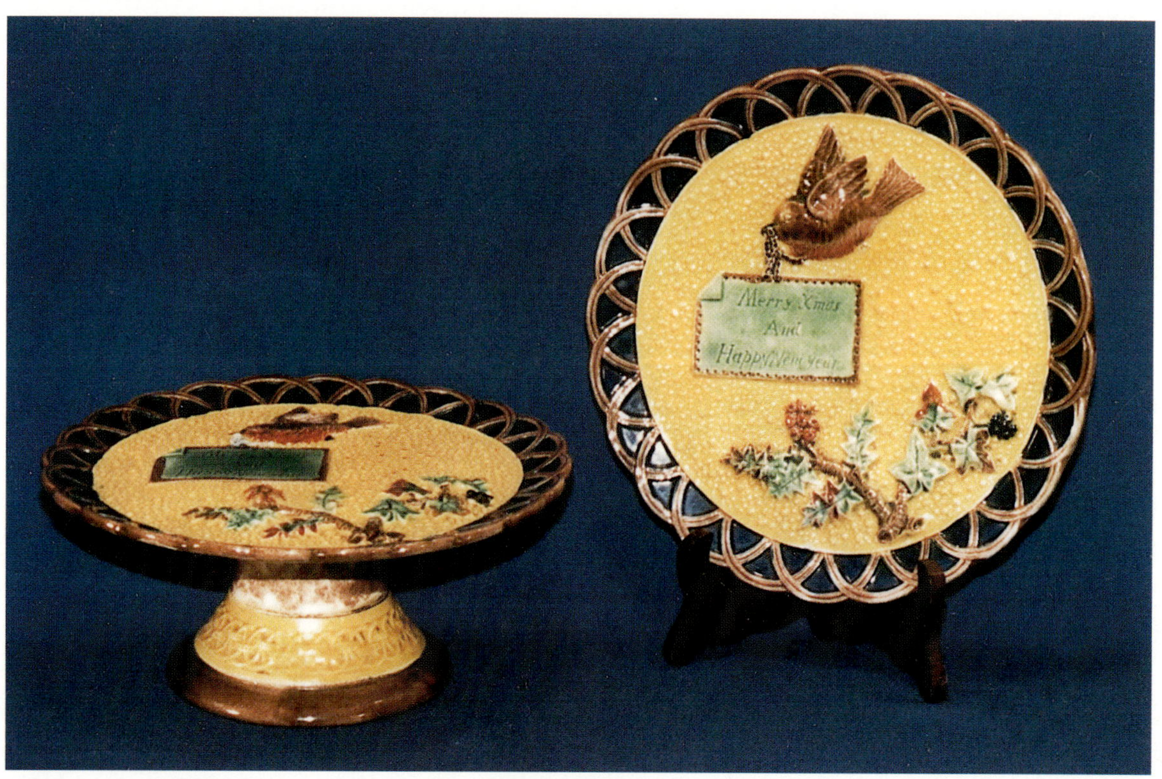

Left to Right:
Eureka pottery "Merry Christmas & Happy New Year" cake stand – **$1200**
Eureka pottery "Merry Christmas & Happy New Year" plate, 9 1/2" – **$1100**

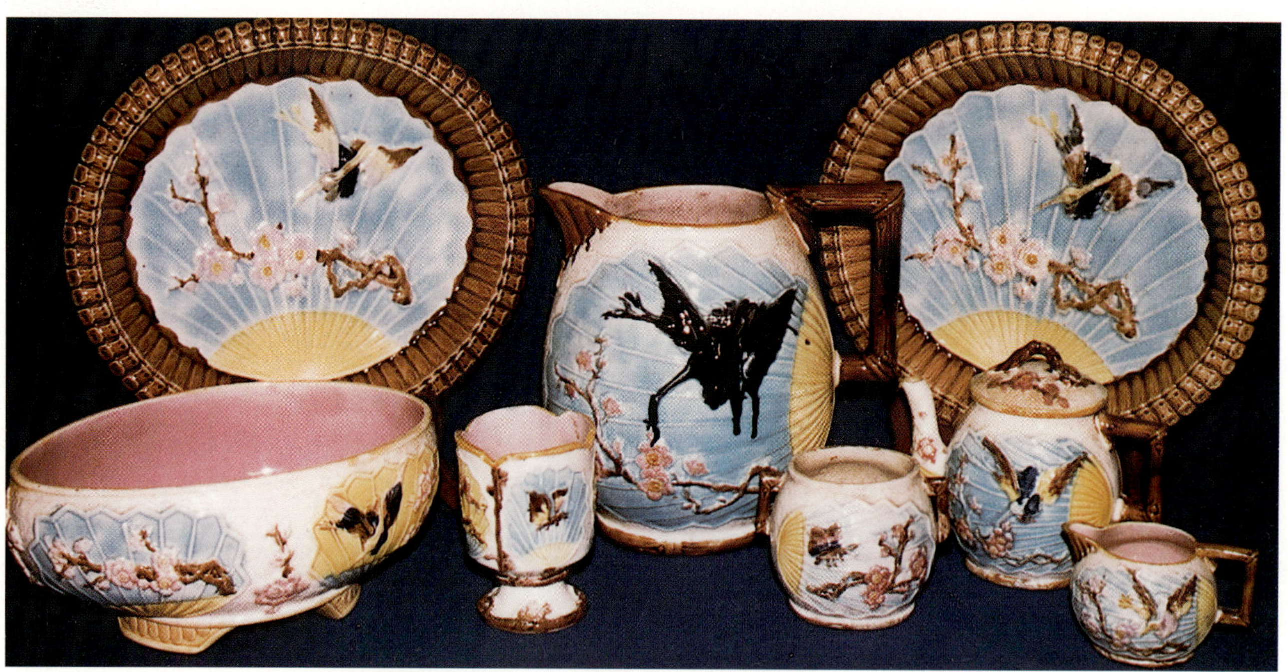

Wardles bird and fan collection included in photo is, two platters 12 1/2", pitcher 9", footed bowl 10 1/2" l, spooner, sugar, teapot, creamer.

Oval footed bowl – **$200** Spooner – **$200** Sugar and Creamer – **$225** Teapot – **$125**
Platters – **$175 each** Pitcher – **$225**

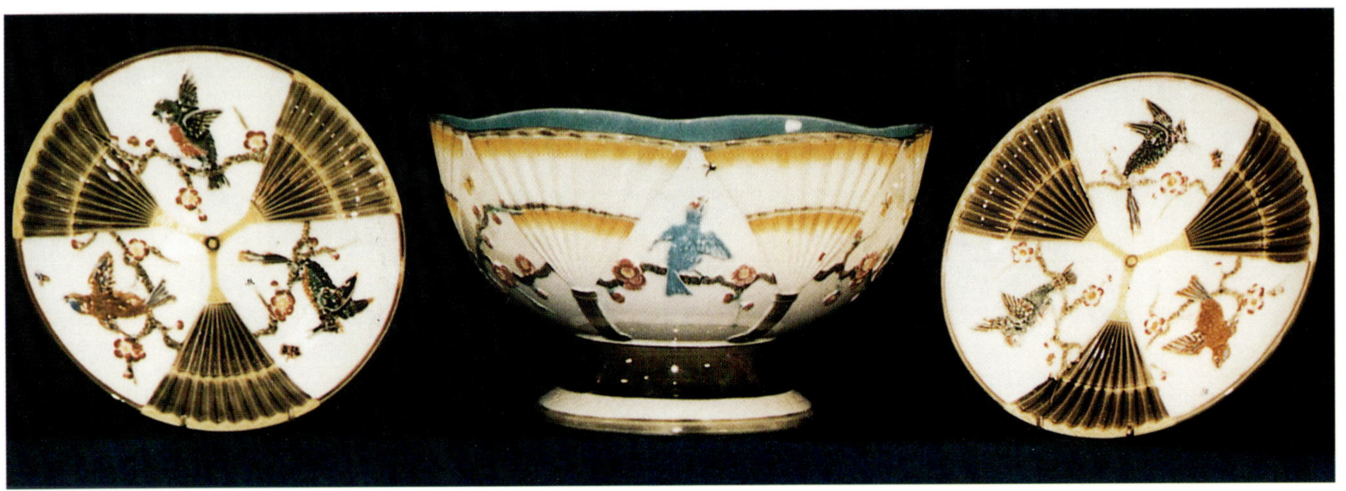

Wedgwood bird and fan plates, 9" (two shown), with a punch bowl 7"h x 12"d in the middle.
$1000 set

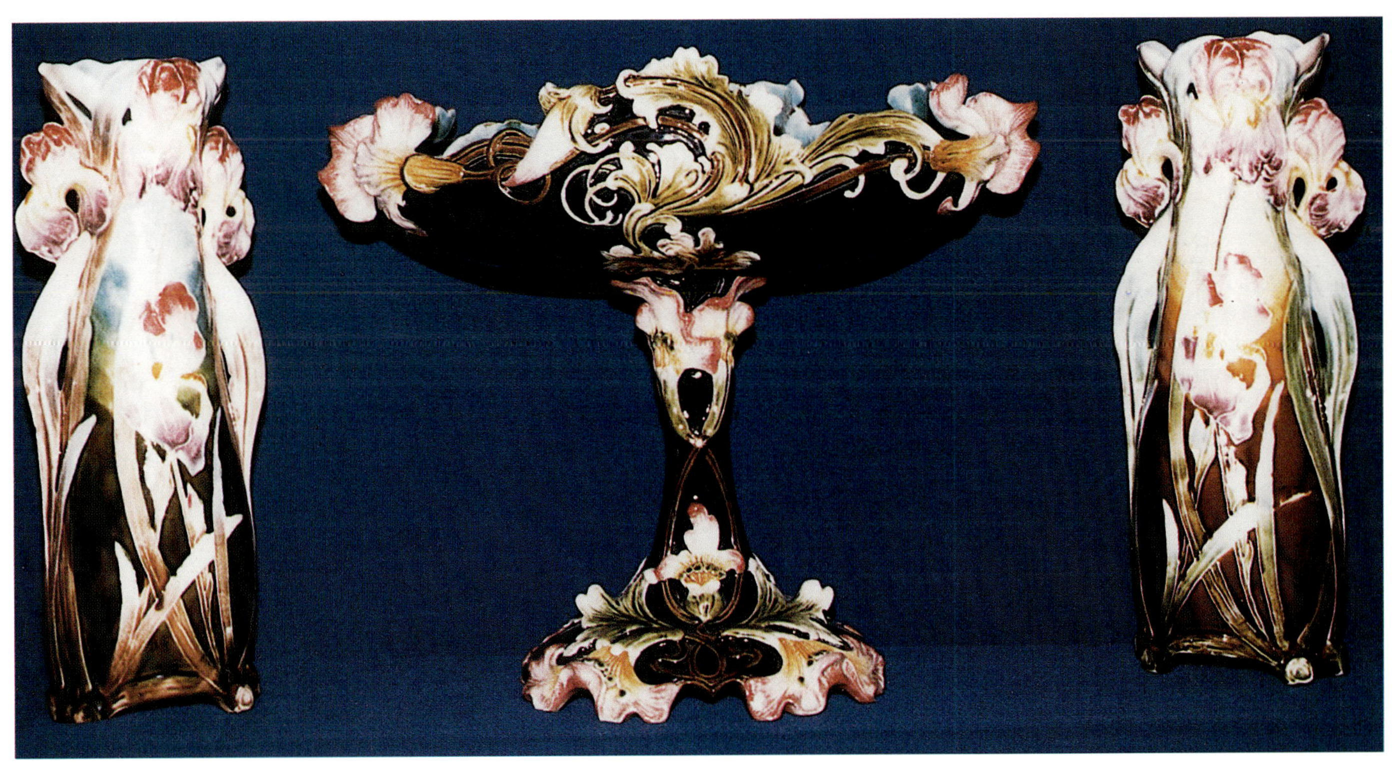

Two continental art noveau style vases, 15" tall – **$325 each**

Wilhelm Schiller & Son art noveau compote, 15" h x 17 1/2" w – **$1000**

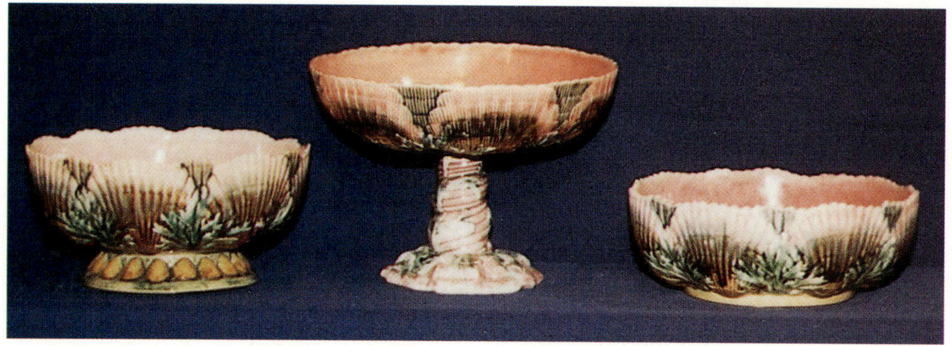

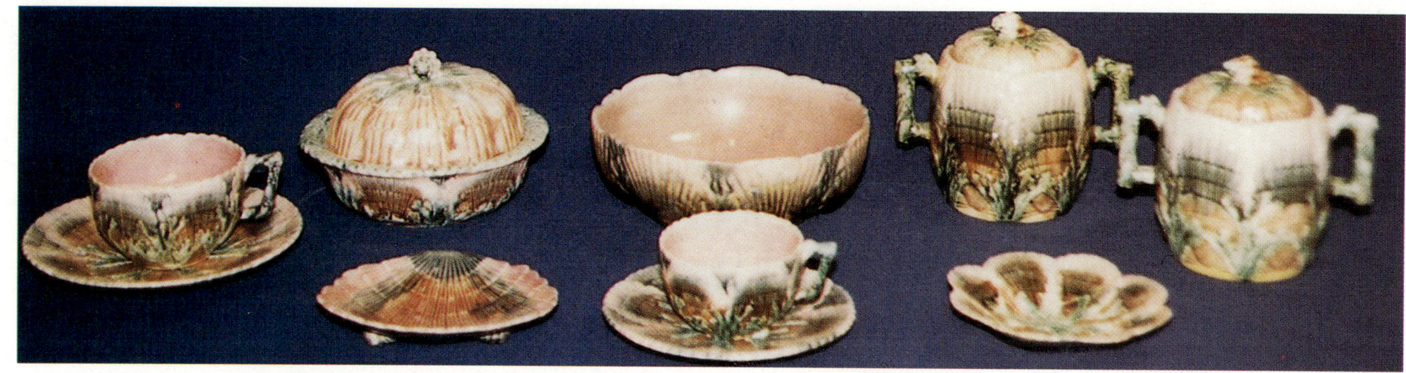

Etruscan shell and seaweed pieces.

Top Picture – Left to Right:

Salad bowl – **$300** Footed compote – **$250** Bowl – **$200**

Bottom Picture – Front Row – Left to Right:

Shell shaped ice cream dish with feet – **$125**
Cup and Saucer – **$150 set** Scalloped edge sauce dish – **$125**

Bottom Picture – Back Row – Left to Right:

Cup and Saucer – **$150 set** Covered butter – **$1000**
Bowl – **$200** 2-Covered Sugars – **$150**

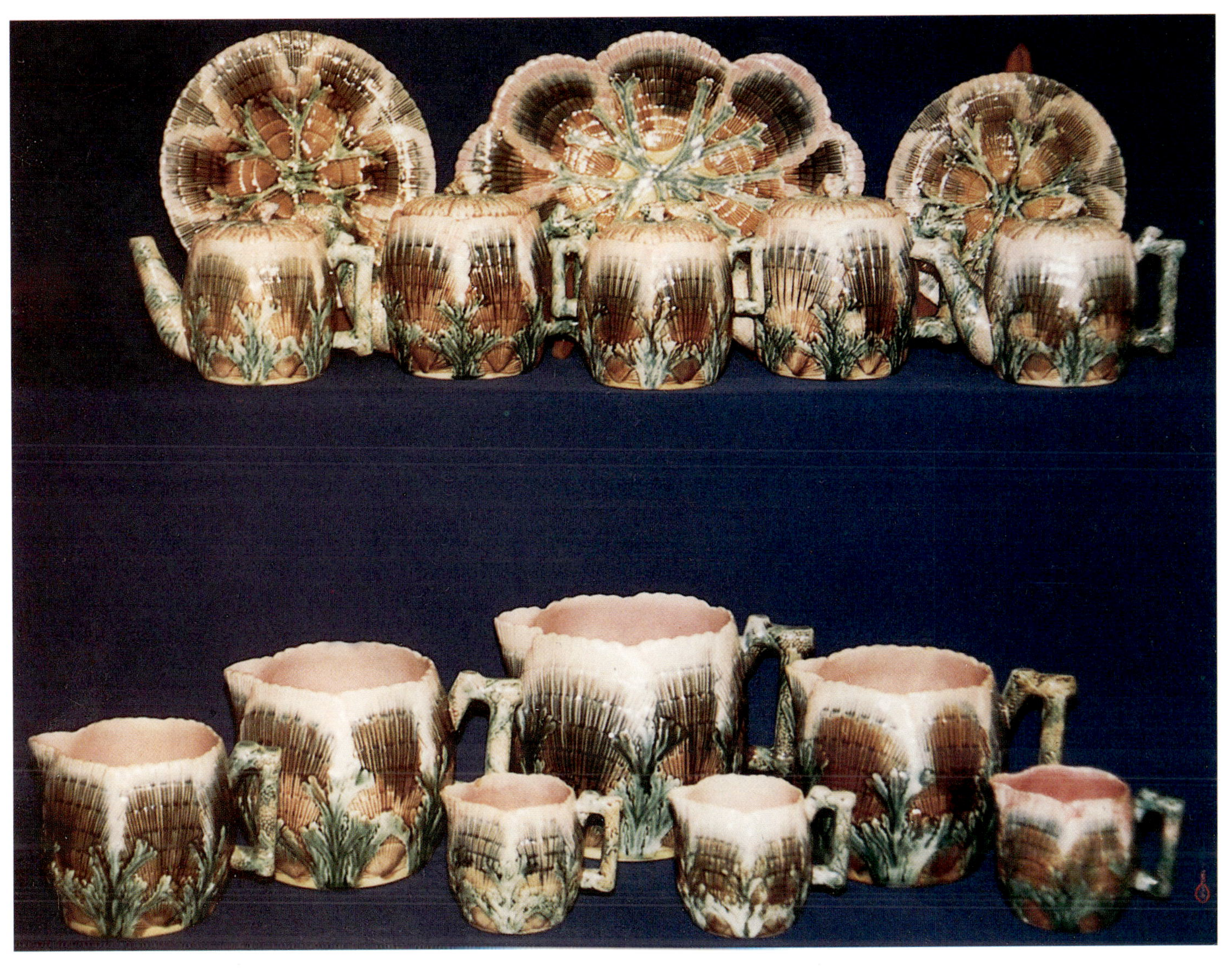

Etruscan shell and seaweed set.

Top of Picture – Front Row – Left to Right:

Teapot with straight spout – **$650** Teapot with bent spout – **$550**
Large Sugar – **$200** Teapot – **$375** Small Coffee Pot – **$650**

Top of Picture – Back Row – Left to Right:

Plate – **$225** Bread Platter – **$600** Plate – **$200**

Bottom of Picture – Front Row – Left to Right:
Three creamers – **$225**

Bottom of Picture – Back Row – Left to Right:
4 3/4 Pitcher – **$150** 5 3/4 Pitcher – **$250** 6 1/2 Pitcher – **$275** 5 1/2 Pitcher – **$300**

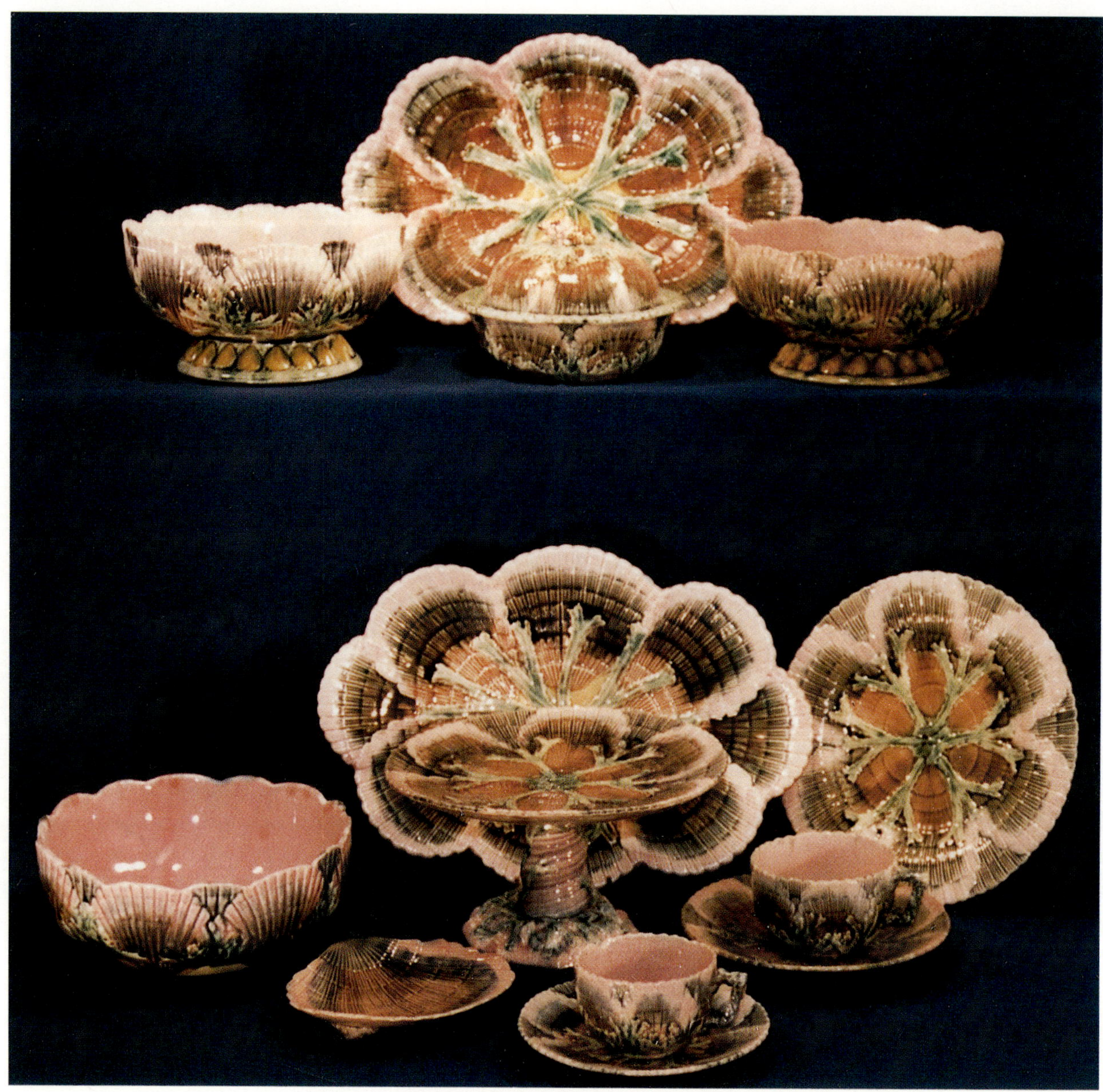

Etruscan shell and seaweed set including:

Top Row:

Two salad bowls, 8 1/4" – **$300 each**
Bread platter, 9 1/2" x 14" – **$600**
Covered butter dish – **$1000**

Bottom Row:

Bowl, 8 1/2" – **$200**
Platter, 9 1/2" x 14" – **$600**
Plate, 9 1/2" – **$200**
Cake Stand, 9" – **$1000**
Shell Shaped dish – **$125**
Two cups and saucers – **$150 each set**

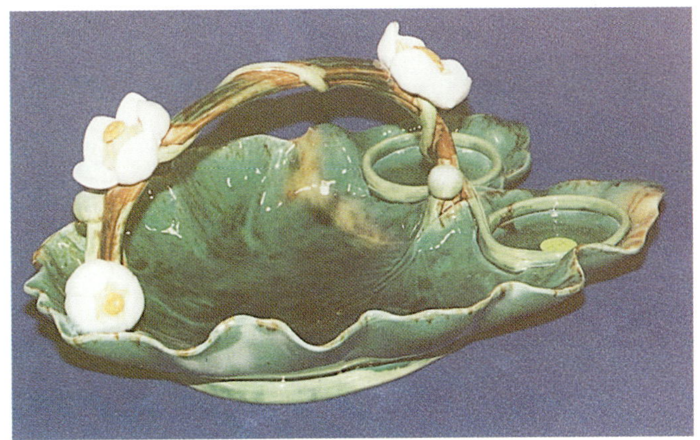

Minton strawberry server with vine handle and strawberry blossoms, 13" long.
$825

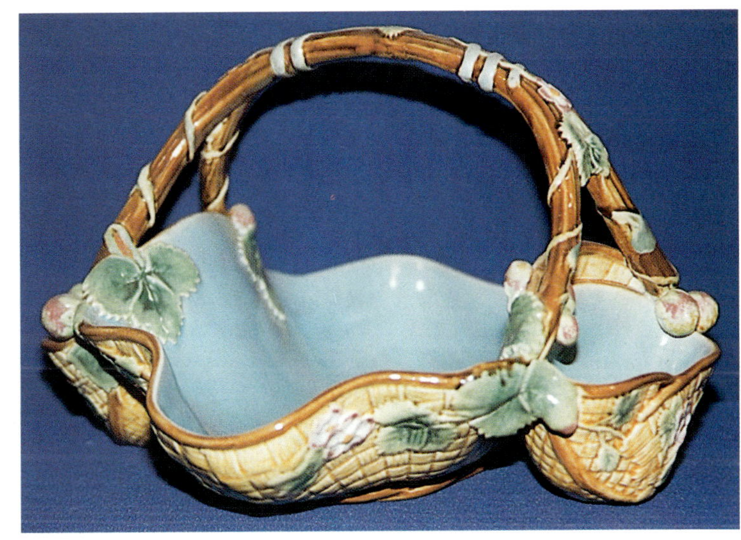

George Jones strawberry server with side pocket cream and sugar. Strawberries in relief, yellow basketweave with blossoms and leaves, turquoise interior, 8" h x 12 1/4" d.
$1200

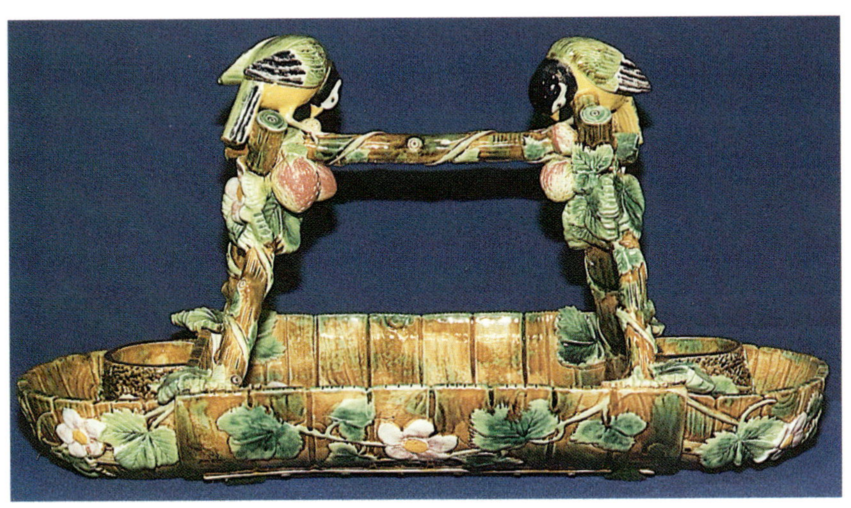

Strawberry server with birds on a branch, 8" tall x 15" long.
$1750

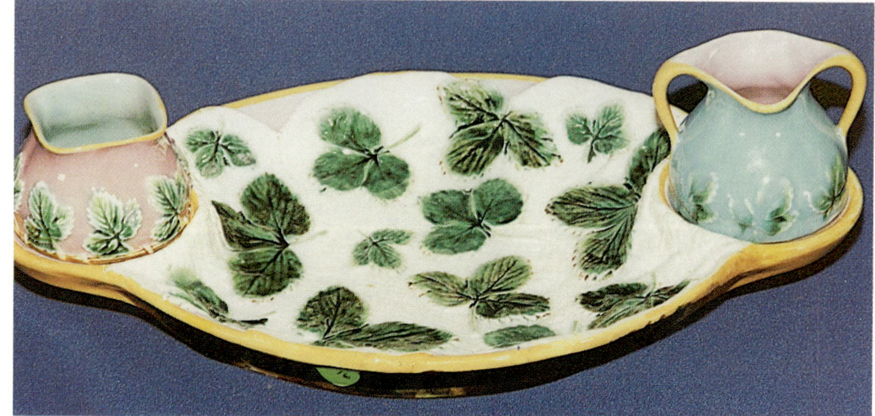

George Jones napkin pattern strawberry server with creamer and sugar.
$350

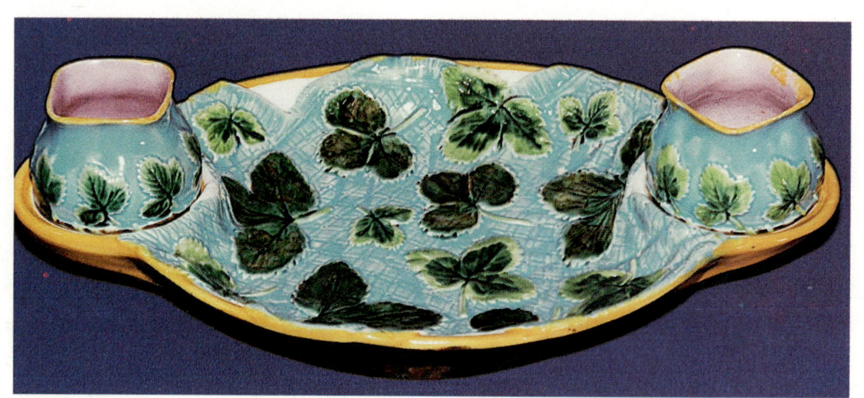

George Jones turquoise napkin pattern strawberry server with creamer and sugar.
$350

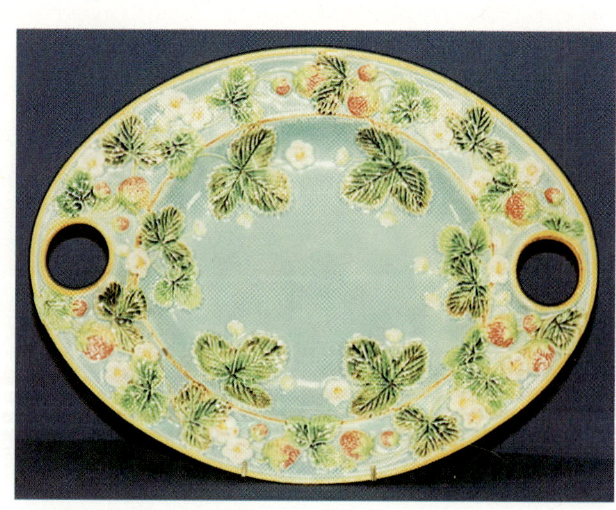

George Jones strawberry serving platter, 11" x 14 1/2".
$550

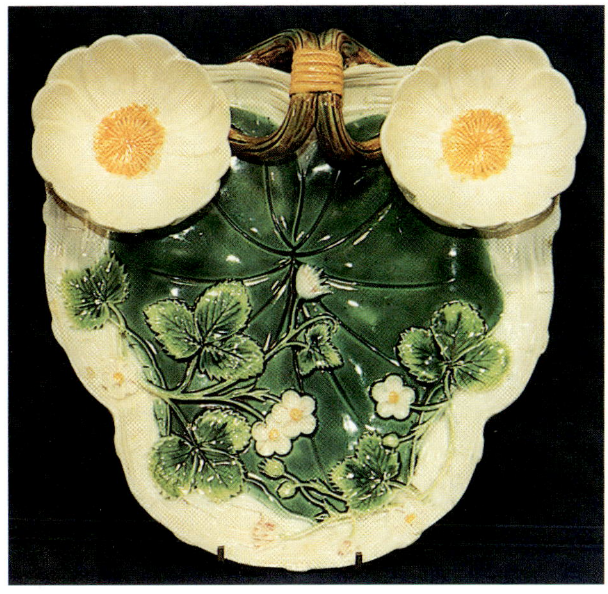

George Jones strawberry server.
$1475

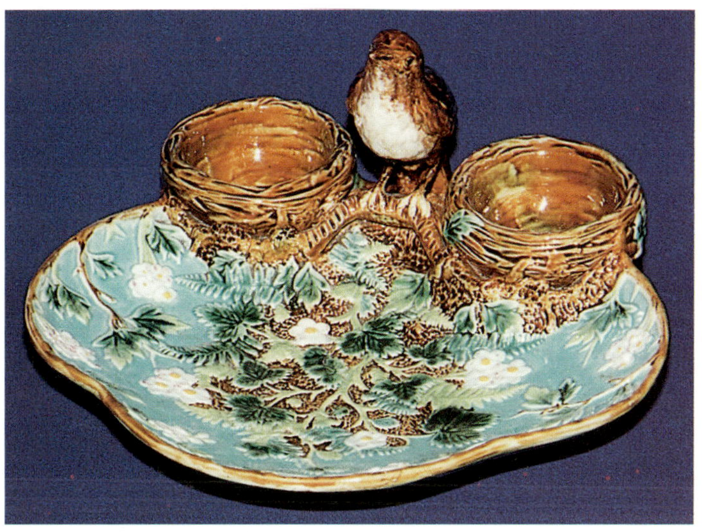

George Jones Strawberry Server with two bird nests, one is a a cream and the other a sugar, with a bird perched on branch.
$2000

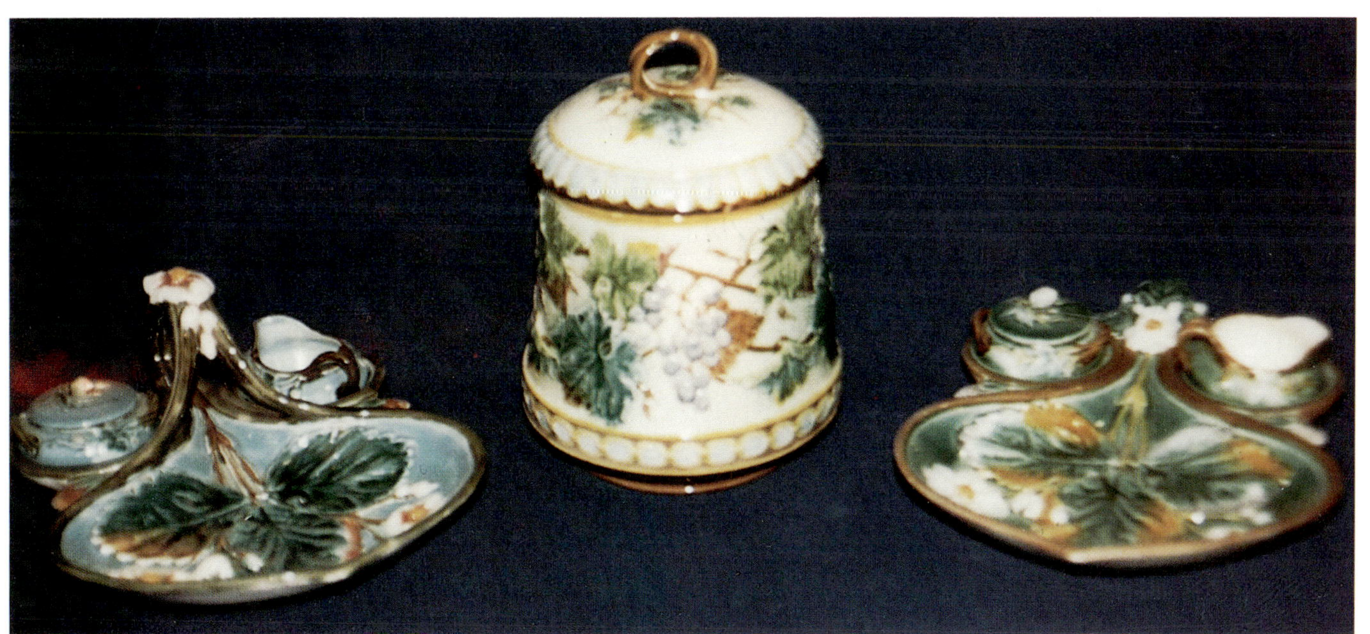

Left to Right:
Wedgwood strawberry server, creamer & sugar – **$1100**

Wedgwood cracker jar, 81/2" – **$1050**

Wedgwood strawberry server, creamer & sugar – **$1200**

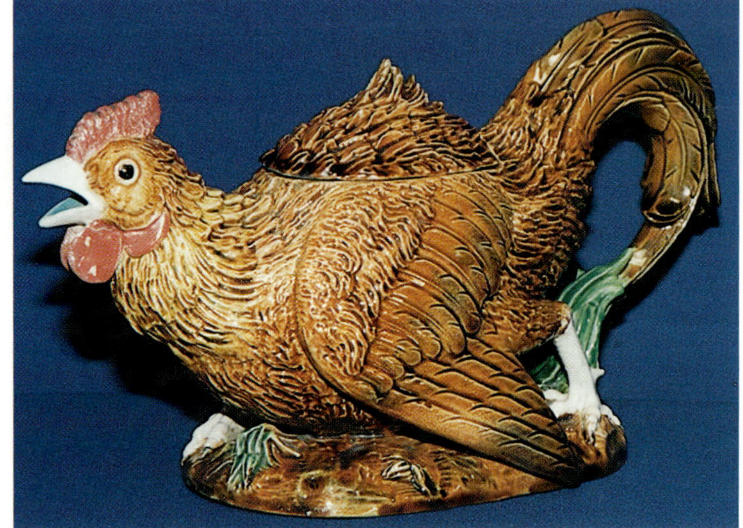

George Jones Rooster Teapot.
$3750

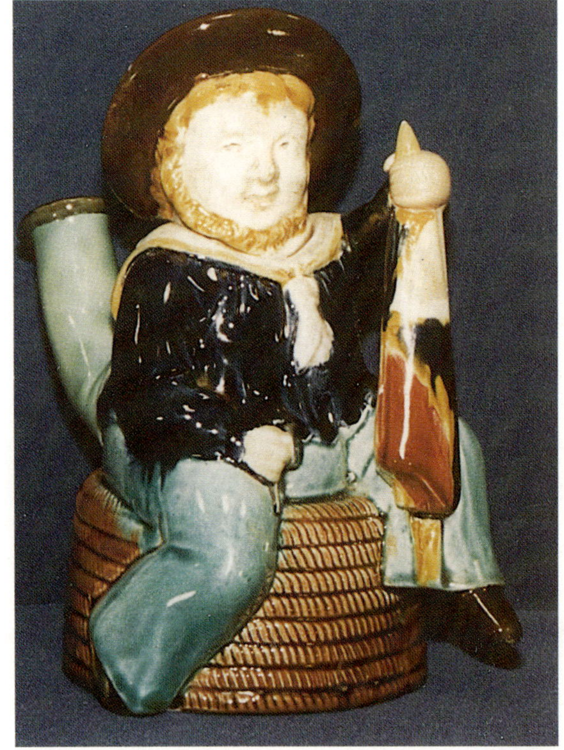

Isle of Man, three legged man figural teapot. The head lifts off to pour. It is marked "W. Broughton, So. Duke St., Douglas which is the capitol of the "Isle of Man" located in the Irish Sea off the coast of Great Britain.
$1400

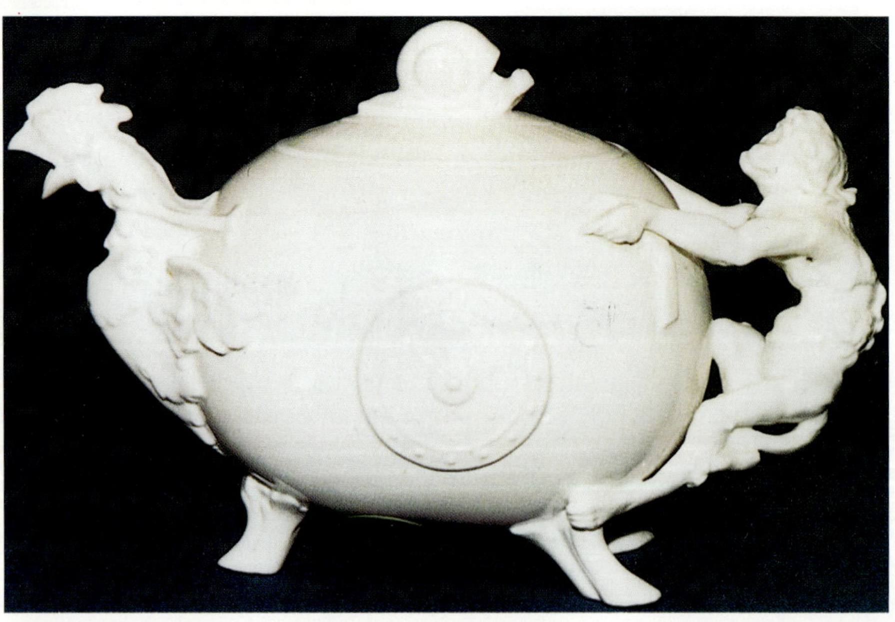

Minton rooster teapot with a monkey as the handle and a snail on the lid, and the rooster head as the spout. Made of white porcelain.
$3000

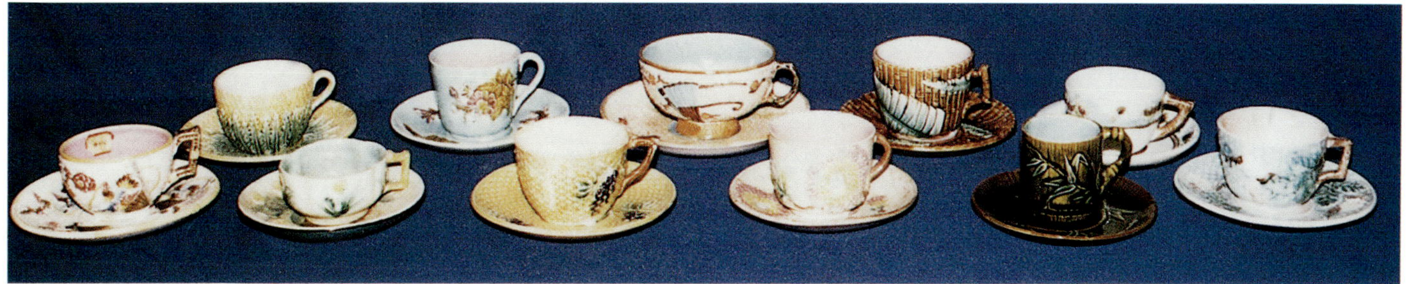

Miscellaneous cup and saucer sets.
Ranging from **$110-250 each set**

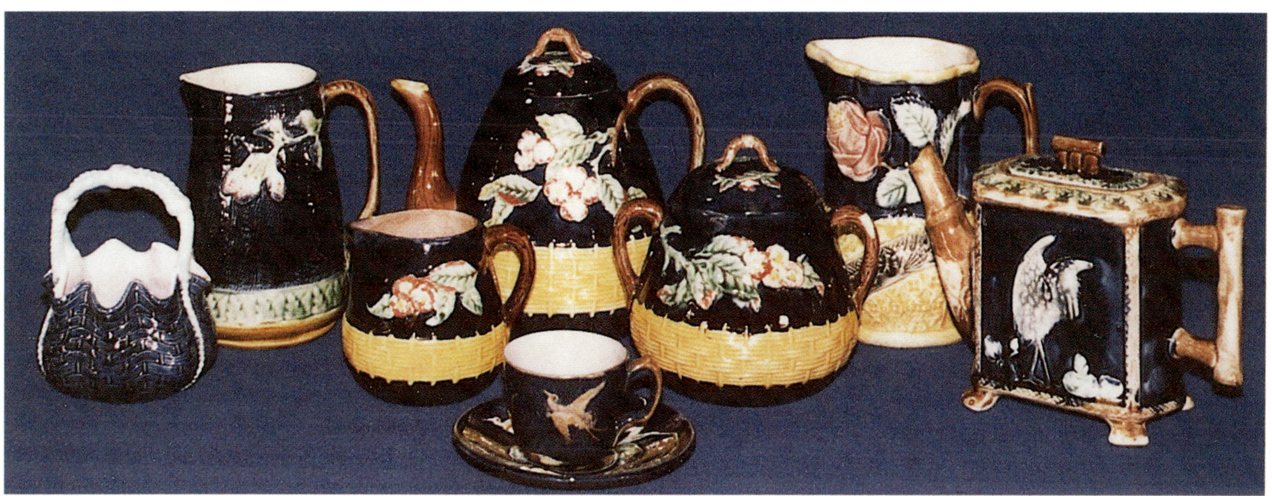

Front:
Cobalt flying crane and water lily cup and saucer – **$200**

Left to Right:
Cobalt basket with turquoise handle trimmed in pink, 6" – **$300**

Cobalt berry pitcher, 7" – **$200**

Three piece cobalt basket and floral coffee service. Coffee pot is 8 1/2" h, Sugar and creamer are 6 1/2" h – **$500**

English rose cobalt pitcher, 7 1/2" – **$225**

Cobalt bird teapot, 7" – **$350**

Minton Teapot, monkey with a coconut, wearing a cobalt jacket and the coconut is yellow, 8 1/2"l x 6" h.
$4000

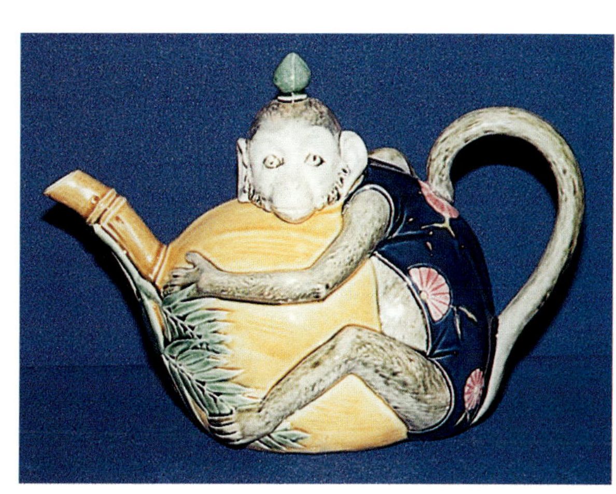

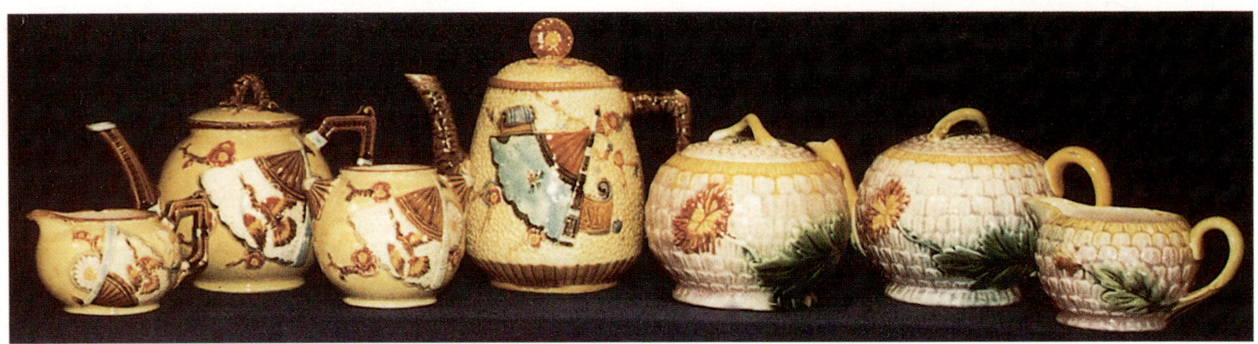

Left to Right:
Three piece tea set with creamer, teapot and sugar. They have an English registry mark and a bird and fan design – **$125**

Scroll teapot with fan and insect design, 7 1/2" – **$275**

Three piece tea set, sugar, teapot, and creamer with lavender interior with red and yellow flowers – **$550**

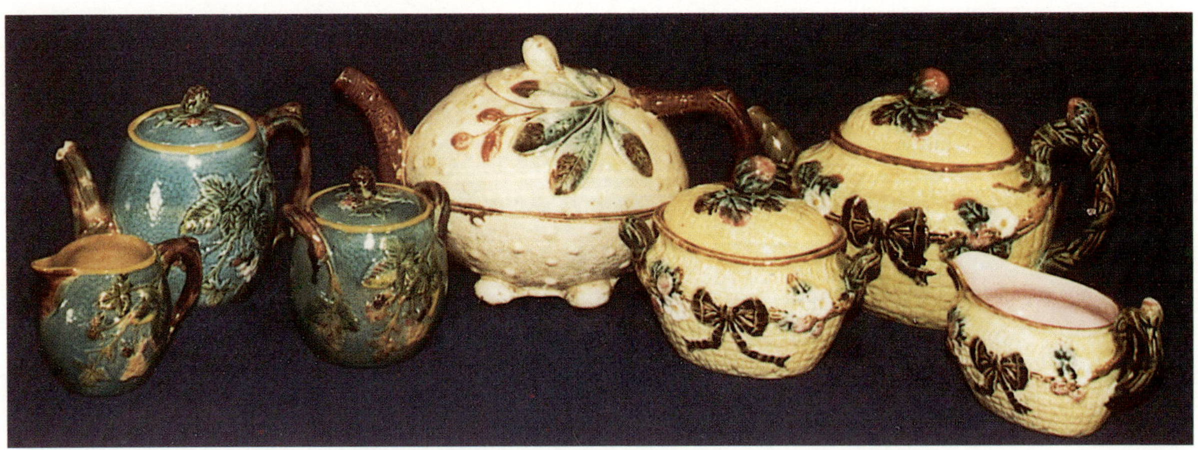

Left to Right:
Three piece tea set, creamer, teapot and sugar. Turquoise and blackberry – **$350**

Teapot shaped as a melon with bumps – **$250**

Tea set, strawberry and bow design, sugar, teapot and creamer – **$325**

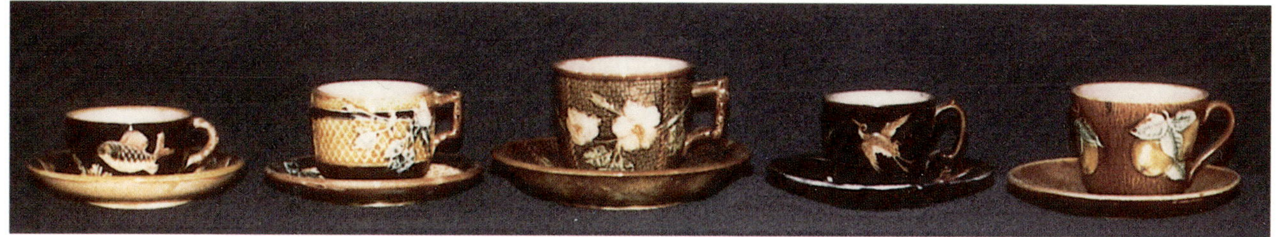

Left to Right:
Cobalt fish and seaweed cup and saucer – **$275**

Wild rose and trellis with cobalt cup and saucer – **$250**

Rose and rope cup and saucer – **$50**

Flying crane cobalt cup and saucer – **$200**

Yellow apple on brown background cup and saucer – **$125**

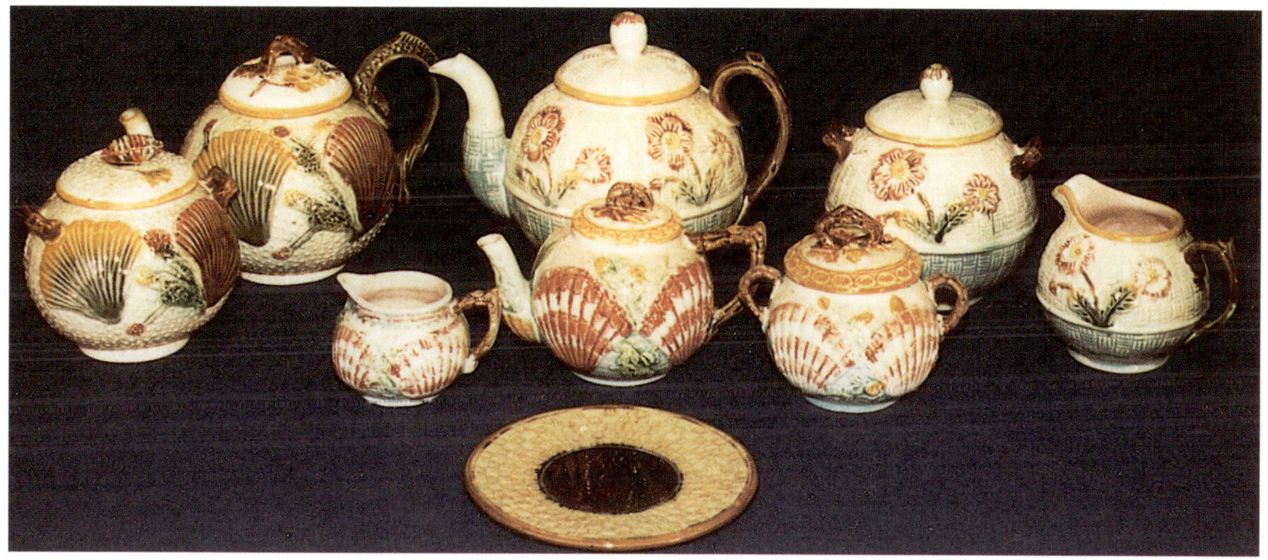

Front:
Teatile basketweave with cobalt blue center – **$75**

Middle Row:
Three piece tea set, shell & seaweed design – **$550**

Back Row:
Shell and seaweed teapot and sugar with fish handle – **$275**

Three piece tea set, floral with basketweave background – **$250**

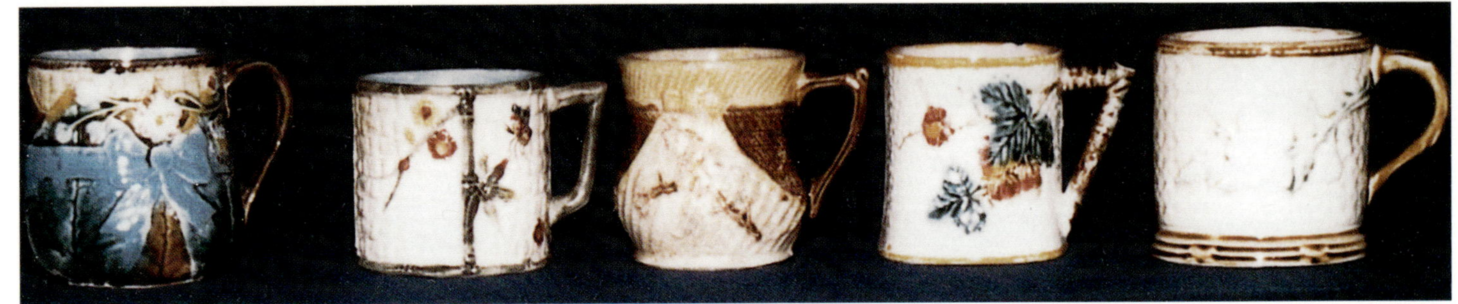

Left to Right:
Fielding leaf and bow mug, has an English registry mark – **$275**

Fielding bamboo, floral and butterfly mug – **$150**

Floral and drapery mug – **$25**

Strawberry mug with white background – **$75**

Floral basket mug – **$25**

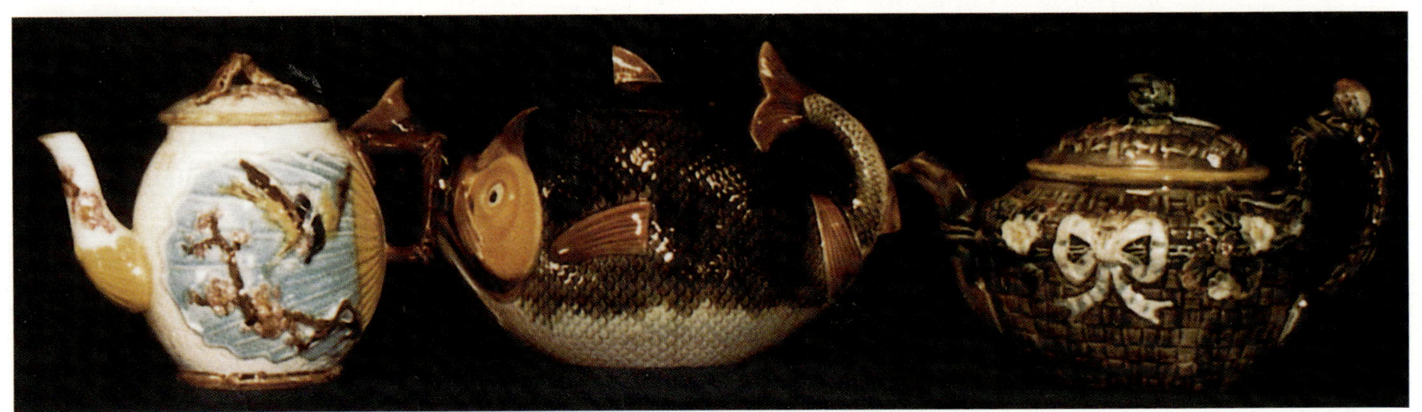

Left to Right:
Bird and fan teapot by Wardles & Co. – **$275**

Figural teapot of a fish swallowing another fish.
$375

Strawberry and bow design teapot, gray background – **$225**

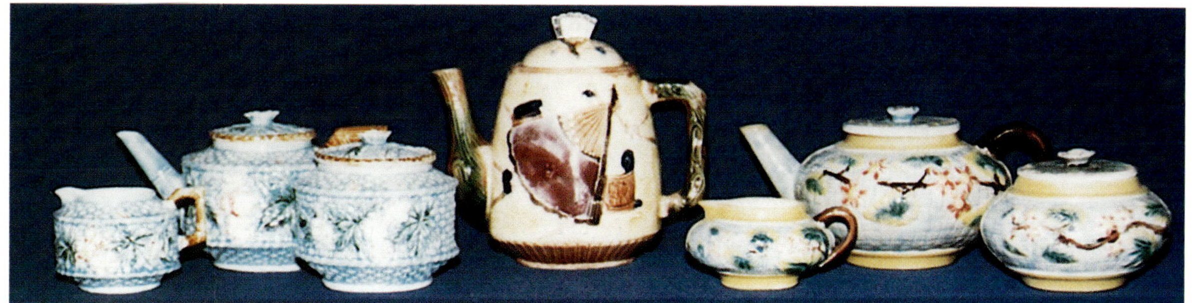

Left to Right:
Three piece tea set, creamer, teapot and sugar, turquoise basketweave design – **$500**

Fielding fan and scroll coffee pot – **$200**

Three piece floral and basketweave tea set with creamer, teapot and sugar – **$300**

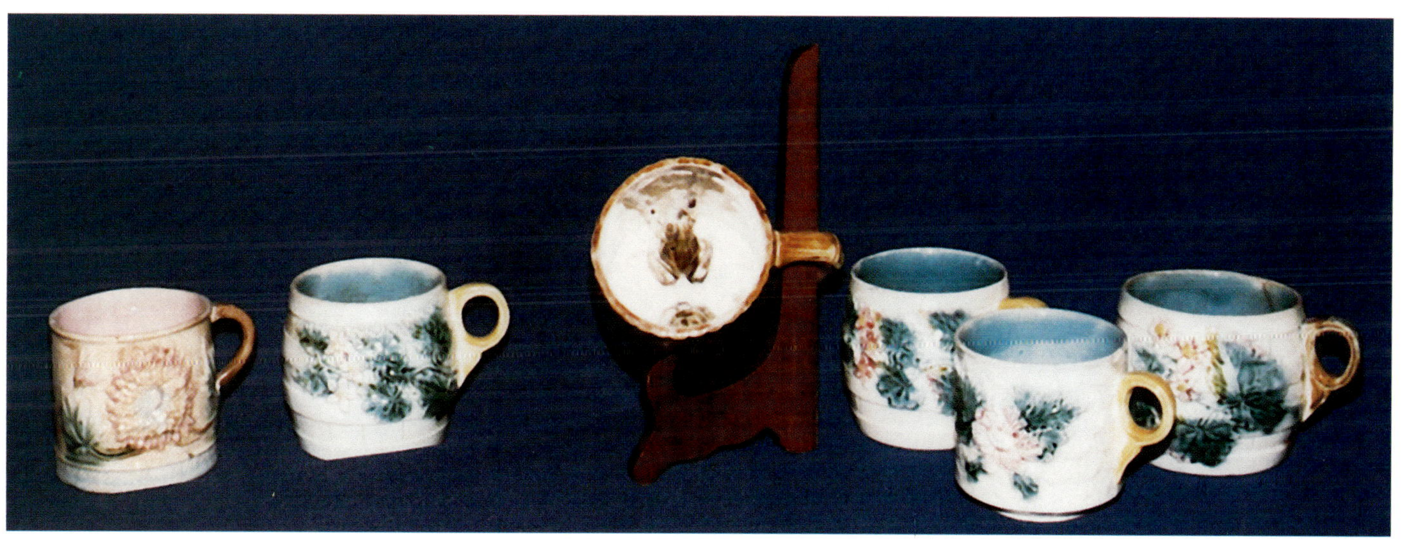

Left to Right:
Aster mug – **$150**

Barrell shape floral mug, light green – **$75**

Bamboo mug with two frogs inside – **$175**

Front cup on right side:
Scale background and floral mug – **$125**

Back two cups on right side:
Two barrel shaped and floral mugs – **$125 ea.**

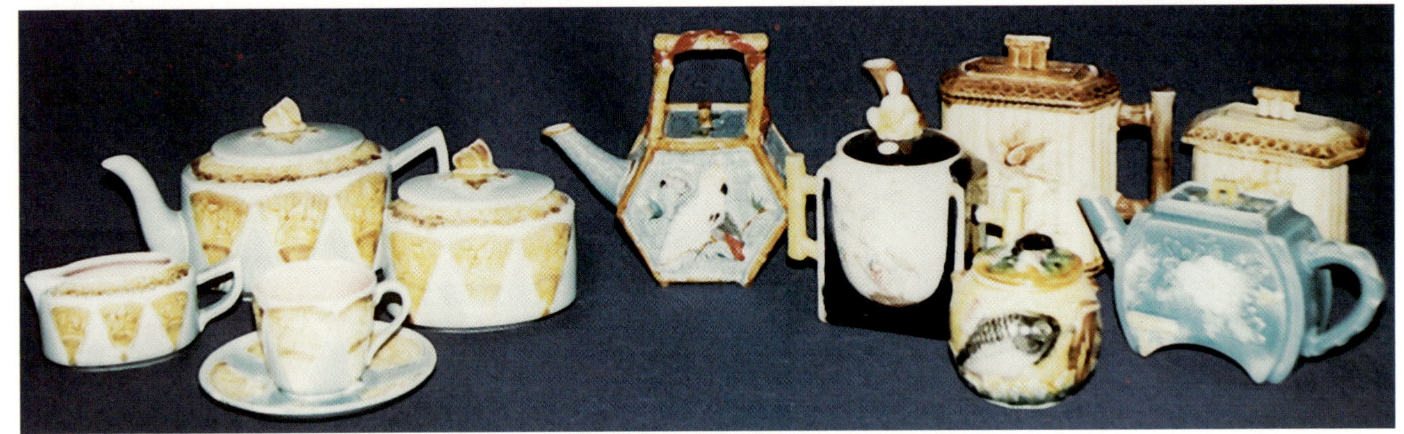

Left to Right:
Three piece tea set, fan and butterfly design – **$275**

Bird and fan cup and saucer – **$110**

Basketweave teapot with two parrots on a branch and a bamboo handle with red ribbon – **$500**

Cobalt blue covered sugar with oriental lady – **$250**

Yellow fish sugar – **$150**

Turquoise floral teapot – **$125**

Bird and Iris and bamboo teapot and sugar – **$225**

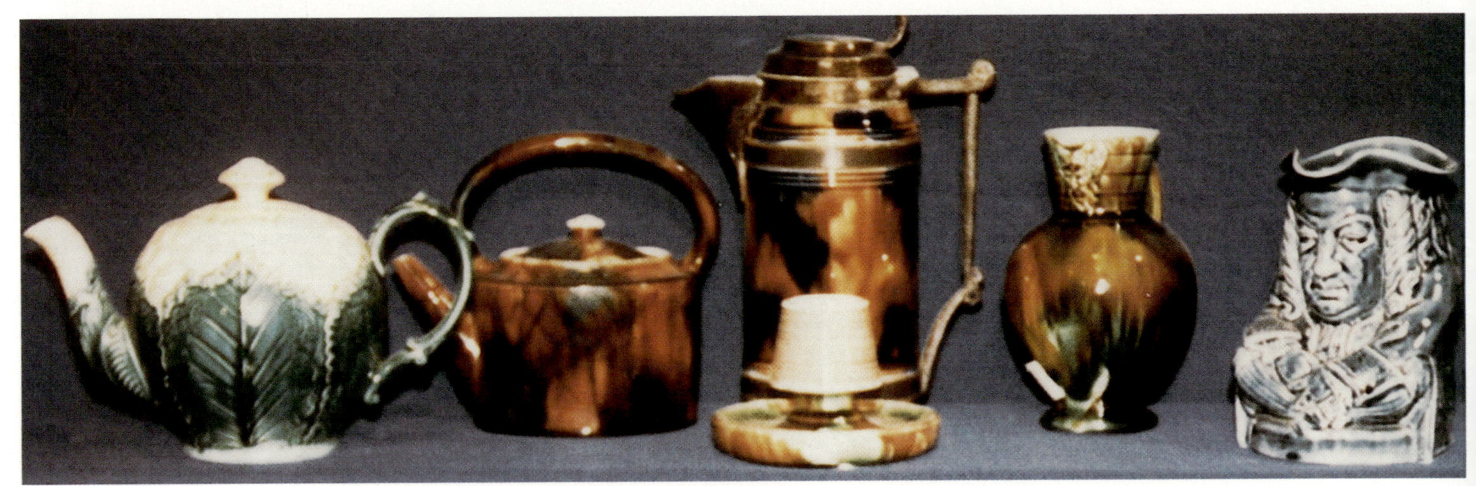

Front:
Wedgwood mottled match holder with striker – **$75**

Back Row:
Wedgwood cauliflower teapot, 6 1/4" – **$375**

Wedgwood mottled teapot, luster finish, 6 1/2" – **$175**

Wedgwood cobalt and brown tankard, 9" – **$225**

Wedgwood Doric jug, face on spout, 6 1/4" – **$75**

Wedgwood Yaleton blue figural jug, 6 1/2" – **$200**

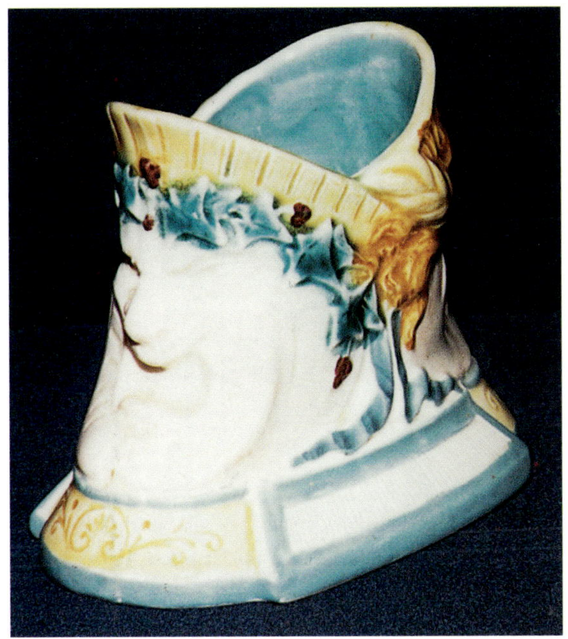

Wedgwood Tragedy & Comedy match holder with striker, 3 1/2" h.
$775

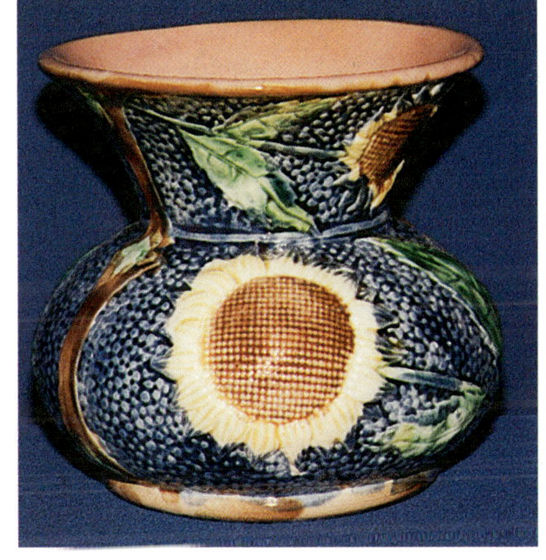

Etruscan sunflower cuspidor, 7" h, rare – **$1200**

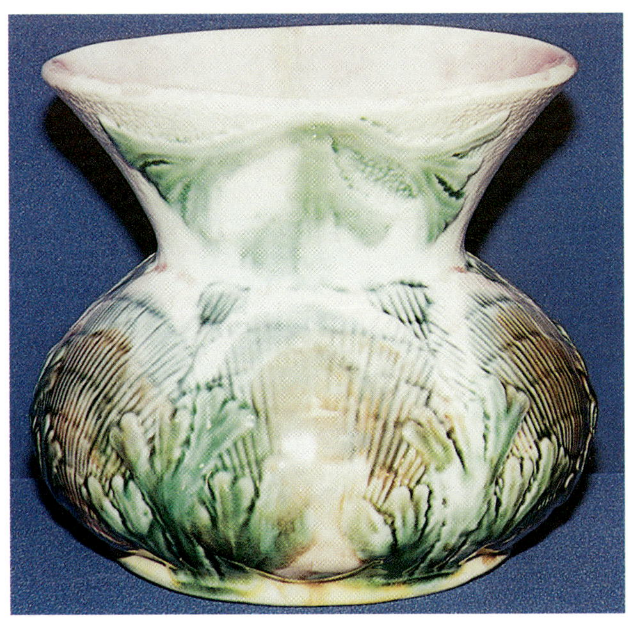

Etruscan shell and seaweed spittoon, 6 1/2" – **$350**

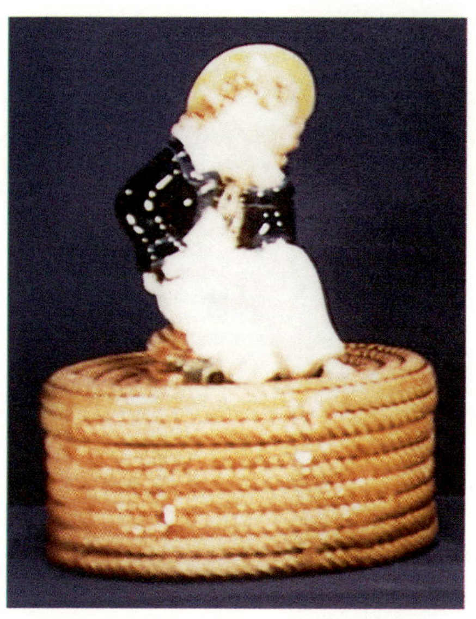

Boy seated on a rope humidor, 7 1/2" h. The boy has a cobalt jacket and a yellow hat – **$225**

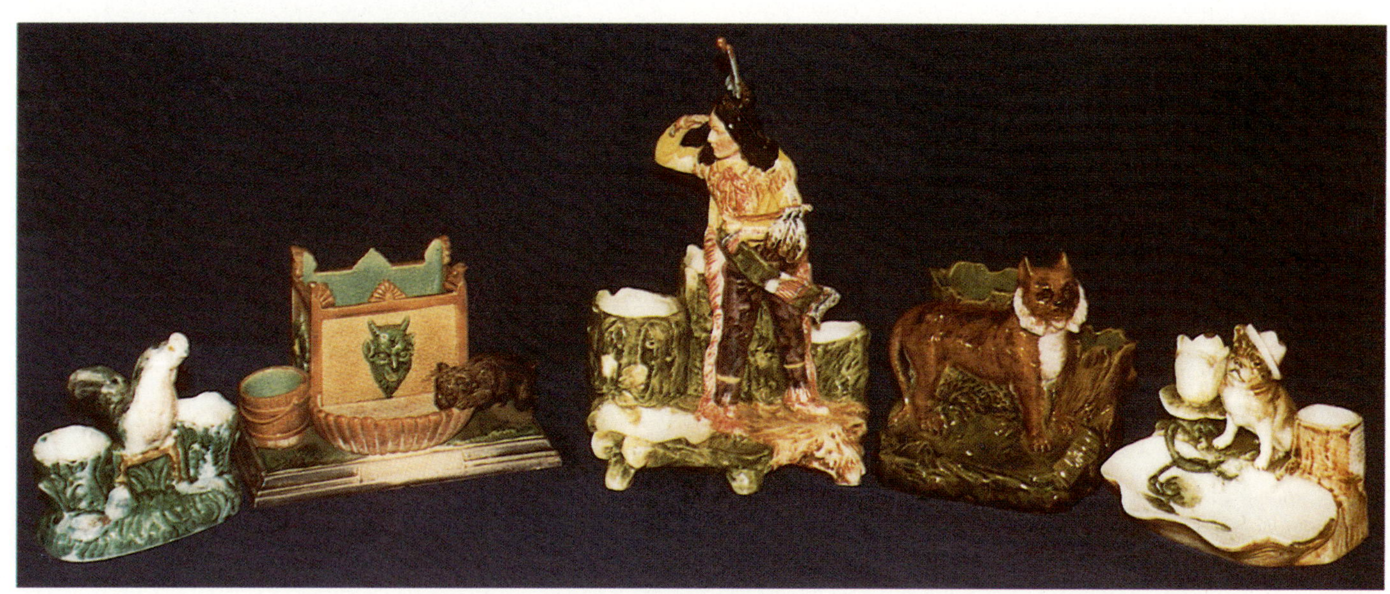

Left to Right:
Toothpick holder, chicken and fern, 5" tall – **$100**

Match holder/striker, dog getting a drink – **$600**

Indian match holder/striker, 11" – **$525**

Mountain lion match holder/striker – **$575**

Bulldog wearing a hat match holder/striker – **$225**

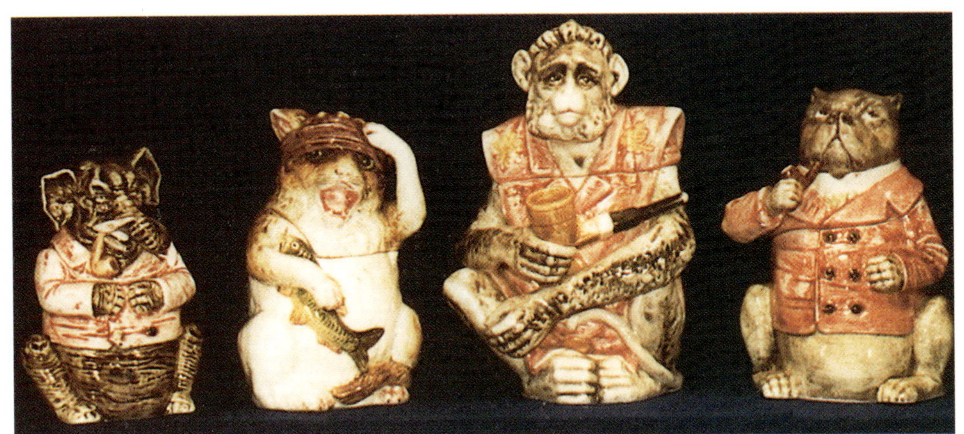

Left to Right:
Elephant wearing a red jacket, 7" tall – **$250**

Cat humidor with bandage on head holding a fish, 7 1/2" tall – **$450**

Monkey humidor with pink jacket, 10" – **$600**

Bulldog wearing a red jacket with a pipe, 8" – **$450**

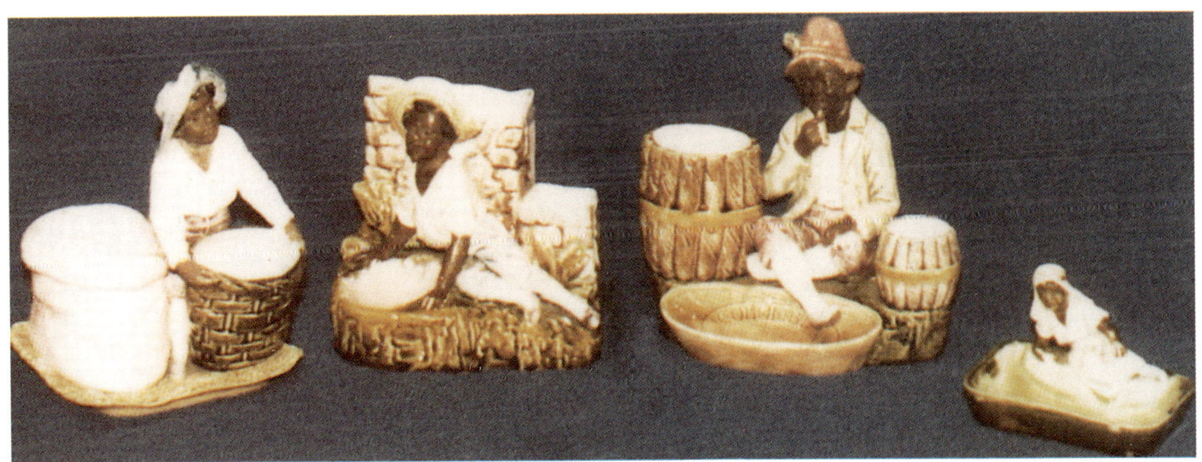

Left to Right:
Match holder/striker with black boy holding a basket – **$175**

Match holder/striker with black boy sitting in front of a brick wall, 6" tall – **$250**

Black man smoking a cigar sitting next to a couple of baskets, marked "Columbia All" – **$225**

Indian laying down on a dish – **$25**

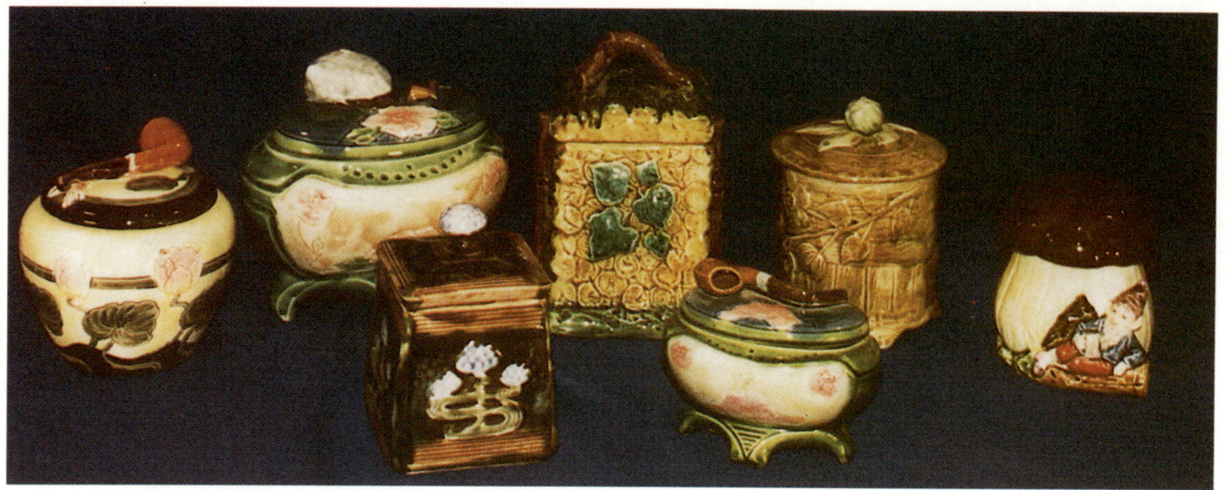

Front Row – Left to Right:
Art noveau floral humidor, 5" tall – **$75**

Continental art noveau humidor with a pipe on lid – **$100**

Back Row – Left to Right:
Art noveau humidor with pipe on lid – **$50**

Continental art noveau humidor with hat on lid – **$100**

Humidor, stacked logs design – **$200**

Picket fence and floral humidor, 5" tall – **$50**

Continental gnome at a mushroom humidor – **$125**

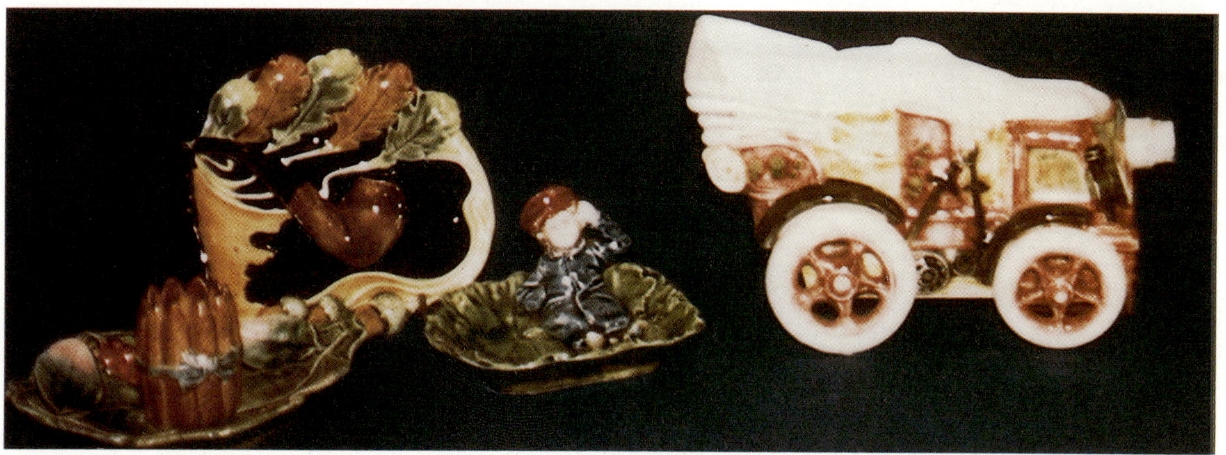

Left to Right:
Bundle of cigars on a leaf match holder – **$75**

Pipe on cobalt dish with oak leaves and acorns – **$100**

A boy on a leaf dish – **$75**

Continental car planter, 5 1/2" x 9" – **$125**

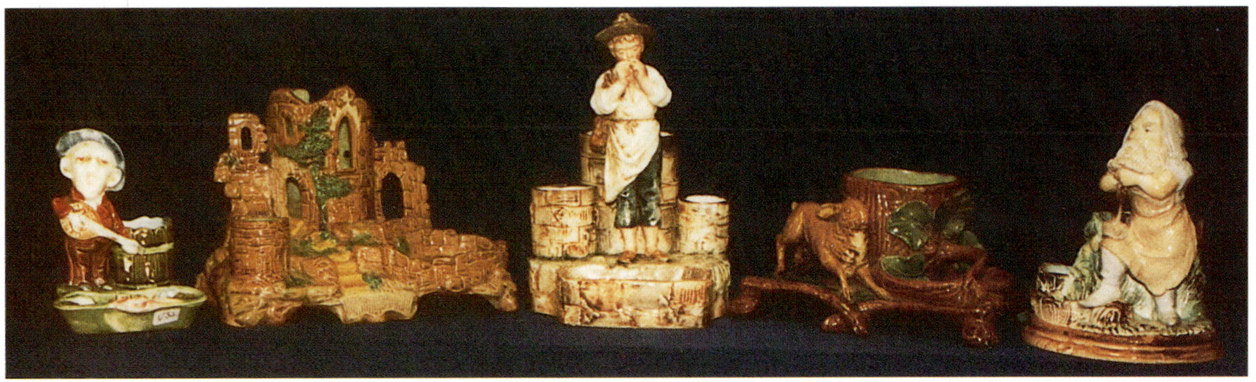

Left to Right:
Match holder/striker with a man singing and playing a mandolin – **$175**

Castle match holder with striker – **$50**

Boot maker match holder/striker, 8 1/2" – **$225**

Rabbit by a tree stump match holder – **$450**

Bearded man match holder/striker, 6 1/2" – **$175**

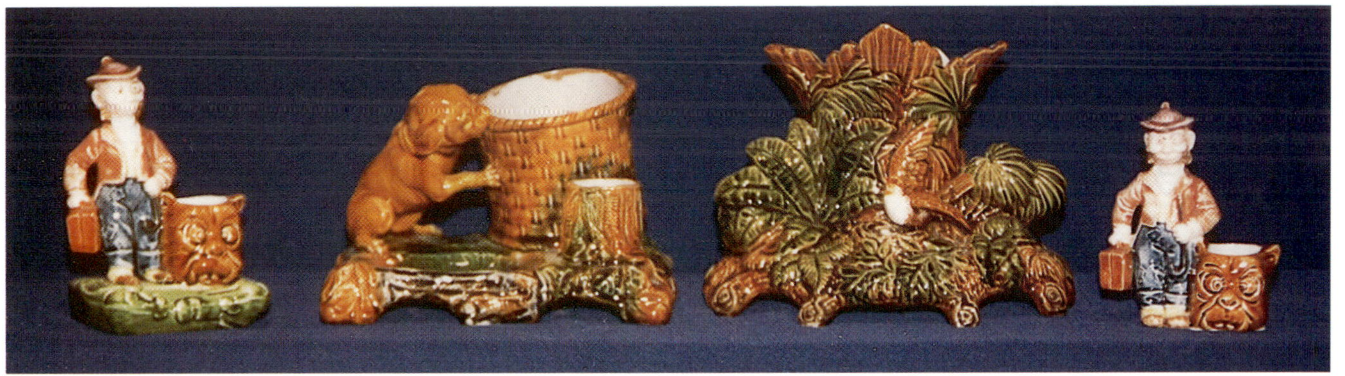

Left to Right:
Happy Hooligan with dogs head match holder/ striker, 5 1/4" – **$50**

Dog with basket match holder and striker – **$250**

Palm trees and birds match holder/striker – **$100**

Happy Hooligan match holder/striker, 4 1/2" – **$75**

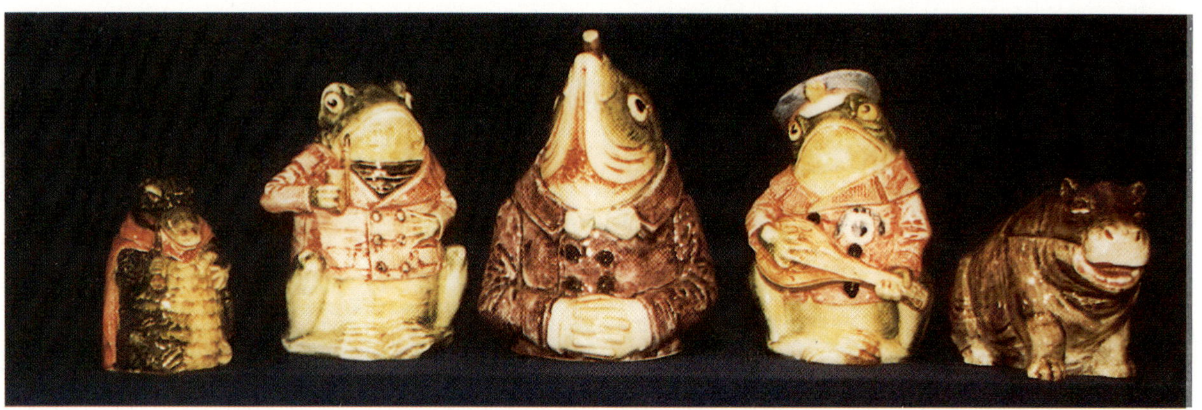

Left to Right:

Alligator humidor with red cap, 5" tall – **$600**

Frog with red jacket & pipe humidor, 7 1/2" tall – **$500**

Fish with a cigar in mouth with purple jacket humidor, 8 1/2" tall – **$550**

Frog playing a mandolin humidor, red jacket and blue hat, 7 1/2" – **$500**

Hippo humidor, 5 1/4" tall – **$650**

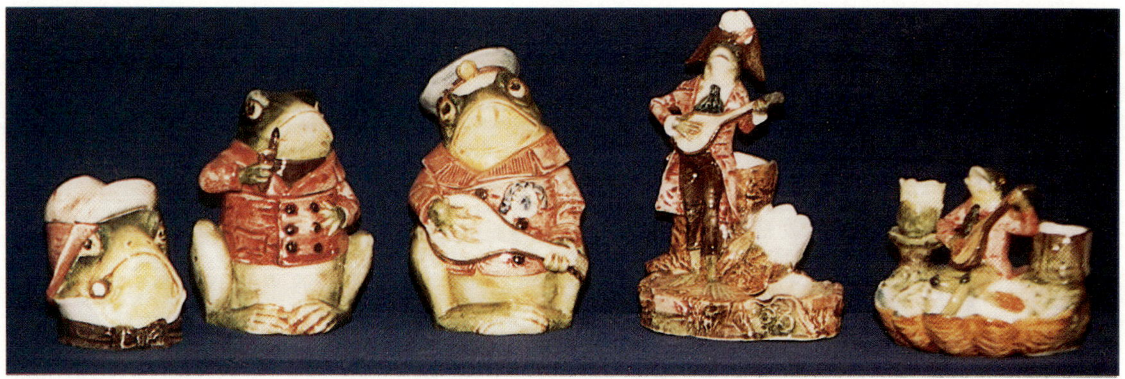

Frog head humidor with a red hat and black bow tie, 5" – **$500**

Frog with pipe and red jacket humidor – **$400**

Frog playing a mandolin humidor – **$575**

Frog playing a mandolin match holder/ striker, 8 1/2" – **$225**

Frog playing a mandolin match holder, 4 1/2" – **$300**

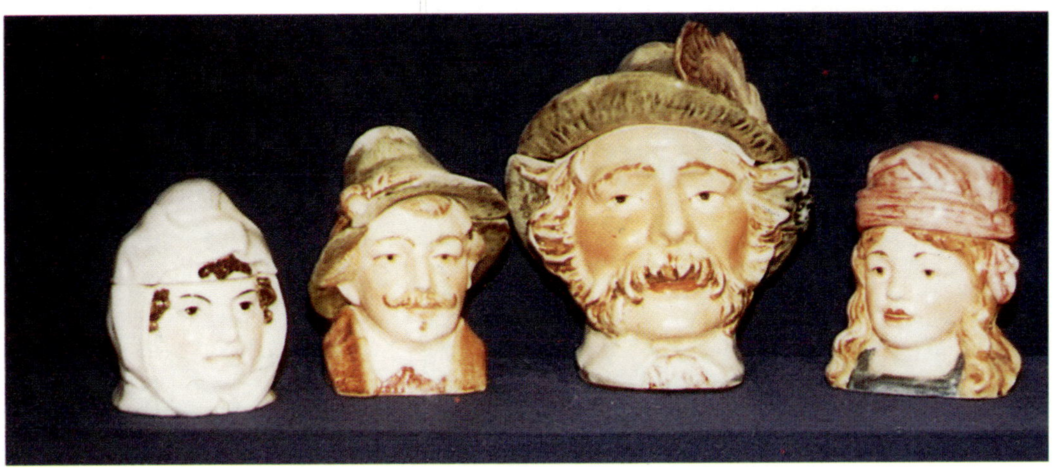

Left to Right:
Lady head humidor, 4 1/2" – **$50**

Scotsman humidor, 5 1/4" – **$50**

Scotsman humidor, 7 1/2" – **$100**

Lady humidor wearing a red turban, 5" – **$125**

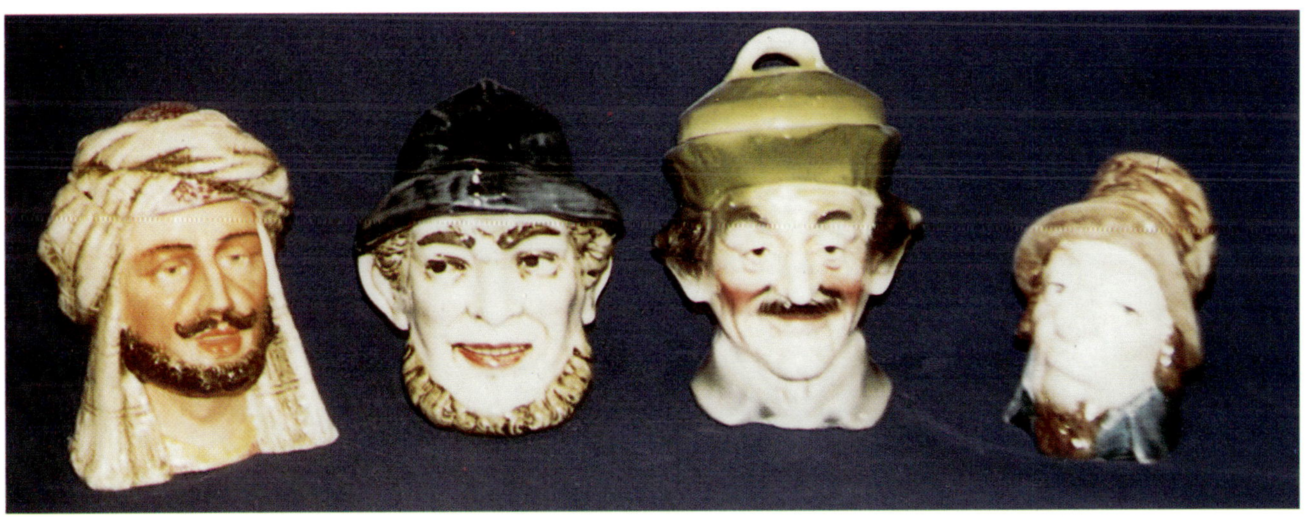

Left to Right:
Arab humidor with turban, 6 1/4" – **$125**

Czechoslovakian man with beard and cobalt hat humidor, 5 1/2" – **$300**

Man with a green hat humidor, 7" – **$75**

Continental humidor man with a funny face, blue collar, beard and brown hat, 4 1/2" – **$100**

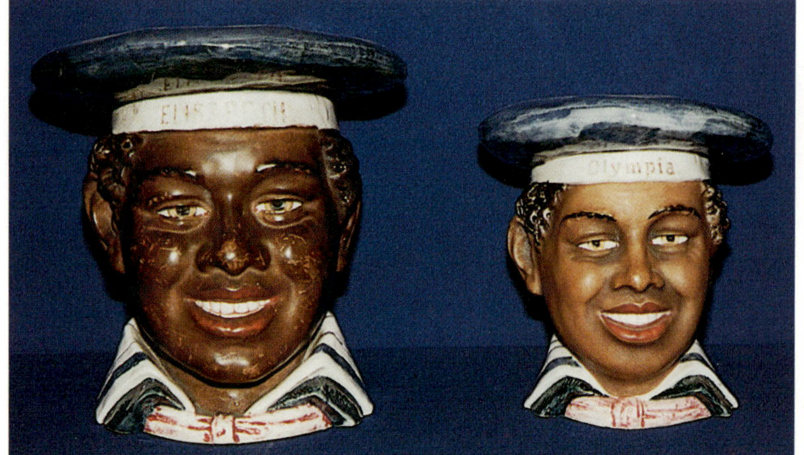

Left to Right:
Large Black Sailor Humidor with Elizabeth on hat band, 7 1/2" h – **$600-800**

Black Sailor Humidor with Olympia on hat band, 6 1/4" h – **$600-800**

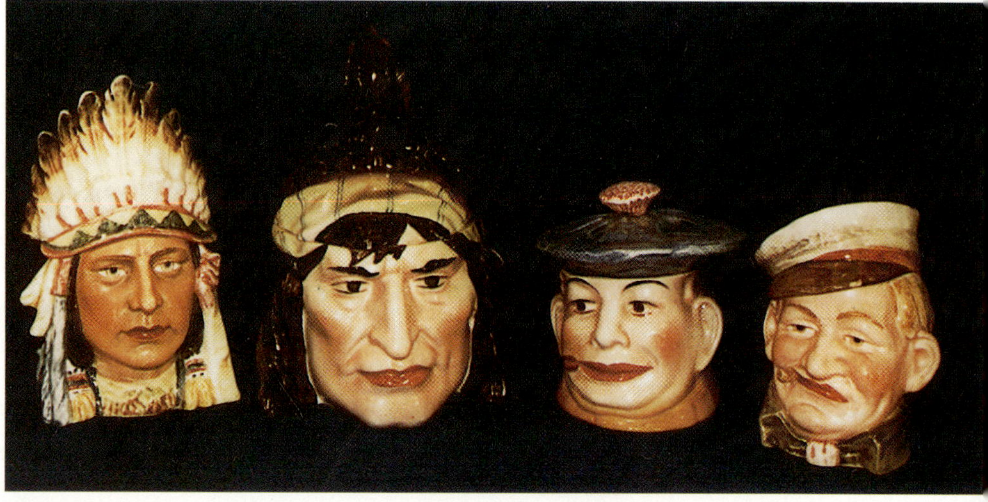

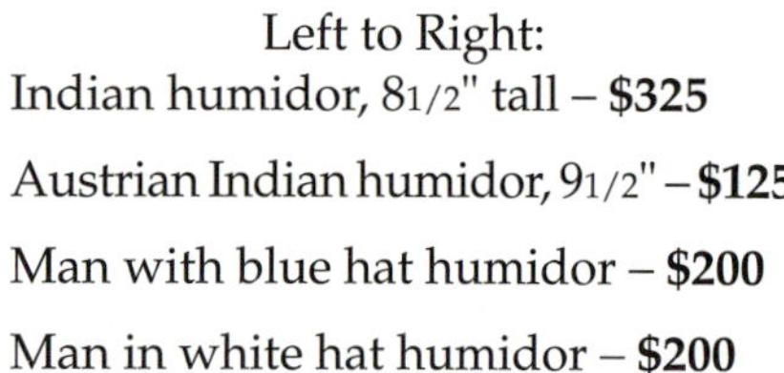

Left to Right:
Indian humidor, 8 1/2" tall – **$325**

Austrian Indian humidor, 9 1/2" – **$125**

Man with blue hat humidor – **$200**

Man in white hat humidor – **$200**

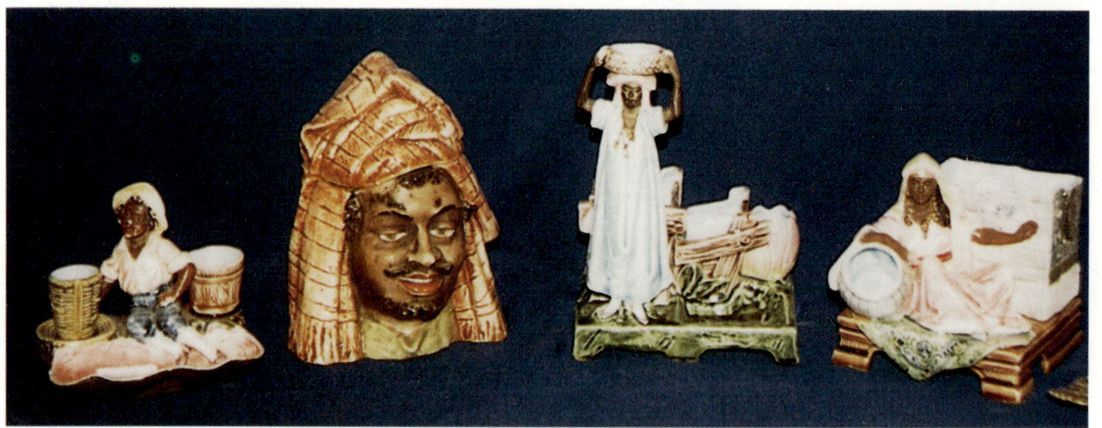

Left to Right:
Black boy with baskets match holder/striker – **$100**

Black Indian humidor, 7 1/2" – **$100**

Black lady, basket on head match holder, 8" – **$275**

Black Indian lady with basket sitting by a brick wall, match holder/striker – **$125**

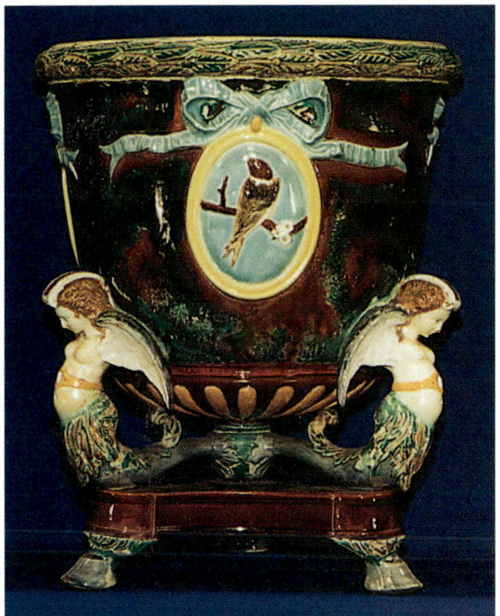

Early Minton jardiniere with three winged ladies and goats feet, three medallions with birds, 13"d x 16"h.
$875

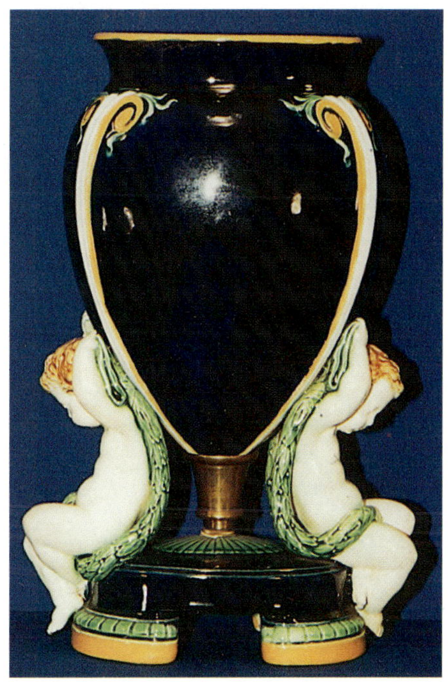

Minton 1873 cobalt vase with two cherubs supporting the vase, (shape #1646), 13 1/2" h.
$825

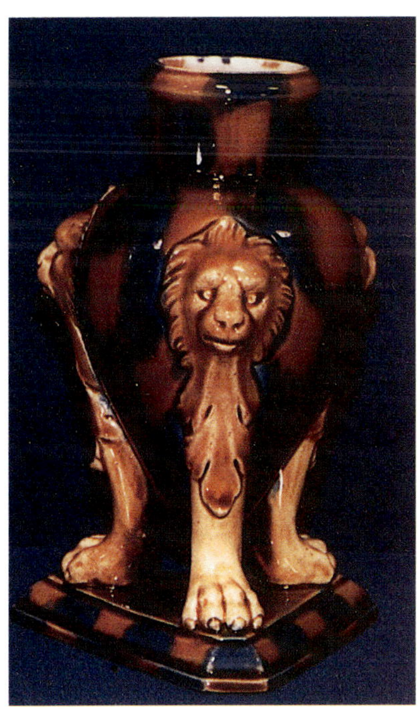

Etruscan three footed lion vase, cobalt and brown, mottled, pink interior.
$450

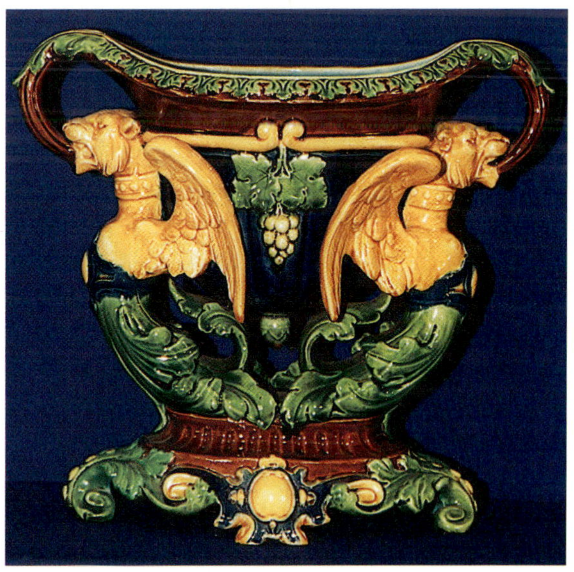

Minton vase with winged griffin on each side. Cobalt base with brown, yellow and green design and leaves, turquoise interior, 10 1/2" h x 12 1/2" w.
$800

VASES, URNS, JARDINIERES, CANDLESTICKS, ETC.

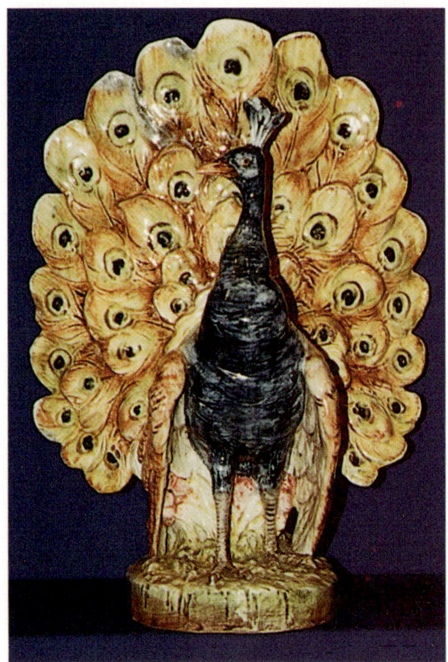

Continental peacock vase, 17 1/2" h.
$700

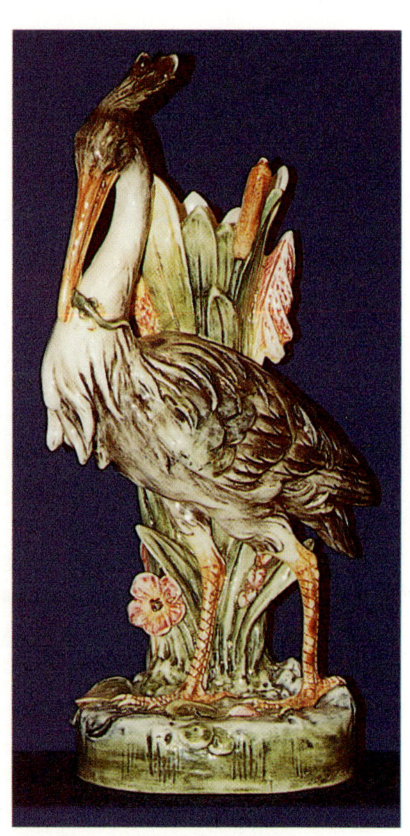

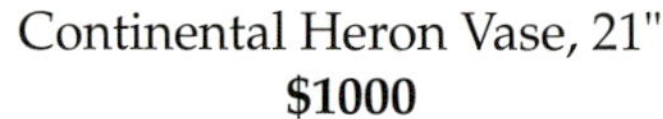

Continental Heron Vase, 21".
$1000

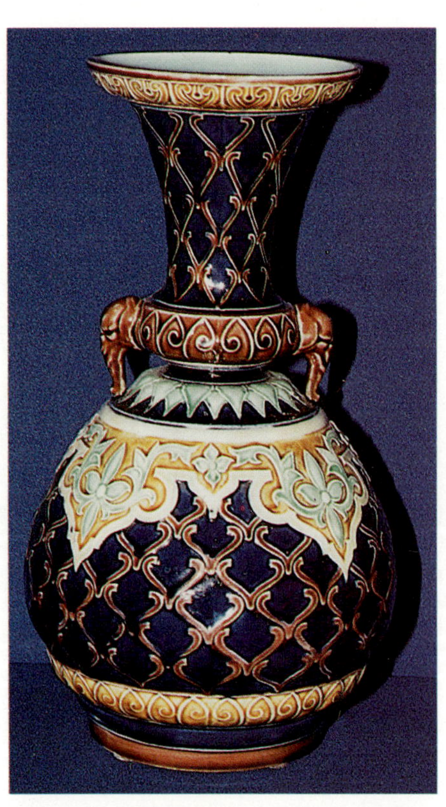

Sarreguemines Vase, cobalt blue with two elephant heads on sides, 12 1/2". **$1000**

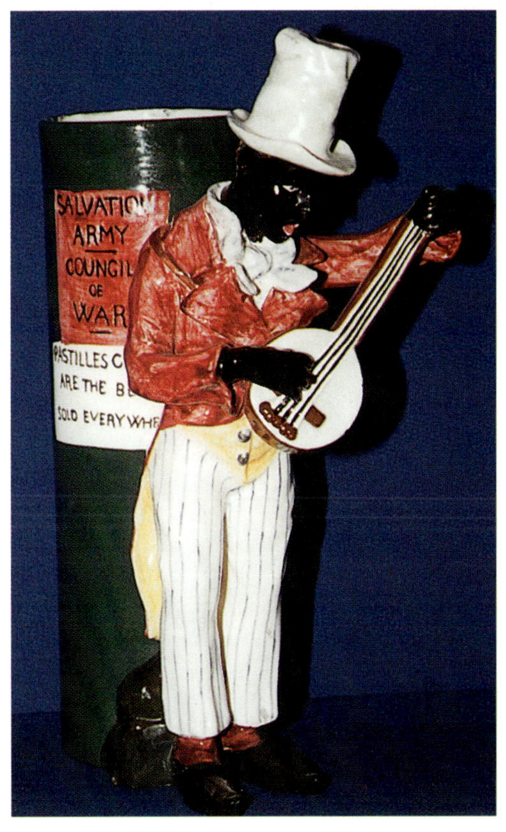

Sarreguemines figural vase with black man playing banjo in front of a post with several signs that read "Salvation Army, Council of War", "Moses Money Lender" and others, 12 1/2".

$1100

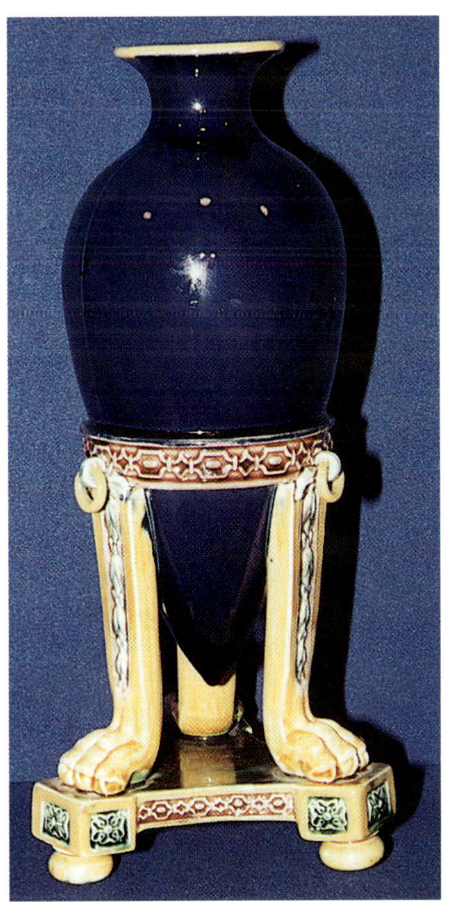

George Jones cobalt amphora vase with claw feet, 13".

$1350

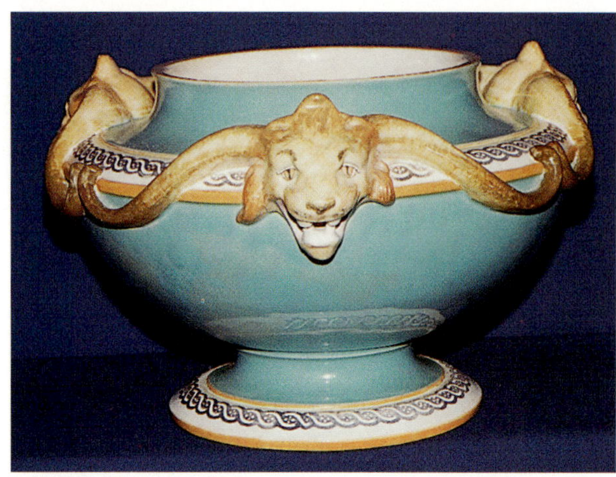

Minton Urn with three griffin heads, 8" h x 14" w.
$1350

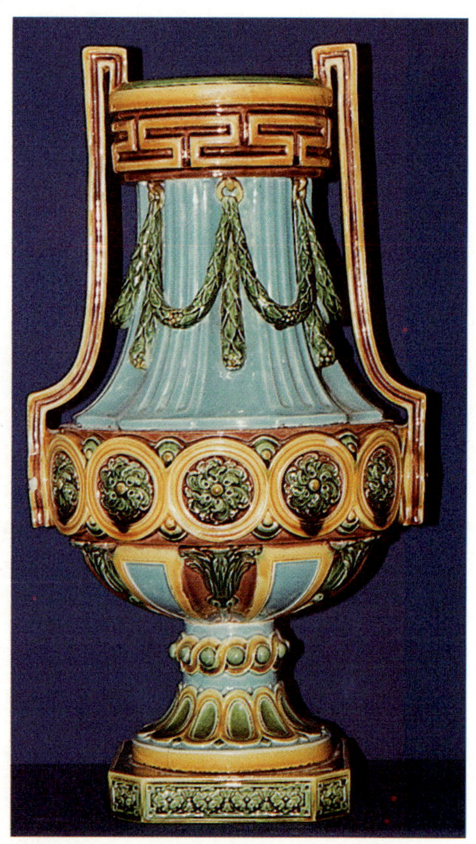

Minton Urn, double handled with drapes of vines, Louis XVI style, 19" h.
$5000

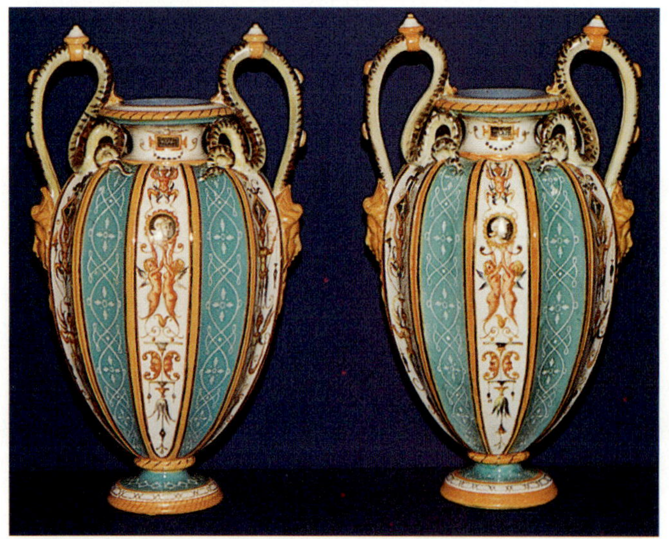

Pair of Minton Egyptian style Urns, with snake handles, marked "Crystal Palace" and "Art Union" on side, 11" h.
$2500

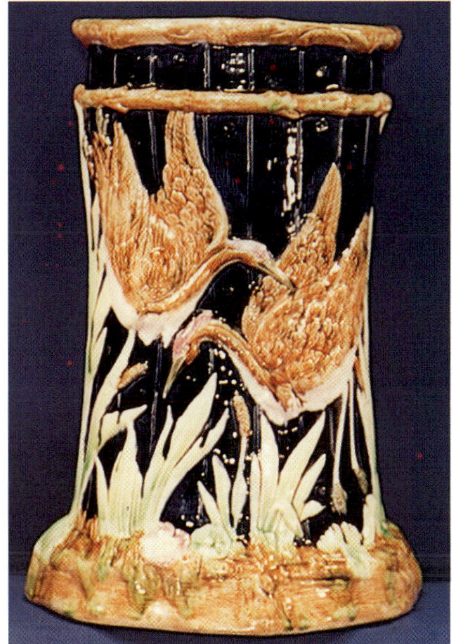

Cobalt blue umbrella stand, with storks in rushes, 20".
$1000

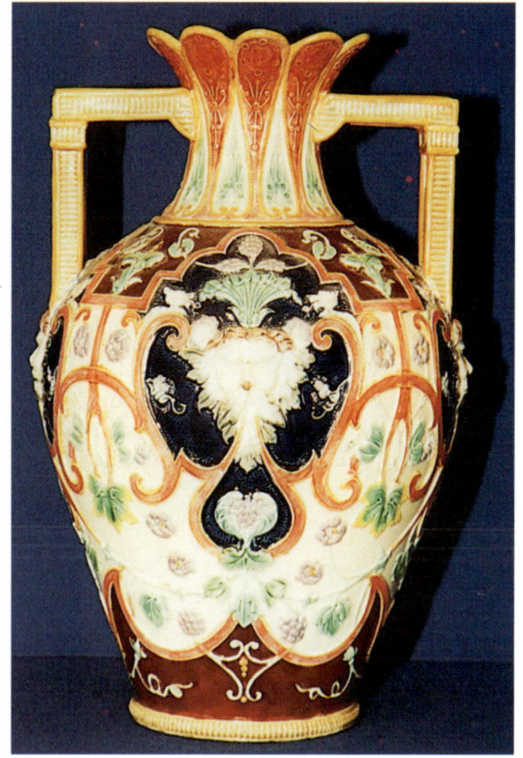

Copeland handled urn, 11 1/2" tall, with Della Robia style faces in relief with floral and vine decor.
$500

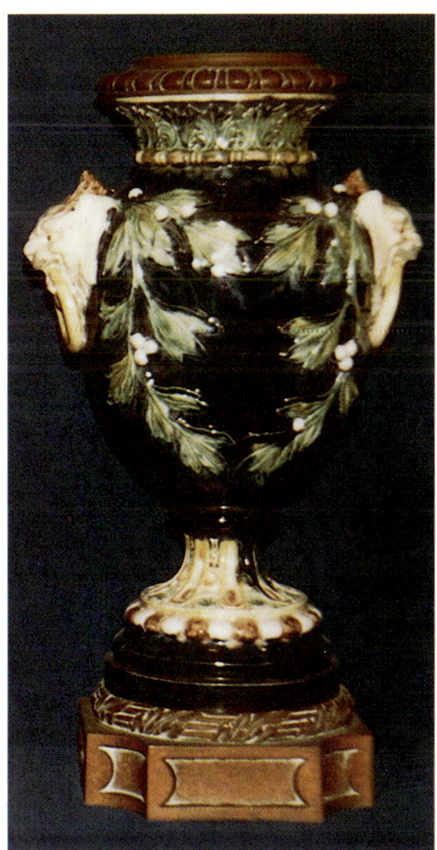

Cobalt urn with green leaves and white berries in relief, animal ring handles, bronze base and rim, 18 1/2".
$775

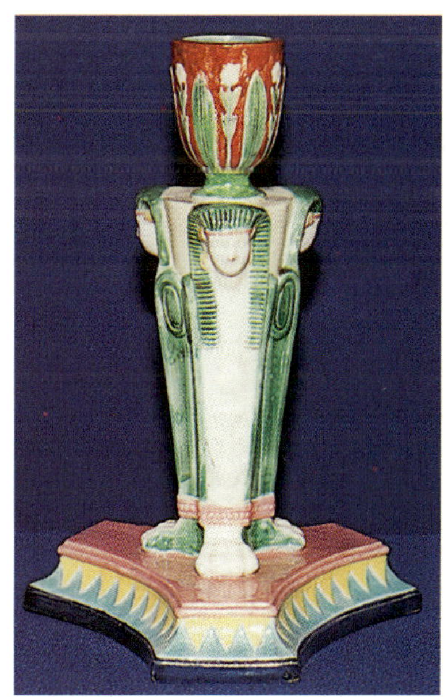

Royal Worcester Egyptian candle holder with three Egyptian faces, 7" h.
$350

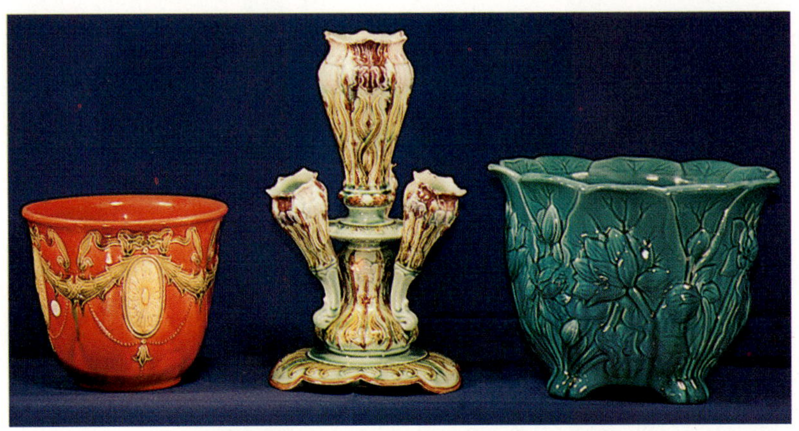

Left to Right:
Red jardiniere, 6 1/2"h x 8" d – **$200**

German four part epergne – **$175**

Minton turquoise water lily footed jardiniere, 8 1/2"h x 11 1/2"d – **$275**

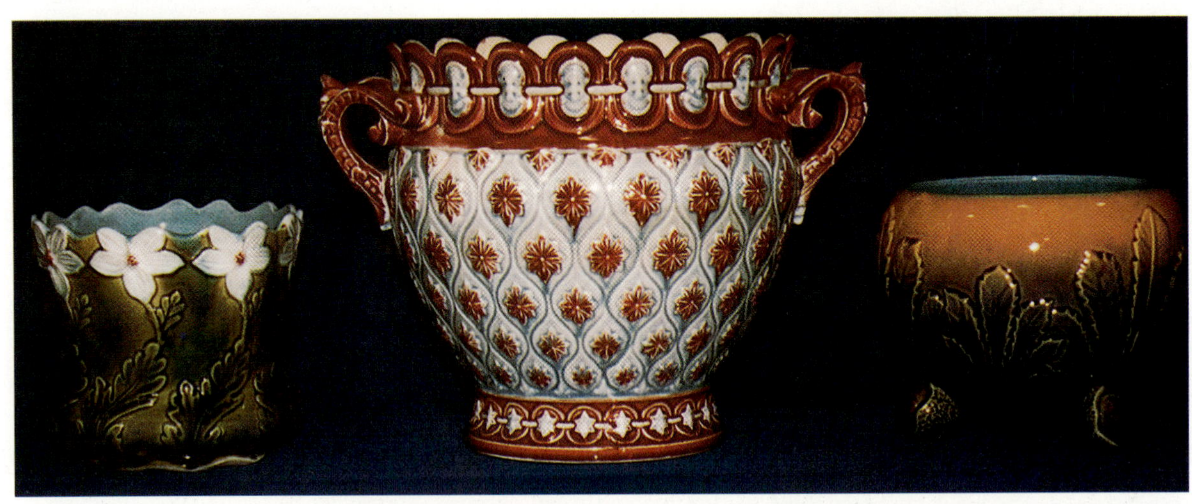

Left to Right:
Floral jardiniere, 6"h x 6 1/2" d – **$100**

Turquoise/red handled jardiniere, 10"h x 14" w – **$550**

Chestnut footed jardiniere 8"d x 6 1/2" h – **$100**

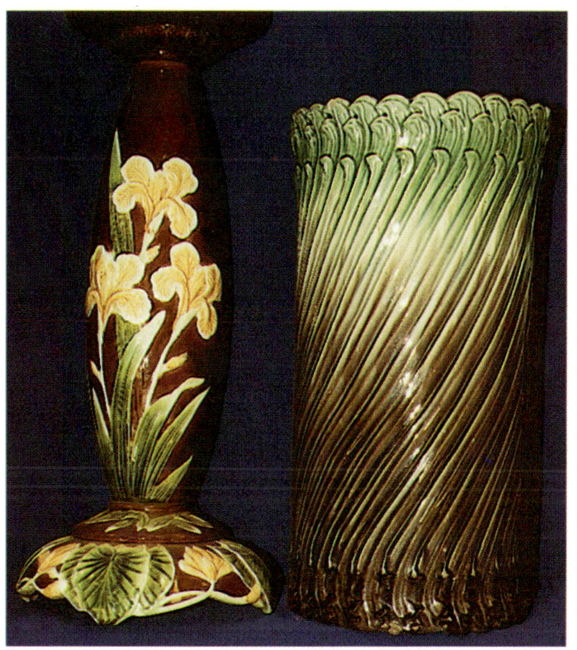

Floral jardiniere, 27 1/2" – **$200**

Umbrella stand, 21 1/2" – **$75**

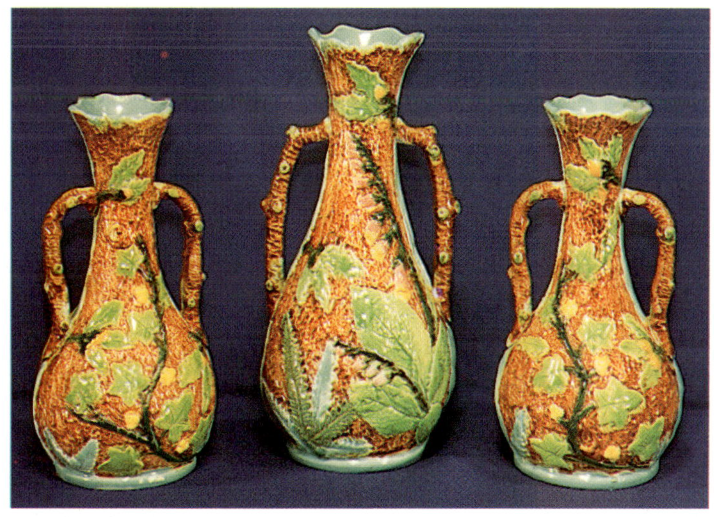

Three handled urns, the two on the ends are 6 3/4" and the middle one is 8".
$475/set

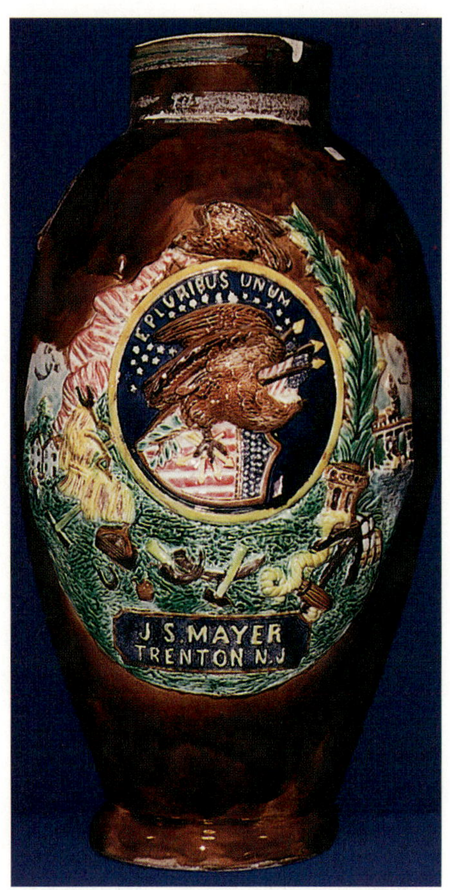

Historical floor vase with an eagle and shield on a scenic background and J.S. Mayer, Trenton, NJ. The other side has corn and flower scenic background of a paddle wheel boat and dock, "Louisiana", 20" tall.
$200

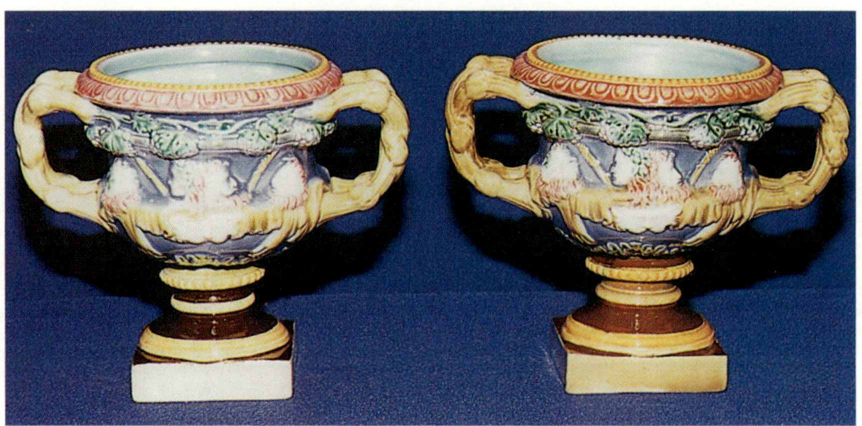

Pair of Copeland urns, 4 1/2"h – **$500 each**

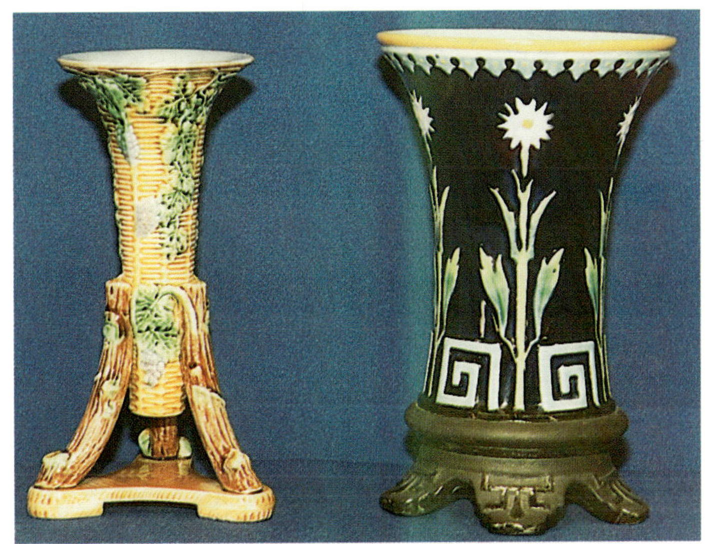

Left to Right:
George Jones trumpet vase supported by three twig legs, 8", turquoise interior – **$500**

George Jones cobalt blue Egyptian vase with turquoise interior – **$700**

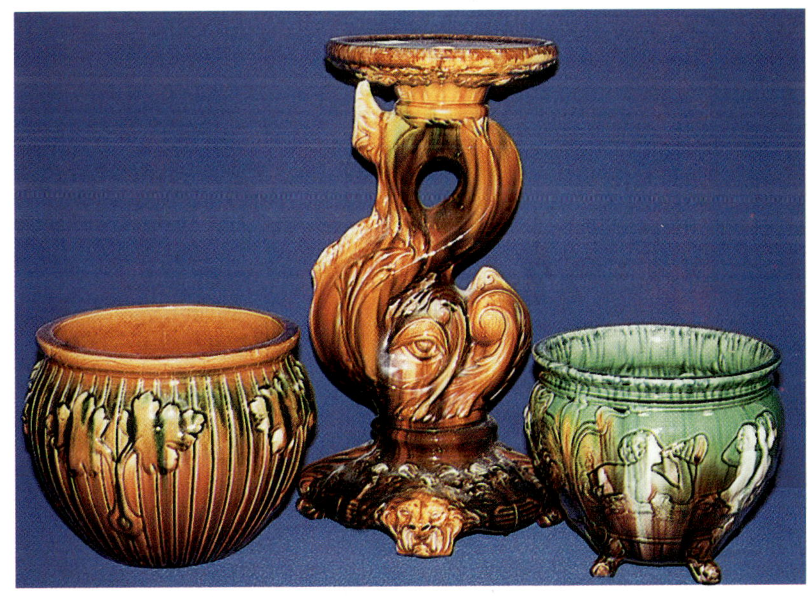

Left to Right:
Jardiniere in green and brown with leaves in relief, 10" h x 12" d – **$50**

Dolphin jardiniere base with lion's head feet, 22" – **$175**

Large brown, green and white jardiniere with people in relief, 8 1/2" h x 11" d – **$75**

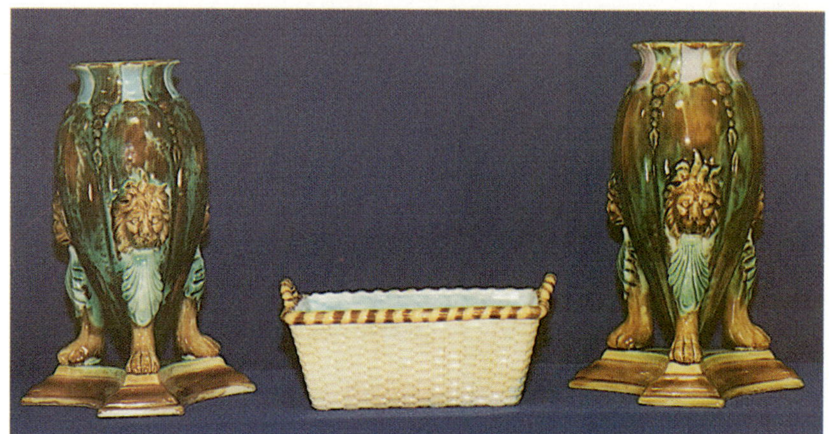

Two lion footed vases, 8 1/2" – **$550**

Minton handled basket, yellow and brown trim, turquoise interior, 3" h x 5 1/2" w x 7" long.

$225

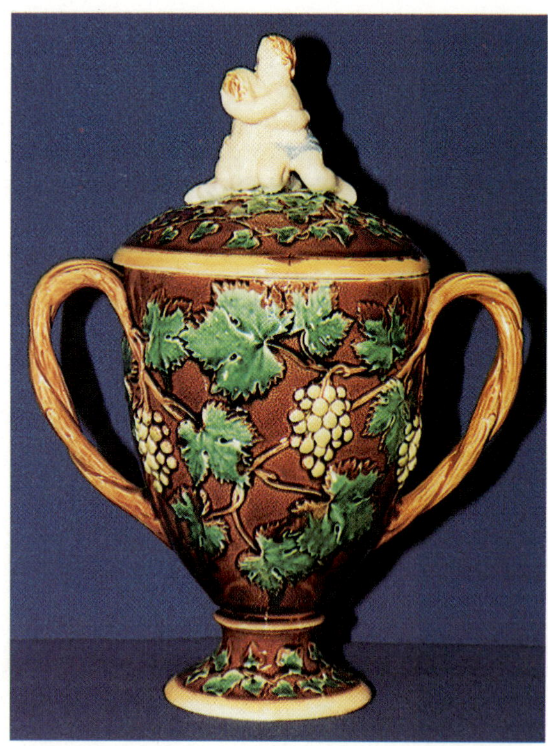

Minton covered urn with two cherubs on the lid with design of grape vines around urn and handles with lavender interior.

$1550

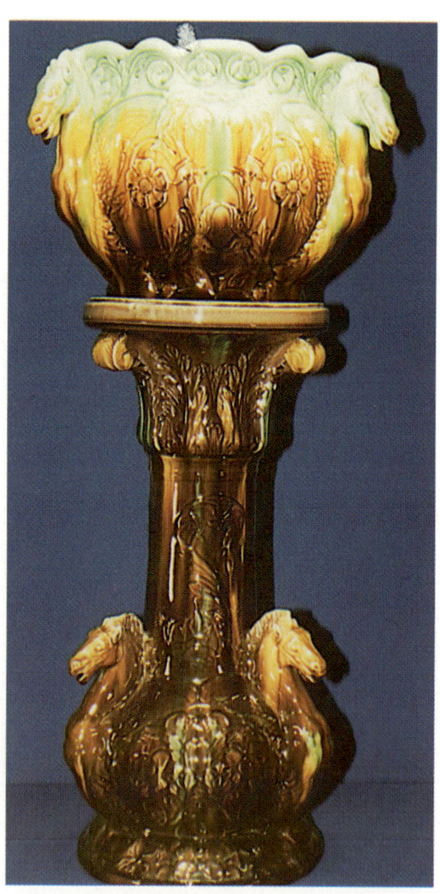

Two piece jardiniere with three horse heads on both pedestal and jardiniere, 34" h.

$475

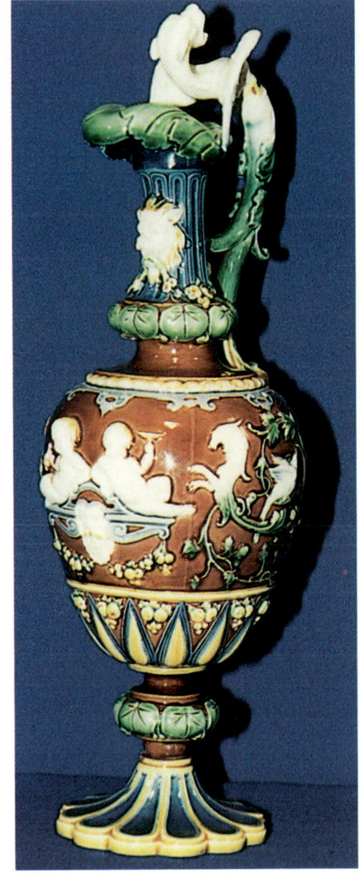

Minton ewer with winged griffin handle, lion face on neck, cherubs and birds on main body of ewer. Cobalt blue accents, 13 1/2" tall.
$1550

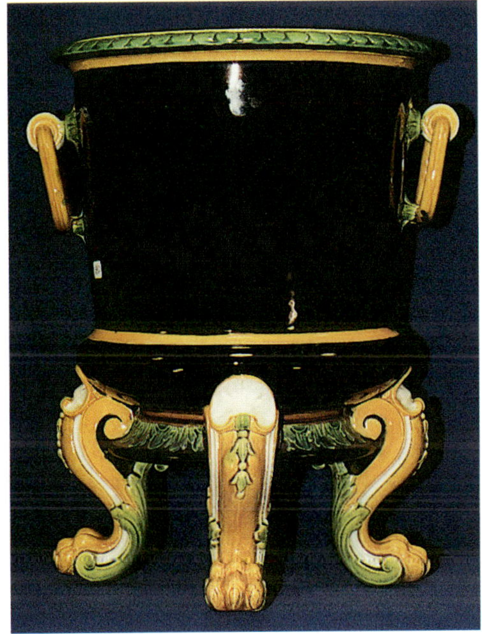

Minton wine cooler with paw feet, cobalt blue and ring handles, pink interior, 11 1/2" d x 16" tall.
$1200

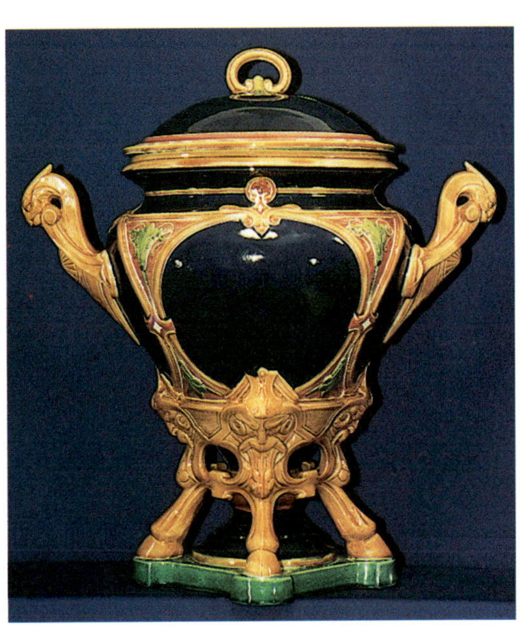

Minton urn, shape #1009, with original paper label on bottom from Mess Daniell London, with griffin handles and hoof feet, 18"w x 20"h.
$2300

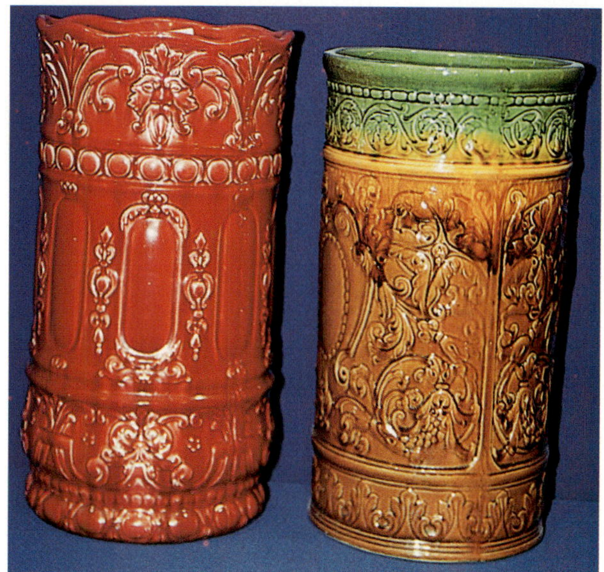

Two umbrella stands with foliage in relief, both are 20" tall, one in red the other is brown and green.
Red – **$110**
Green/Brown – **$150**

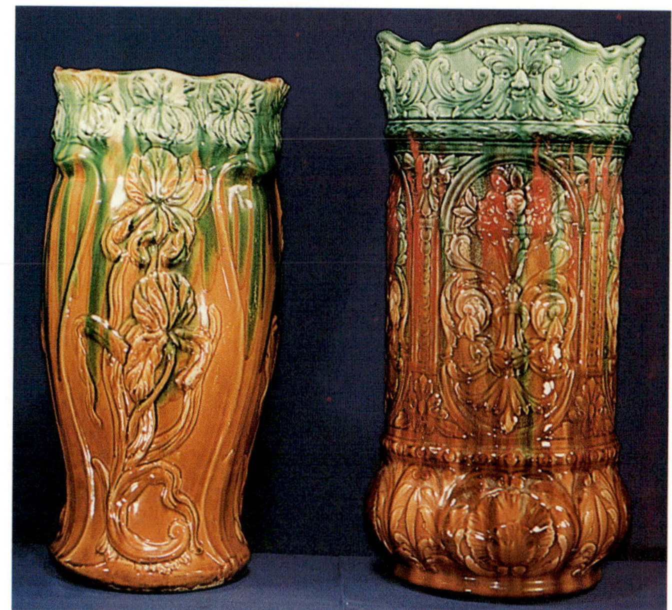

Two umbrella stands, the one on the left has an orchid design and is 20" tall. The one at the right has foliage in relief and with Old Man Winter faces around the top.
$325 each

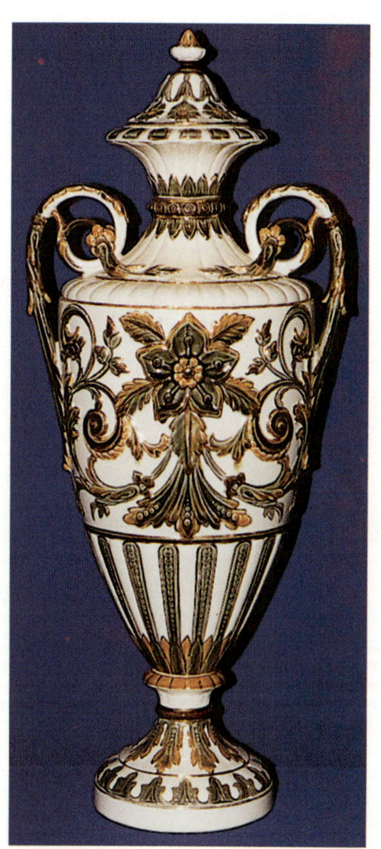

Rorstrand ivory covered two handled urn with lid, with flowers in relief, 25 1/2" h.
$225

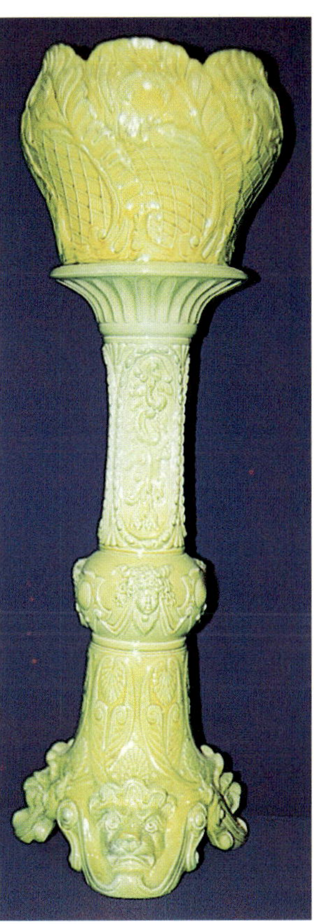

Two piece jardiniere and stand signed England. The piece has foliage in relief and the base has cherub faces and lion faces also in relief, 37 1/2".
$200

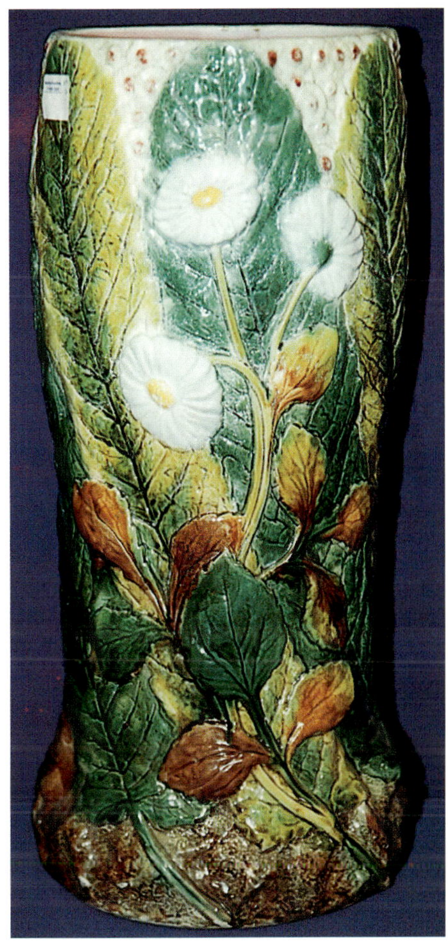

Tobacco leaf and floral with rosettes, umbrella stand, 21".
$375

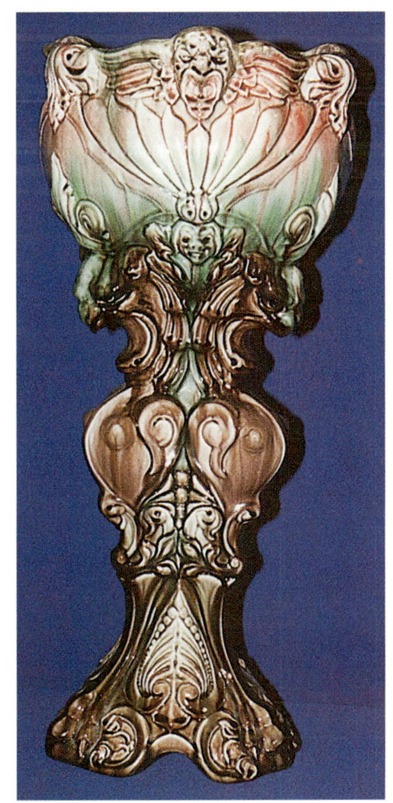

A floor jardiniere, 27", mottled pink, green and brown with jesters, grotesque and claw feet in high relief.
$300

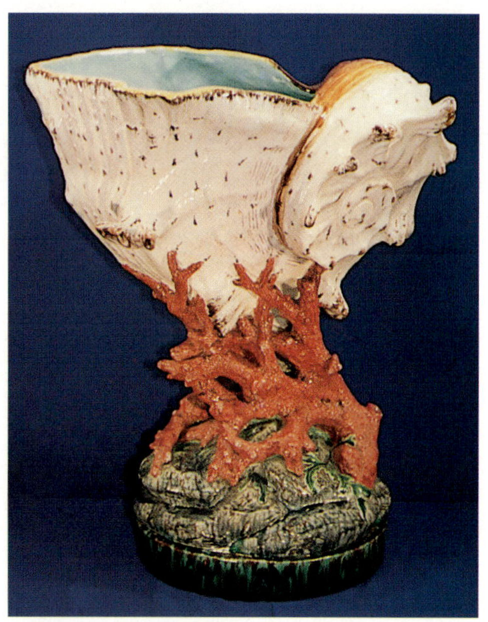

1866 Minton coral shell urn, (shape #966), 25" h, the shell is 18" x 23". The shell is supported by coral with seaweed and rock at the base – **$7000**

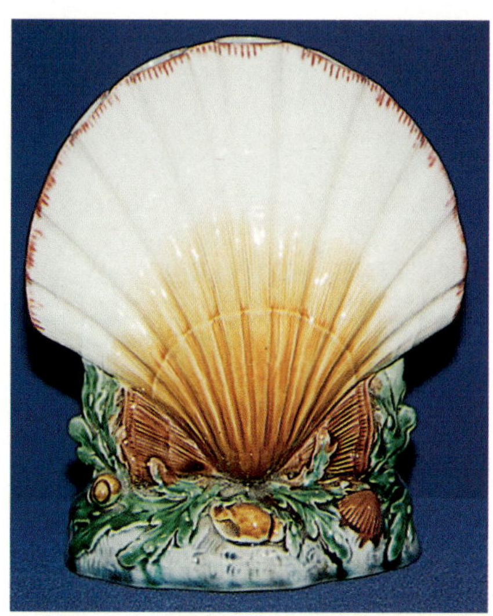

Minton shell, five hole vase, 7" h.
$1750

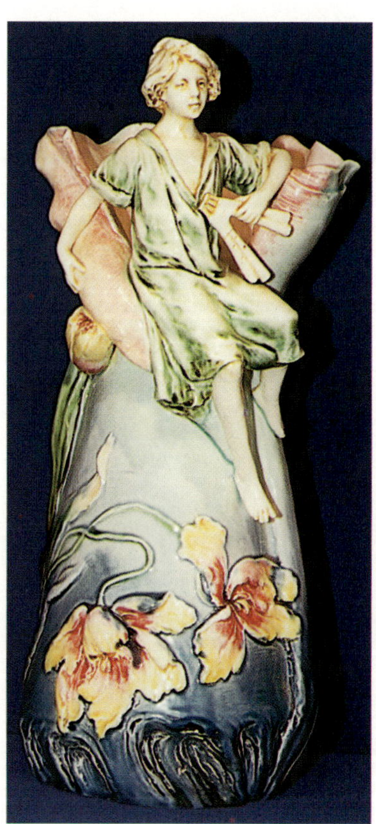

Art noveau vase with lady seated on the rim, 15 1/2" tall.
$875

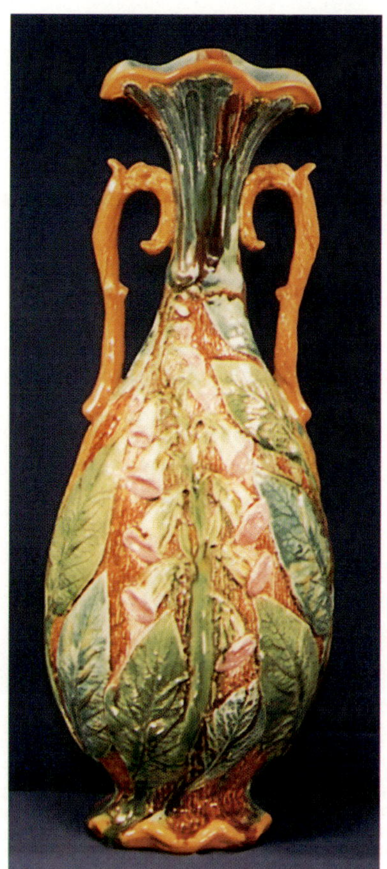

Fox Glove vase with handles, 17 1/2" – **$325**

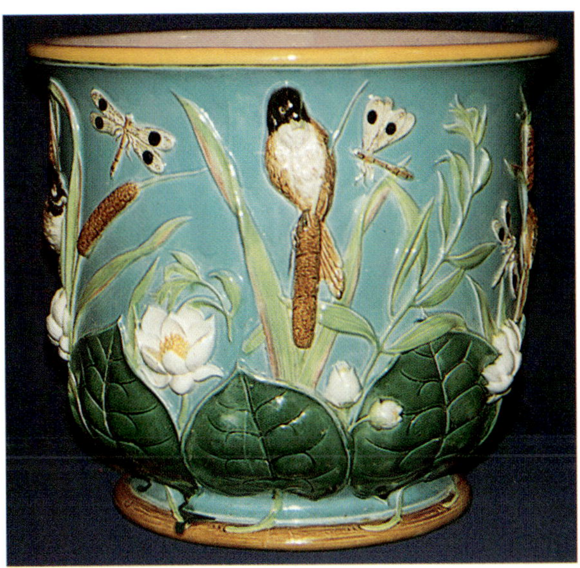

George Jones turquoise water lily jardiniere with cattails, birds and dragonflies, 17 1/2" d x 15 1/4"h – **$8500**

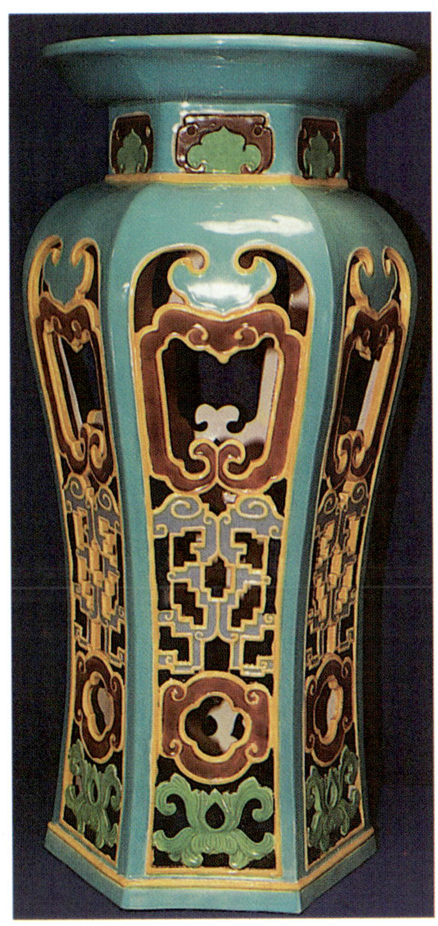

Minton jardiniere chinese taste. The top is 14 1/2"d x 31 1/4" tall.
$2000

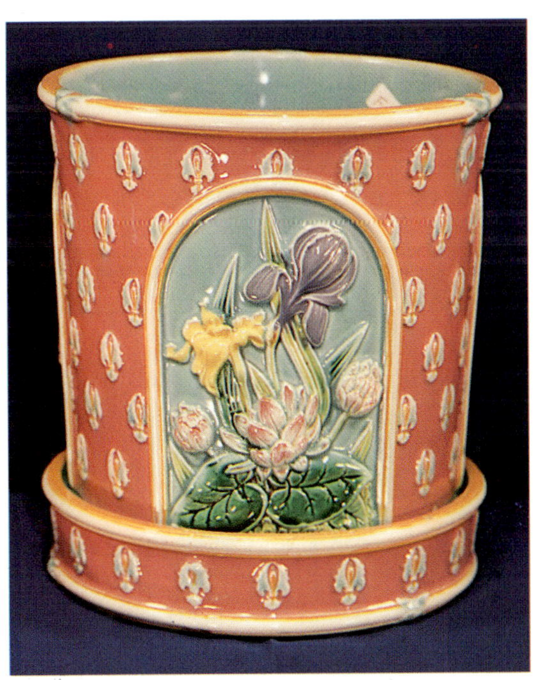

George Jones, two piece jardiniere, pink with iris in center.
$800

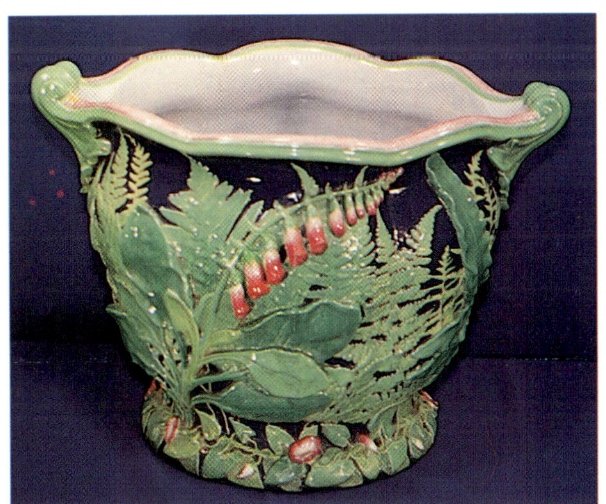

Minton 1851 fox glove jardiniere, cobalt blue background, 14 1/2"h x 21 1/2"w.
$3700

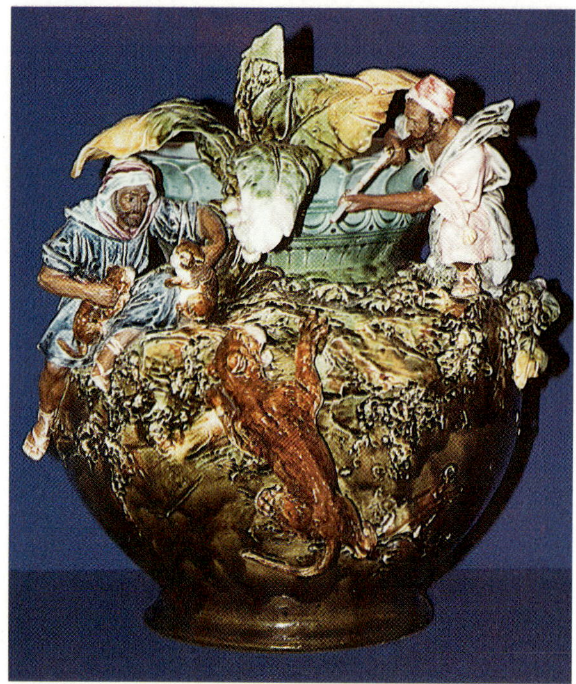

Continental Jardiniere with two black hunters taking tiger's cubs while the adult tigers are climbing up the tree after them, all in relief, 16 1/2" h x 14" w.
$2500

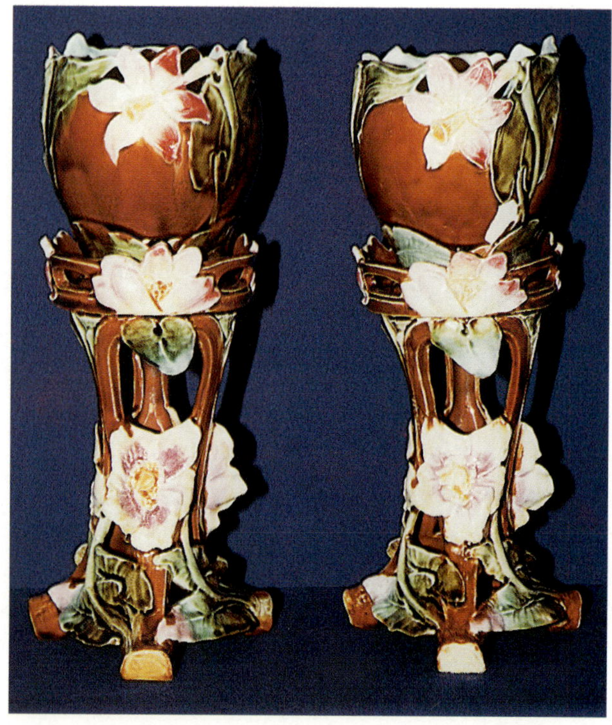

Pair of French Jardinieres and Stands, miniature salesman samples, 12" h.
$1250 pair

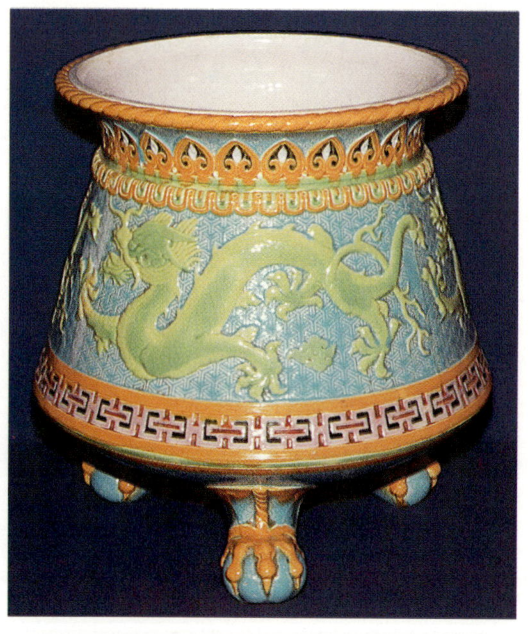

Minton Jardiniere, dragon footed, 14" h x 12" d.
$4500

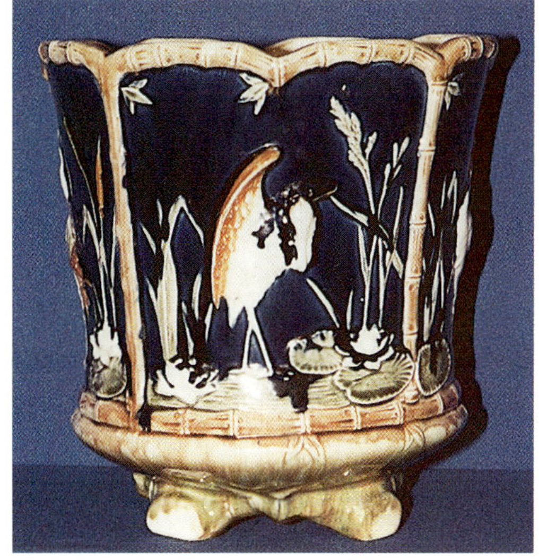

Jardiniere, cobalt blue, footed with stork in lily pads, 10" h x 10" d.

$1000

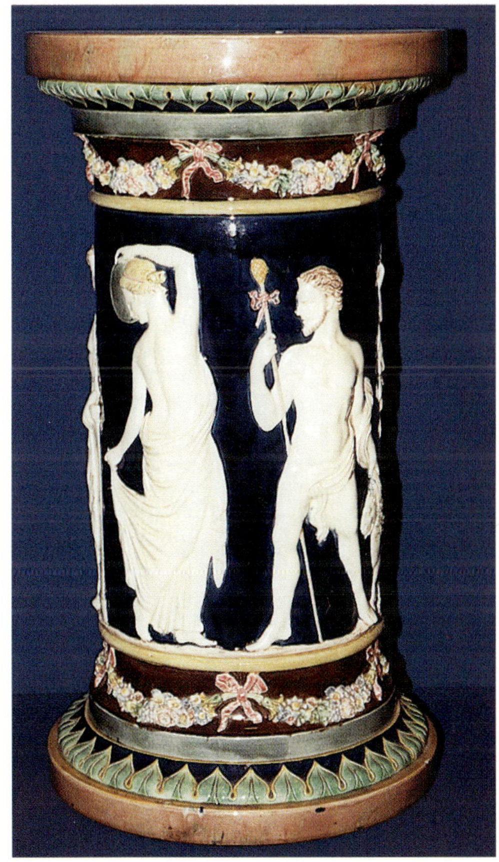

Copeland Jardiniere Stand, cobalt blue with mythological figures around center with drapes of flowers, ribbons and bows, 25 1/2" h x 14" d.

$3000

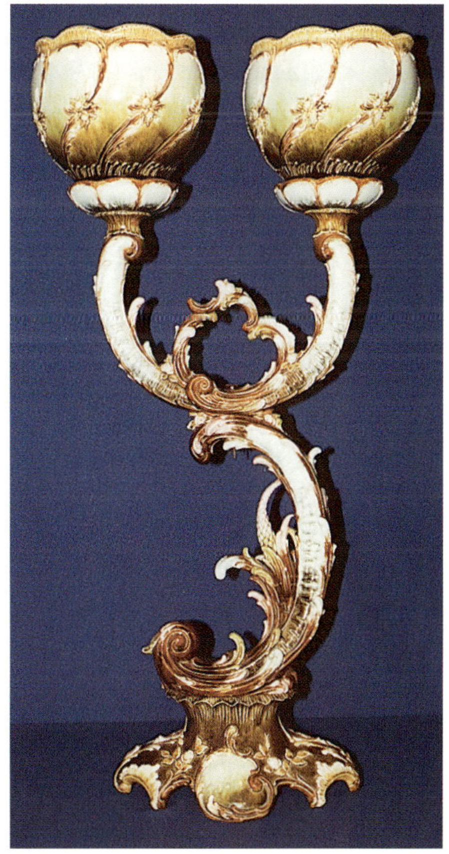

Austrian Jardiniere #6654, five piece double pedestal 45" h. The jardinieres are 10 1/2" d x 8" h.

$2500

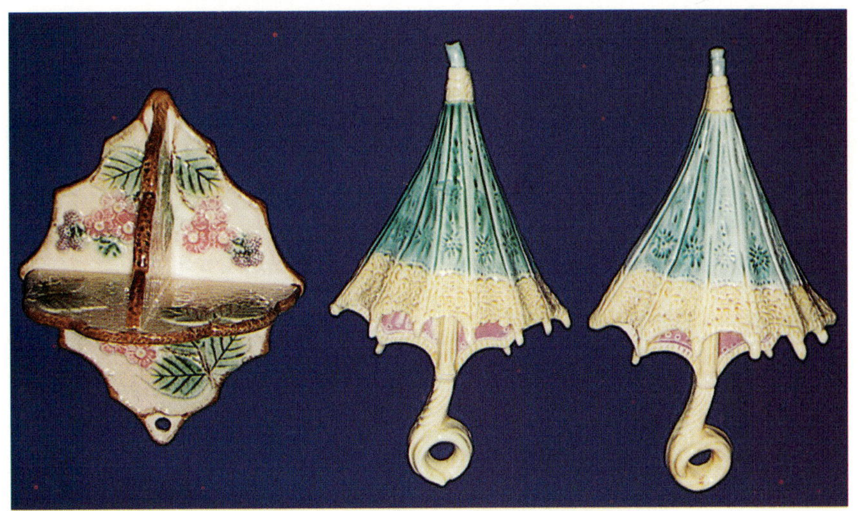

Left to Right:
Wall Bracket Shelf, with flowers and blackberries and leaf designs – **$400**

Pair of Parasol Wall Pockets, 12" h – **$700 pair**

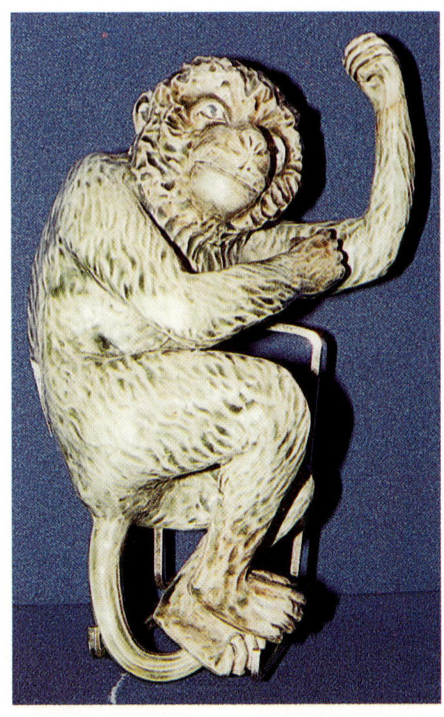

Hanging Monkey, mottled colors, with holes through hands and feet to hang on a string, 9" tall.
$600

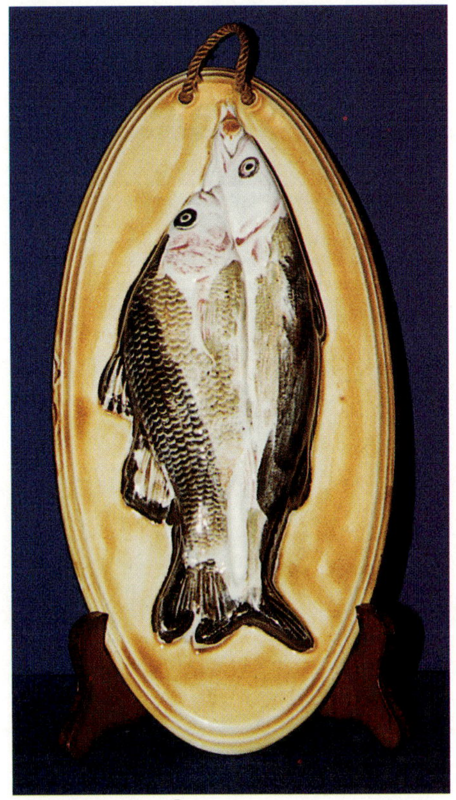

Wall hanging fish plaque, 13 1/2", George Morley's Majolica East Liverpool, OH.
$700

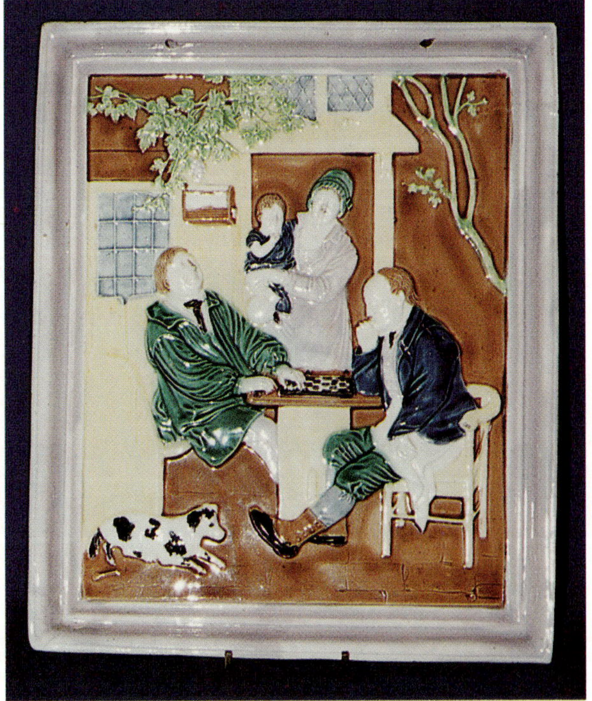

English Wall Plaque of two men playing checkers with a woman and child in the background, 13" x 11".
$1000

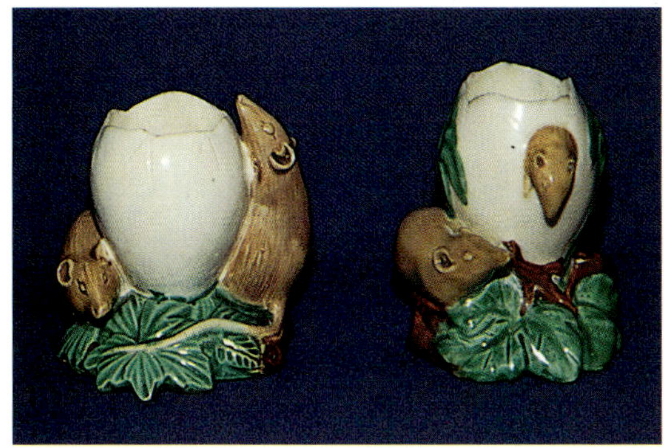

Pair Toothpick Holders, Royal Worcester mice figural, 2 1/2" h.
$1750 pair

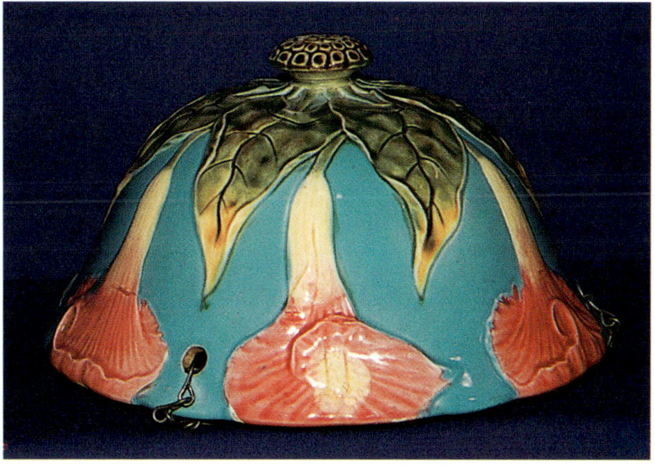

French Calla Lilly Hanging Planter, with turquoise background, pink and yellow calla lillies and green leaves, 10" d.
$1000

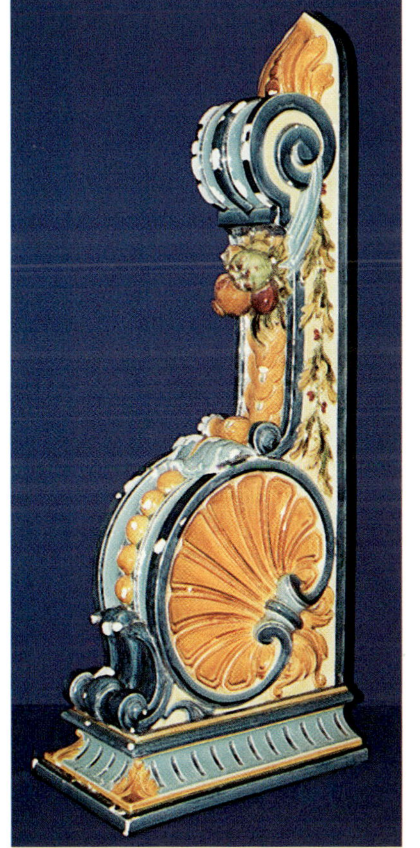

Table Bracket Base for foyer entry wall table, 42" h x 16" d x 10" w.
$700

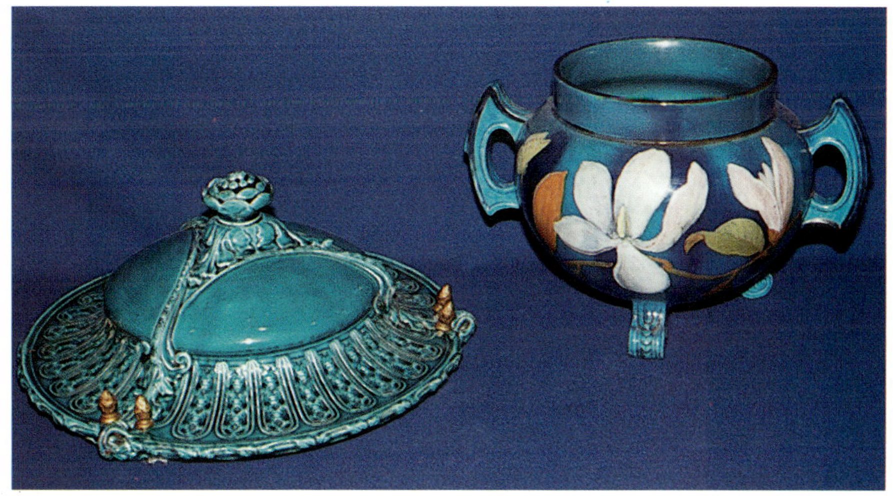

Left to Right:
Minton Hanging Planter, blue, date code for 1878, 15" d – **$500**

Minton Jardiniere, two handled with iris flowers and a butterfly, three footed, 9" h x 14" w – **$500**

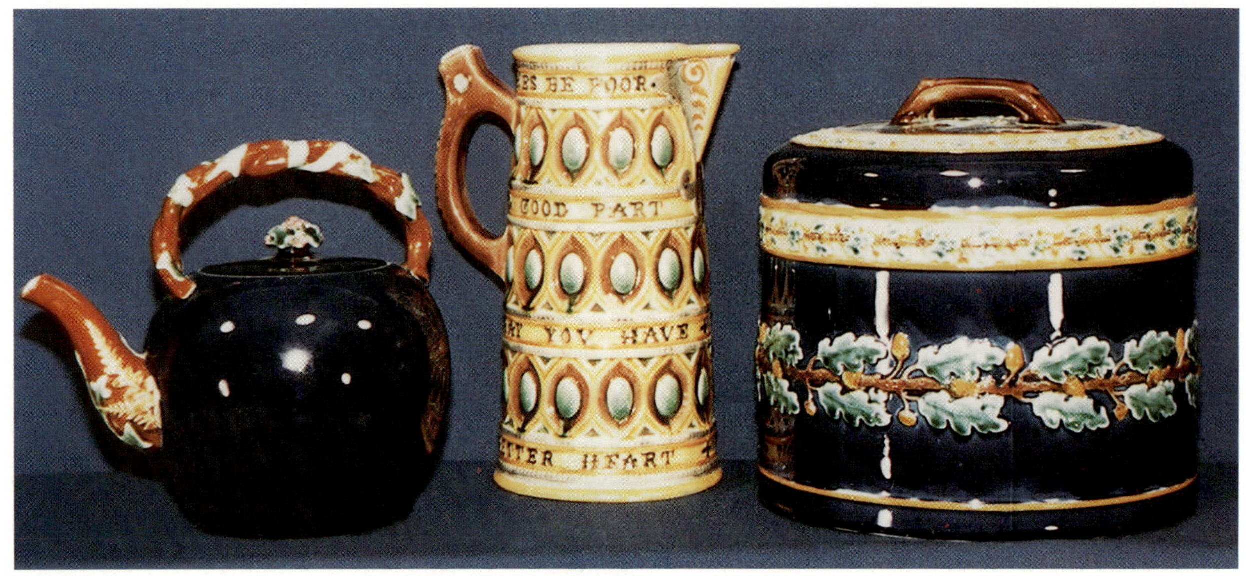

Left to Right:
Wedgwood cobalt blue teapot, with brown spout and handle, 7" – **$500**

Wedgwood caterer pitcher, 8 1/2" – **$450**

Wedgwood cheese keeper, cobalt blue with oak leaf and acorns, 7 1/2" h x 8"d – **$875**

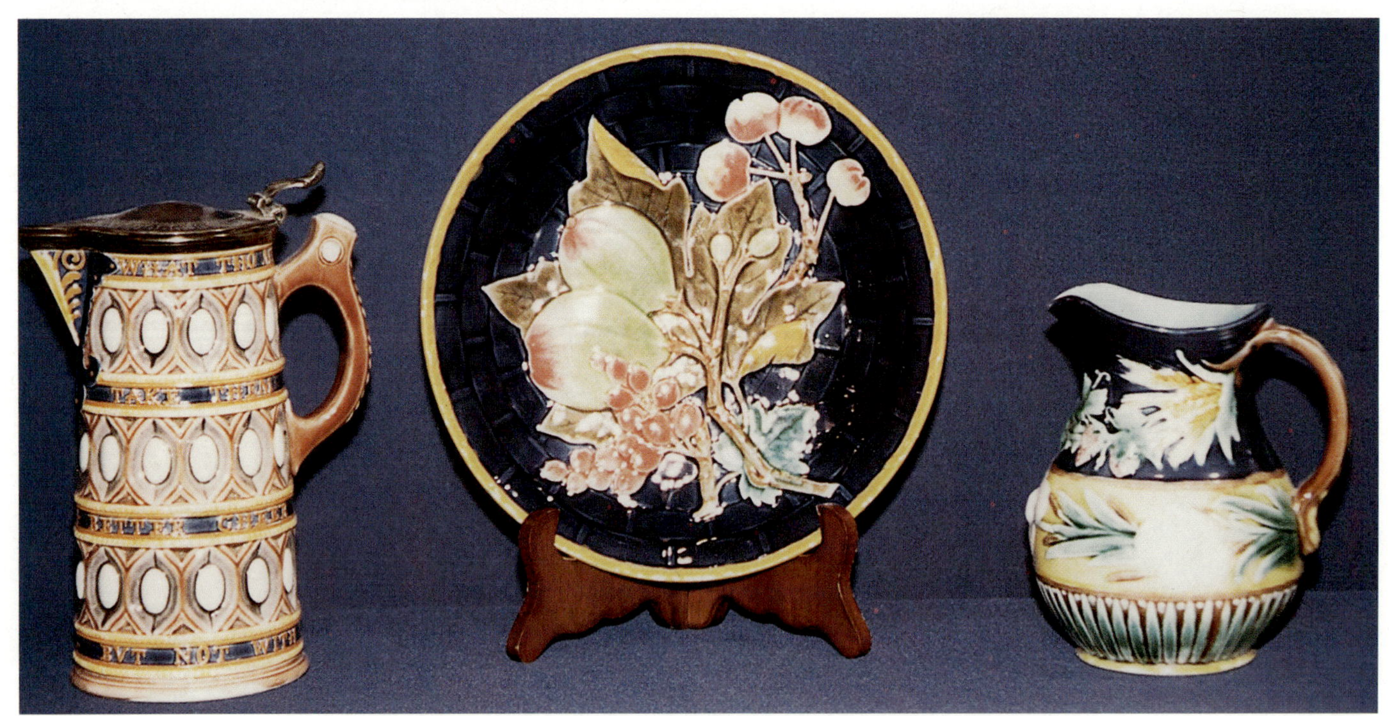

Left to Right:
Wedgwood caterer jug with cobalt and turquoise accent pewter top with hinged handle, 8 1/2" – **$775**

Wedgwood cobalt blue plate with three kinds of fruit, 9" – **$700**

Wedgwood cobalt blue and yellow pitcher with strawberries, wheat, and cattails, 6" – **$650**

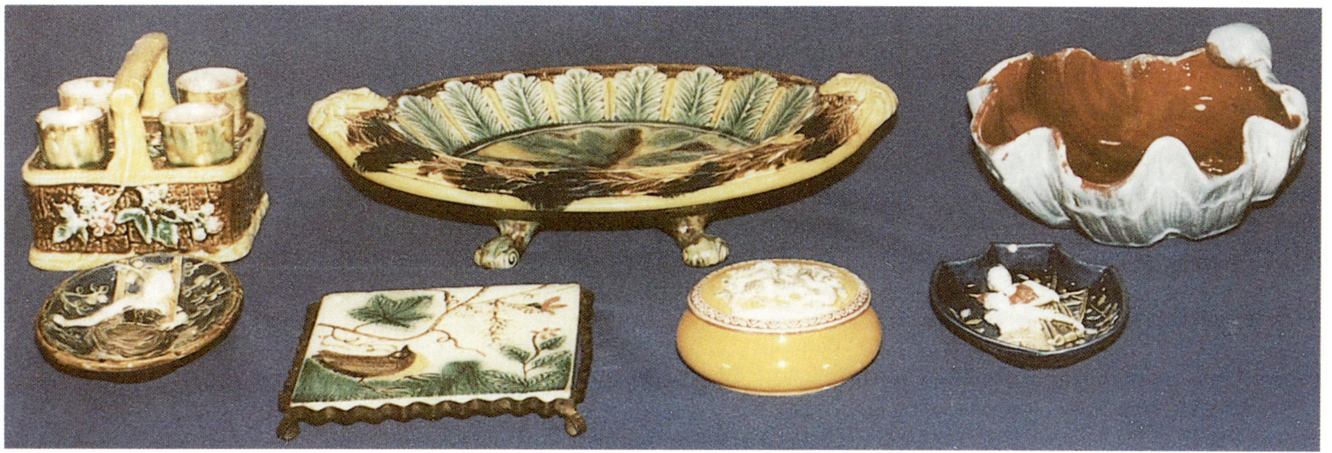

Front Row – Left to Right:
Lady on a ladder dish – **$125**

Tile with a bird and fly in a metal trivet – **$50**

Powder jar, Eichwald w/puttis, ram in relief – **$75**

Cobalt dish with lady and man on ladder – **$125**

Back Row – Left to Right:
Egg cup holder – **$500**

Footed bread platter w/ladies heads as handles – **$225**

Shell shaped bowl, turquoise w/red interior – **$75**

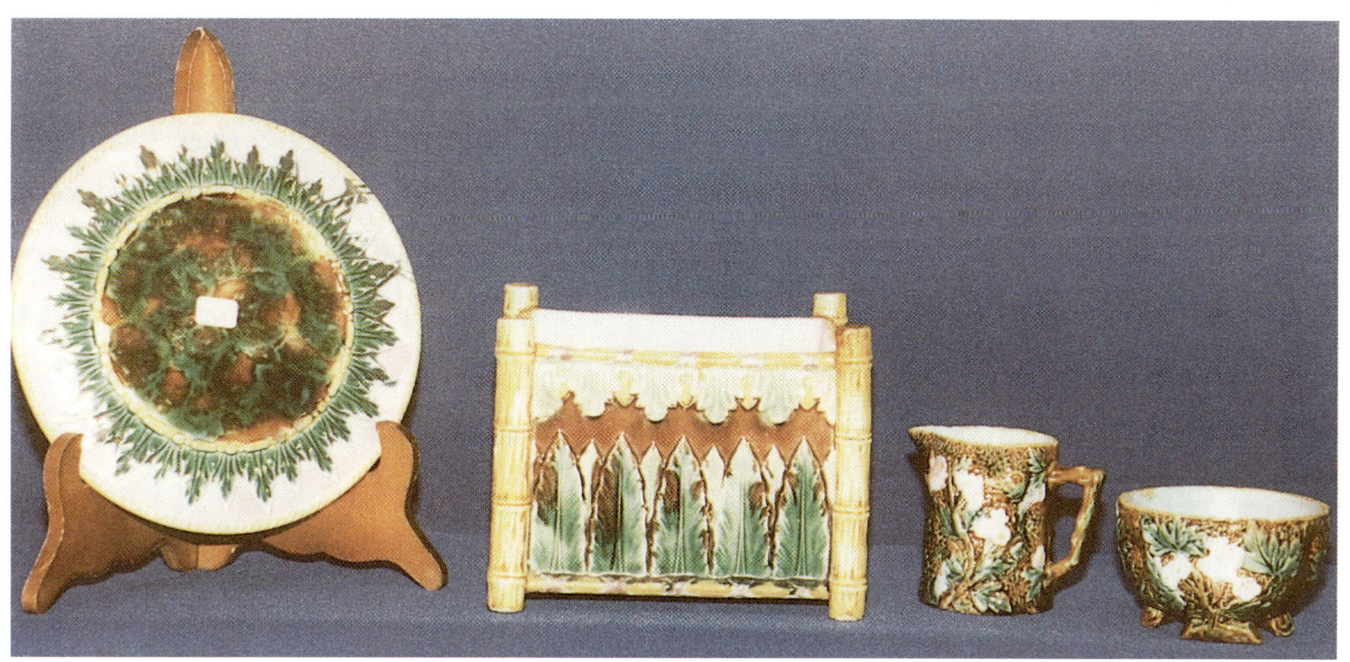

Left to Right:
George Jones round underplate, 8" – **$175**

George Jones bamboo footed planter, lavender interior, 61/2" sq. x 51/4"h – **$875**

George Jones rustic cream and sugar, turquoise interior. **$325**

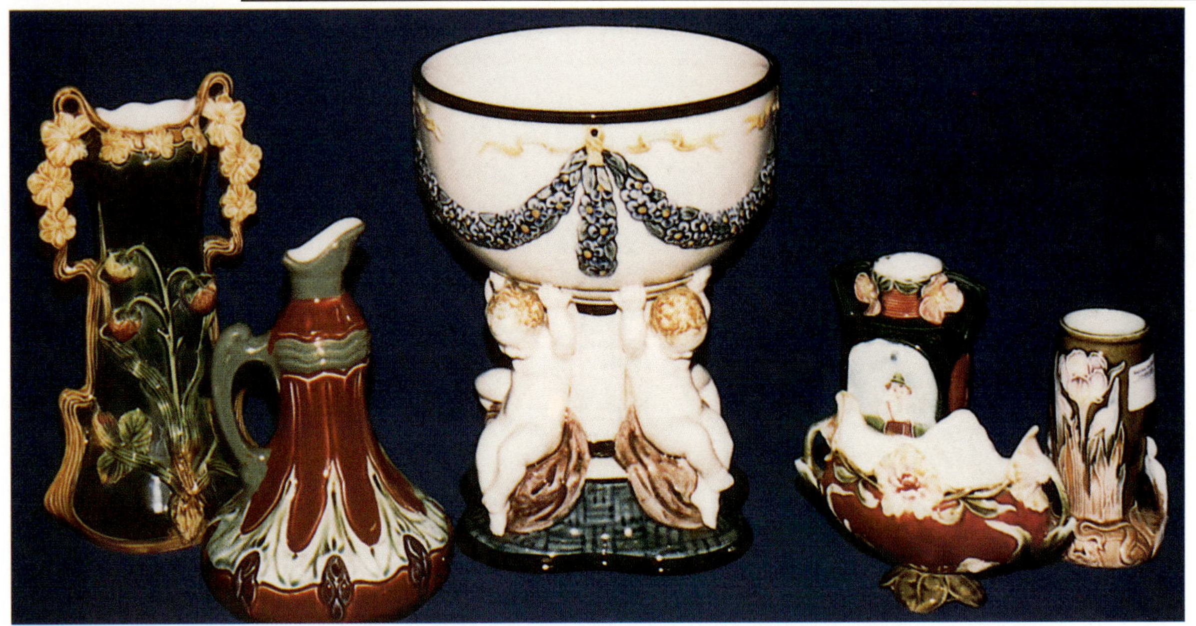

Left to Right:
JS continental vase, dark green w/applied strawberries and leaves, 10 1/2" – **$175**

Art noveau ewer, red background, 8" – **$175**

Baden compote supported by four cherubs, 8 1/4"d x 10 1/2" h – **$100**

Three small continental vases, (two art noveau styles and one with a boy and a wagon) – **$175**

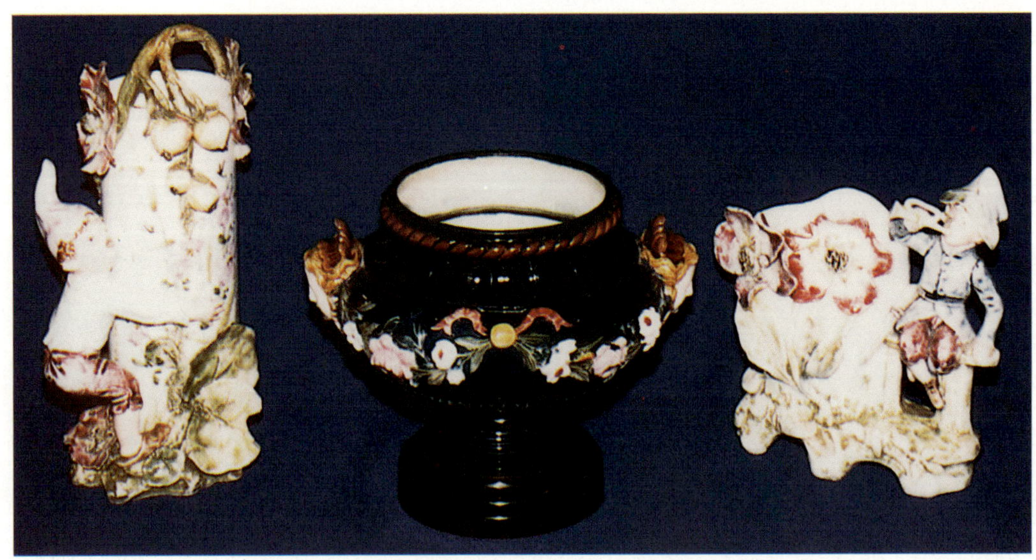

Left to Right:
French figural vase with boy on the side and applied flowers and fruit, 11 1/2" – **$100**

Cobalt footed bowl on a wooden base, two ladies heads and flowers in high relief, 8" h – **$350**

French vase with boy blowing a bugle and applied flowers, 8" – **$75**

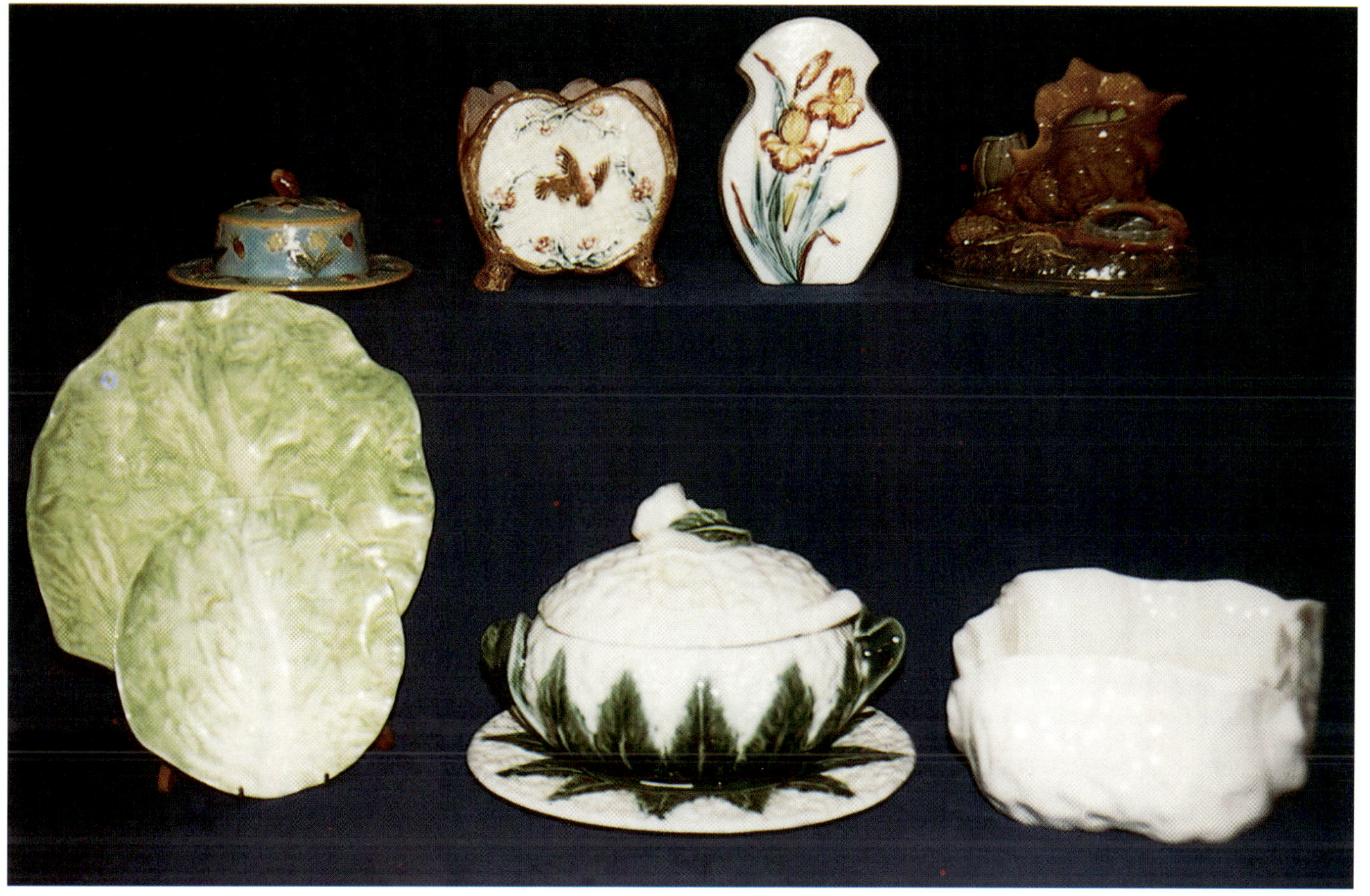

Top Row – Left to Right:
Covered butter, strawberry design – **$275**

Three sided bird on a basket footed jardiniere, 61/4" – **$225**

Vase with flowers in relief, 81/4"h – **$175**

English shell spill vase, "BB2379", 7"h x 10"w – **$250**

Bottom Row – Left to Right:
Wannopee "Lettuce Leaf" charger 12" and a matching plate, 8" – **$125**

Portuguese cauliflower soup tureen with underplate and ladle – **$225**

Wannopee white "Lettuce Leaf" salad bowl – **$25**

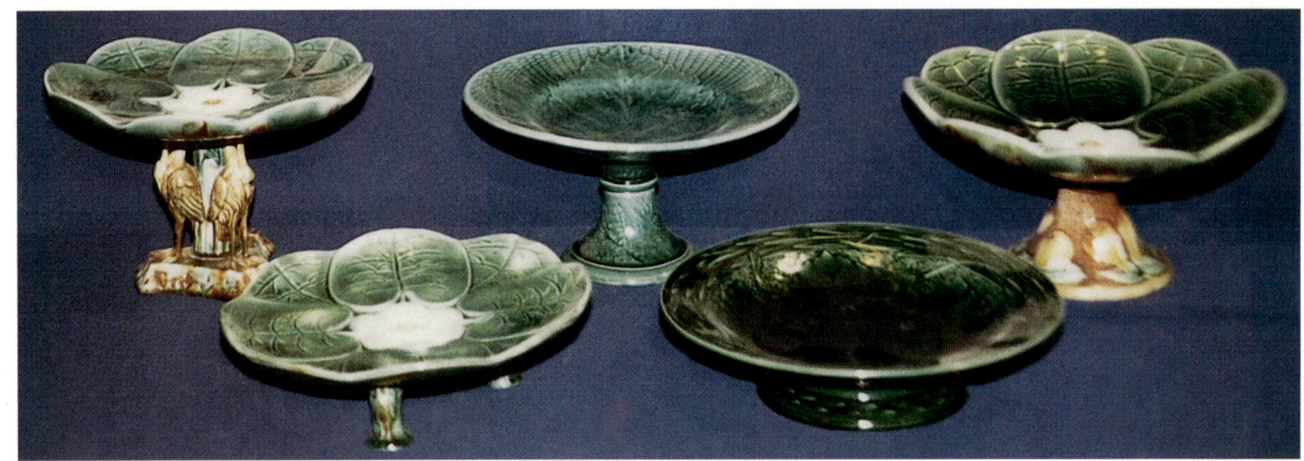

Front Row – Left to Right:
Pond lily plate with three storks at the feet, 9 1/4" d – **$175**

Dark green maple leaf footed bowl, 10" x 12 1/2" – **$75**

Back Row – Left to Right:
Pond lily cake stand with three storks on the foot of the stand, 6"h x 9" d – **$325**

Dark green maple leaf on basket compote, 5" h x 9 1/4" d – **$50**

Pond lily compote with brown pear base, 3 1/2" h x 10 1/2" d – **$175**

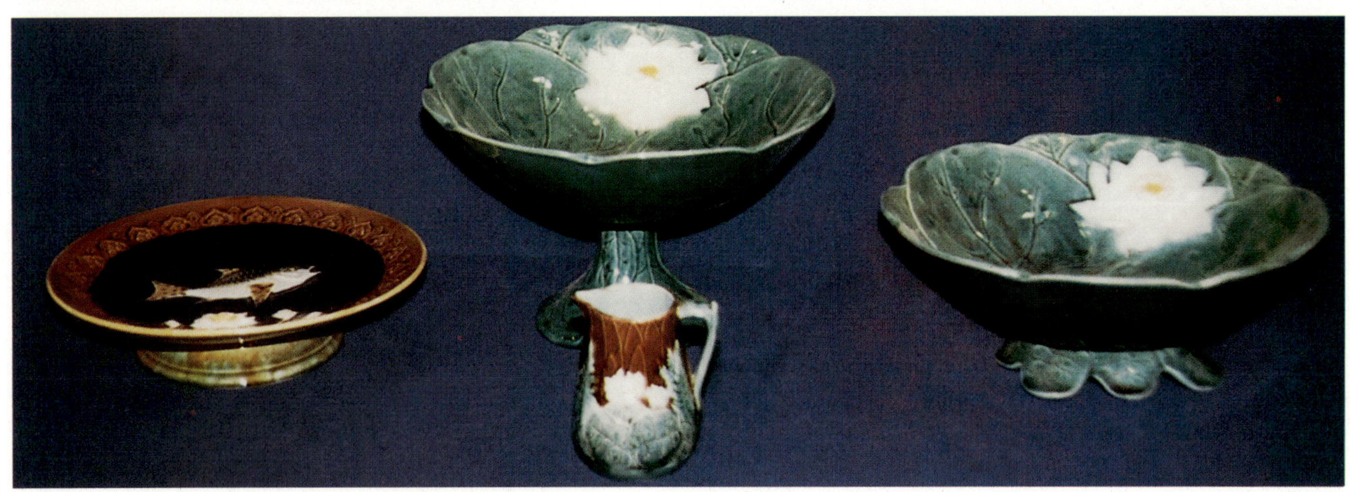

Front:
Holdcroft brown lily pitcher, 4" – **$200**

Back Row:
Holdcroft cobalt blue fish and daisy footed plate, 9 1/2" d – **$400**

Holdcroft pond lily compote, 6 1/2" h x 10 3/4" d – **$225**

Holdcroft pond lily footed bowl, 11"d – **$100**

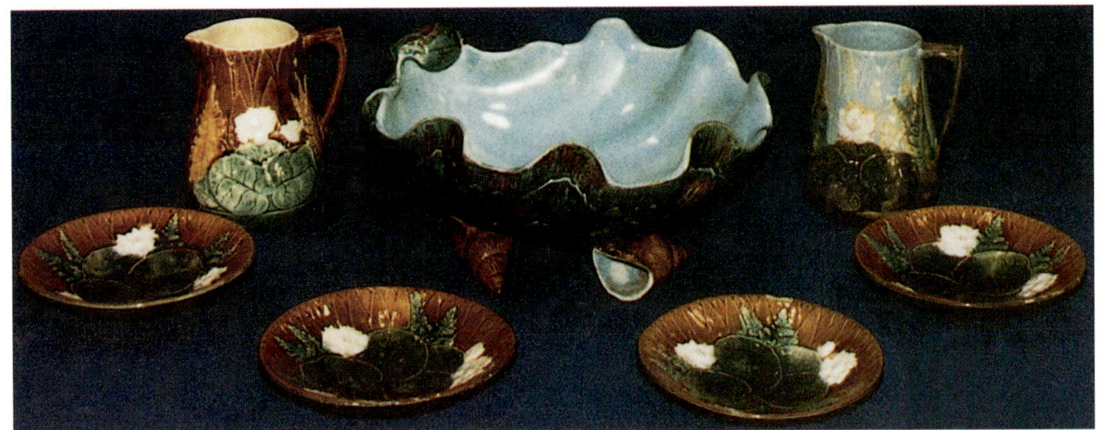

Front:
Set of four pond lily sauce bowls, 5 1/2" – **$50 ea.**

Back Row – Left to Right:
Holdcroft pitcher, lily design, 5" tall – **$225**

Holdcroft shell, turquoise interior, mottled exterior – **$450**

Holdcroft pitcher, turquoise, lily design, 4 3/4".
$75

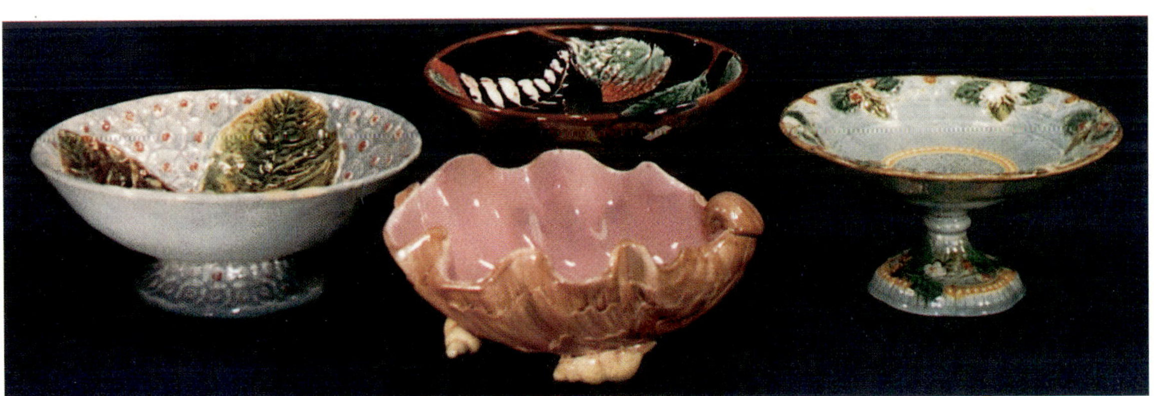

Front:
Holdcroft type shell bowl, with three shell feet, 10"d – **$200**

Back Row – Left to Right:
Footed bowl, banana leaf design, 4" x 10 1/2" d – **$225**

Cobalt blue bellflower compote, 9 1/4"d – **$450**

Sarreguemines turquoise strawberry compote, 5"h x 9 1/2" d – **$225**

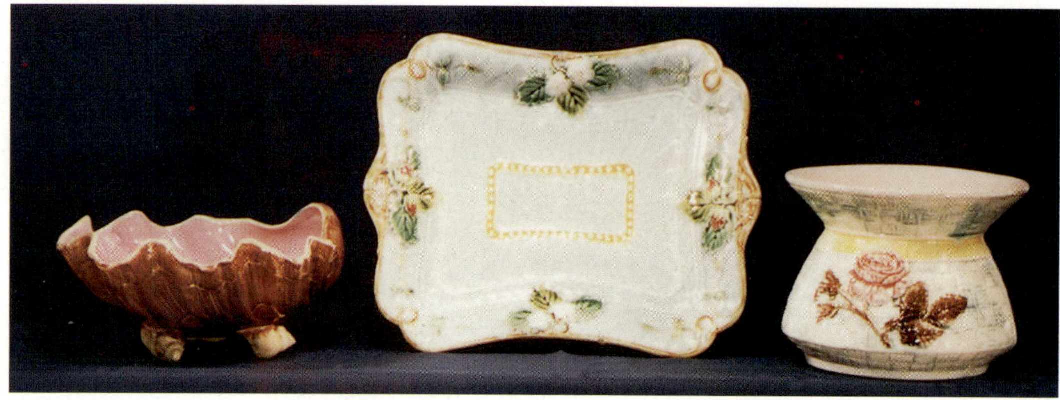

Holdcroft shell form bowl, with three shell feet, 9 1/2" d – **$200**

Sarreguemines turquoise strawberry platter, 10" x 12 1/4" – **$375**

Basketweave spittoon – **$225**

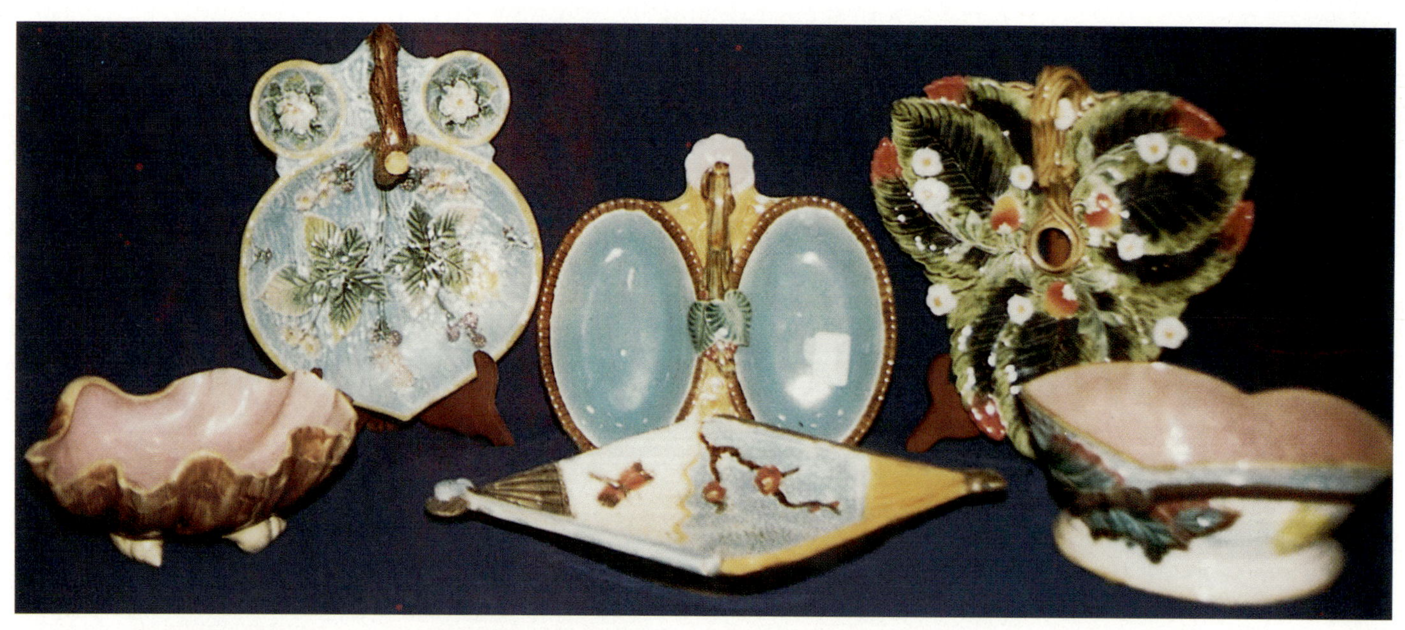

Front Row – Left to Right:
Shell footed bowl, pink interior – **$200**

Eureka bird and fan platter, 16" – **$225**

Oval bowl with picket fence and flower belt buckle, english registry mark, 11" l – **$125**

Back Row – Left to Right:
Tree bark berry server with twig handle, 12" l – **$350**

Two part handled condiment, 11" w – **$325**

Czechoslavakian three part condiment dish with vine handle – **$75**

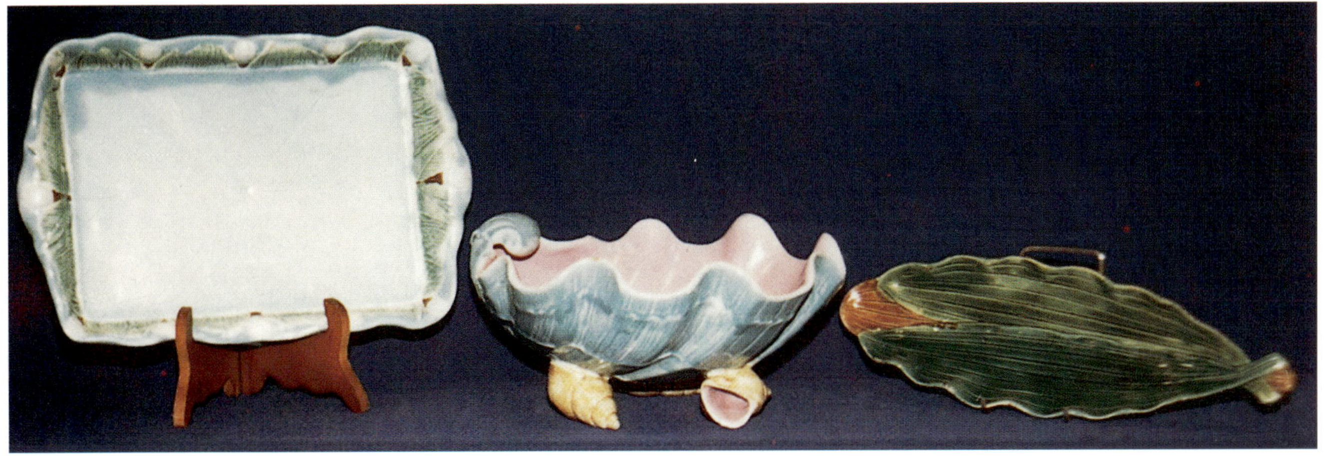

Left to Right:
Holdcroft rectangular platter with water lilies, 13". **$375**

Holdcroft shell footed seashell bowl, turquoise with pink interior – **$400**

Holdcroft corn leaf dish, 13 1/2" l – **$50**

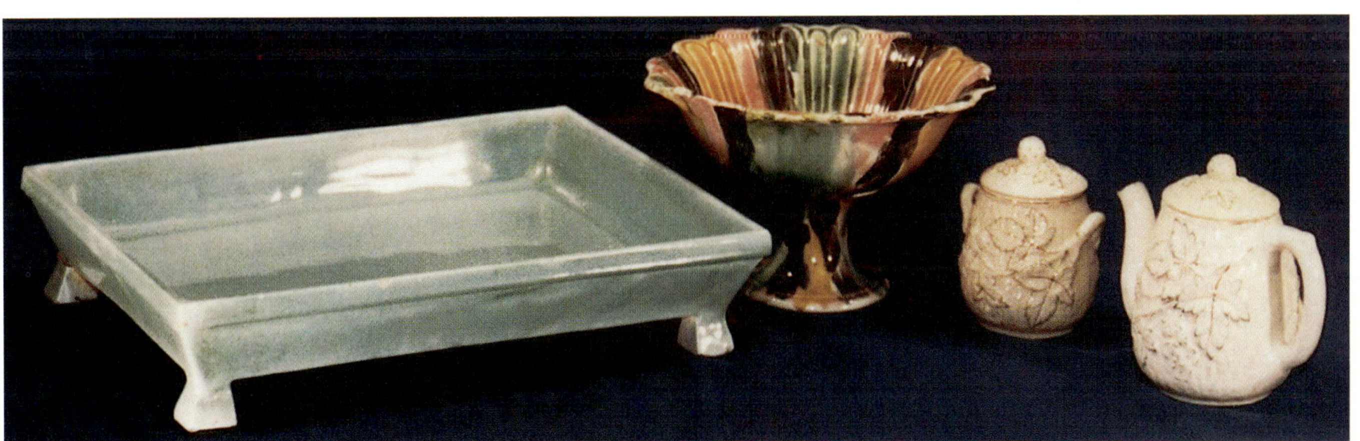

Left to Right:
Footed tray, turquoise, 12" x 16" – **$100**

Morley & Company compote, 6" h x 9 1/2"d – **$50**

Avalon leaf and berry sugar – **$75**

Avalon leaf and berry teapot – **$175**

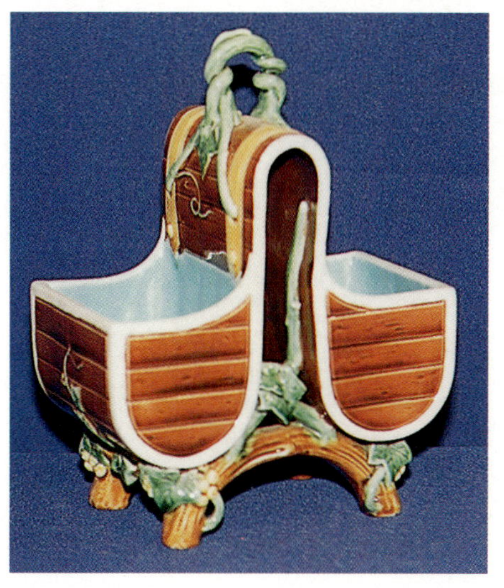

Minton two part card holder, 8" high – **$600**

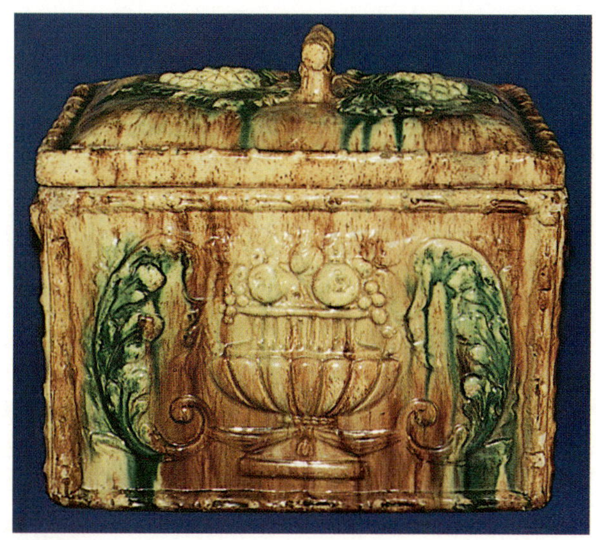

Bread dough box, mottled brown and green with grapes and fruit in relief, 11 1/2" d x 13" h x 16" w – **$400**

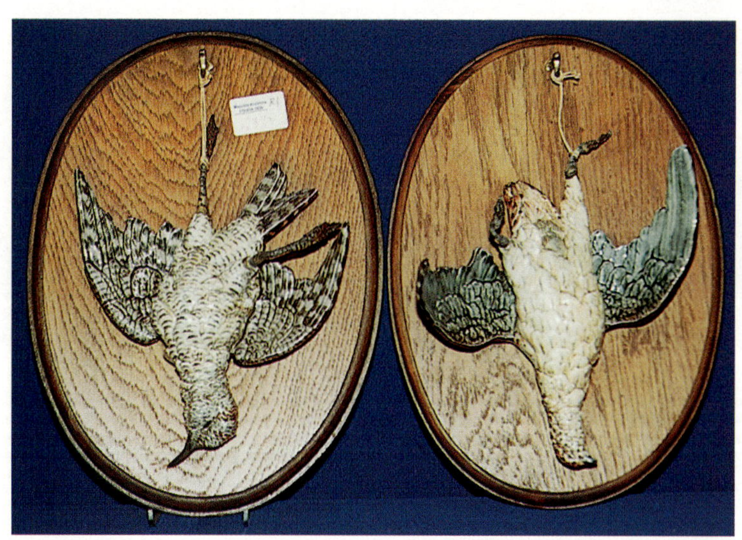

A pair of quail hanging on oak boards, 9 1/2" w x 13" l – **$550/set**

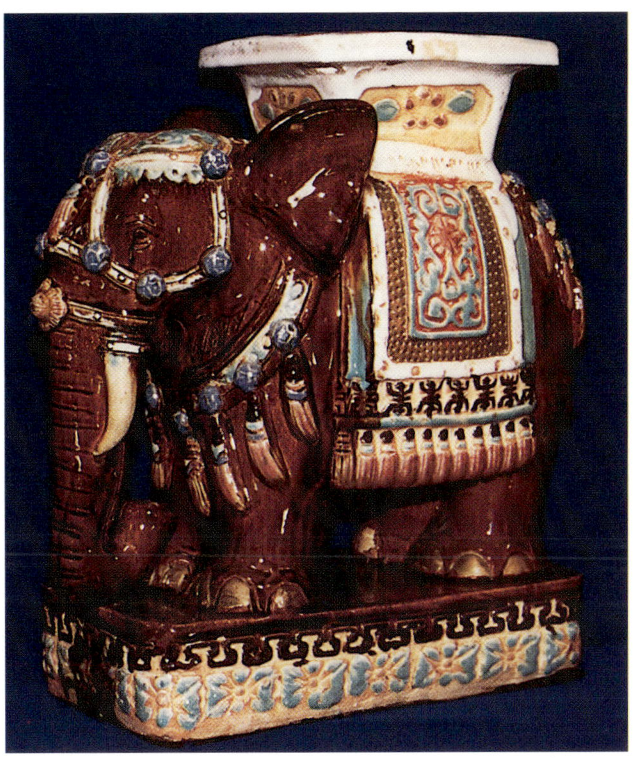

A Chinese majolica elephant garden seat,
17" tall – **$450**

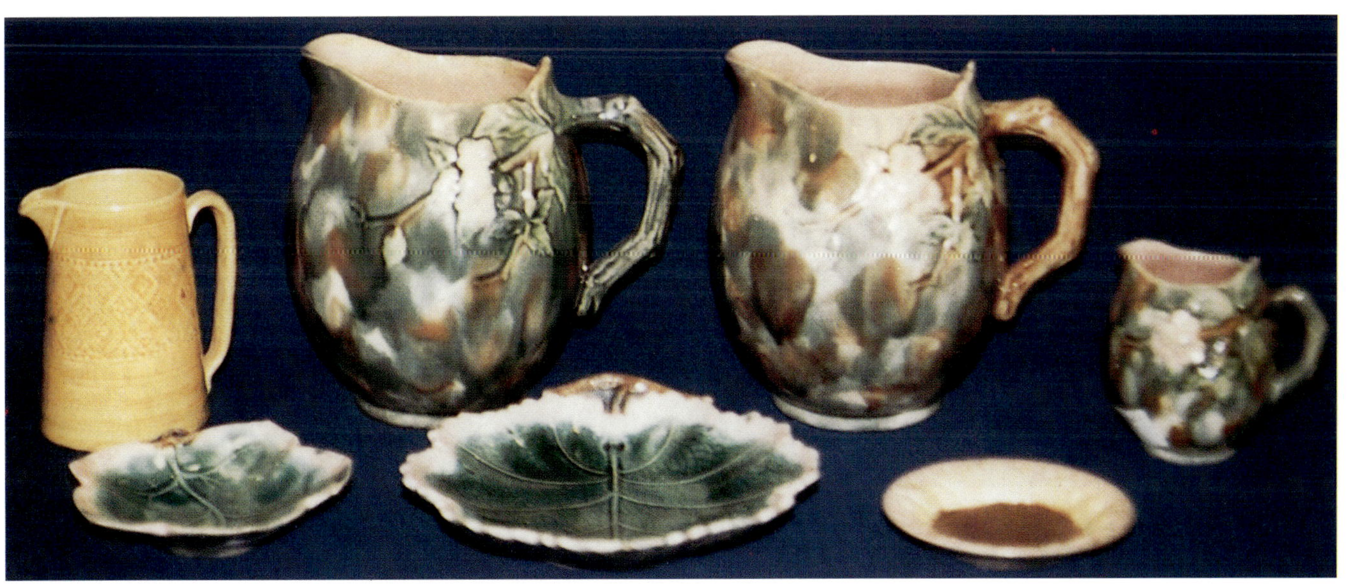

Front Row – Left to Right:

Etruscan leaf dish with a pink border – **$175**

Etruscan leaf dish, cobalt accent, 8 1/2" – **$100**

Pink sunflower Etruscan sauce dish – **$225**

Back Row – Left to Right:

A conventional Etruscan jug, 5 1/2" – **$25**

Two Etruscan Hawthorne jugs, 8" – **$100 each**

Etruscan Hawthorne creamer, 4 1/4" – **$100**

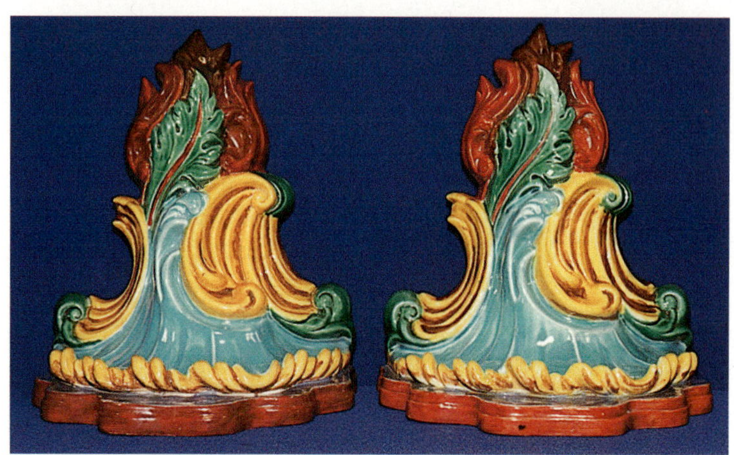

A pair of bracket wall shelves, (Royal Worchester) 6" d x 81/2" h – **$775**

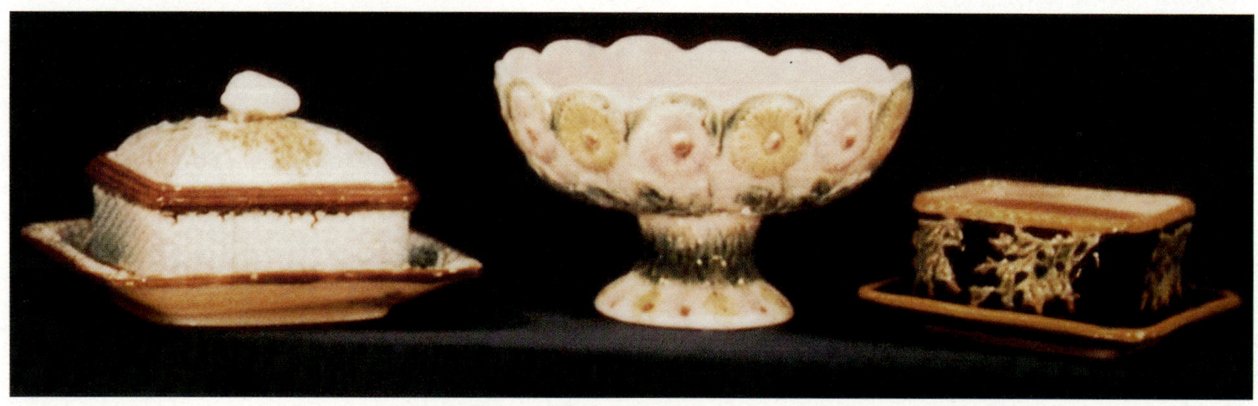

Left to Right:
Conch shell basketweave sardine box with underplate – **$550**

Etruscan daisy compote – **$450**

Cobalt blue shell and seaweed sardine box – **$300**

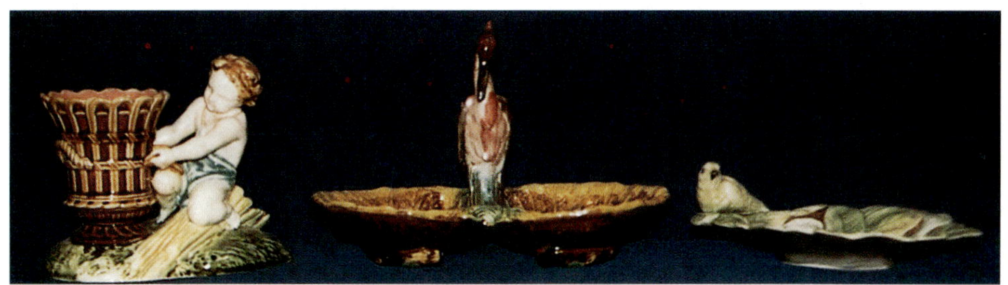

Sarreguemines cherub with basket, 6 1/2" h x 8" l – **$500**

Two part condiment with stork handle and twig base, 7 1/4" h x 11 1/2" l – **$400**

Bird on a floral leaf dish, 10" l – **$275**

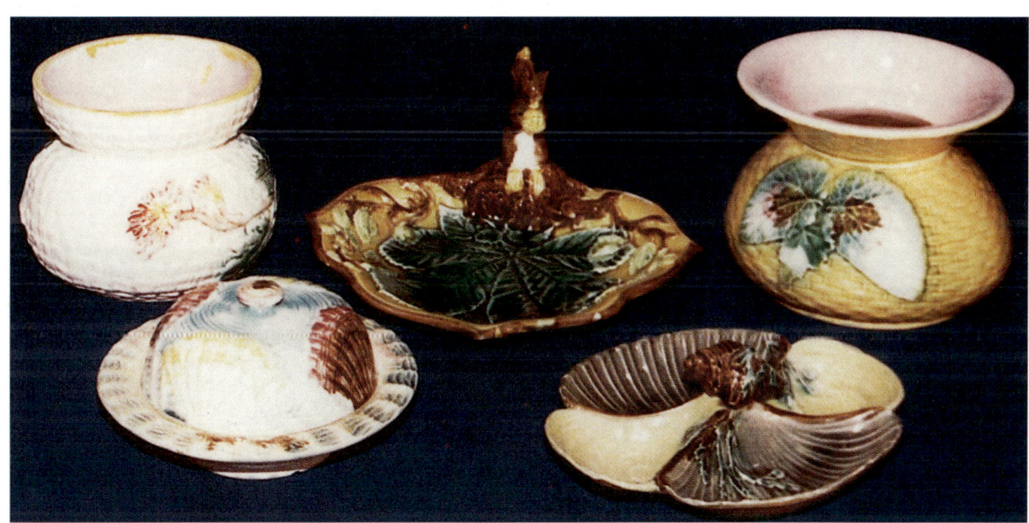

Front Row – Left to Right:
Butter dish designed after a shell and waves with seaweed – **$125**

Shell condiment dish – **$75**

Back Row – Left to Right:
Basket spittoon with flower – **$175**

Leaf dish with a squirrel holding a nut sitting on dish – **$250**

Yellow basket spittoon with begonia leaf – **$200**

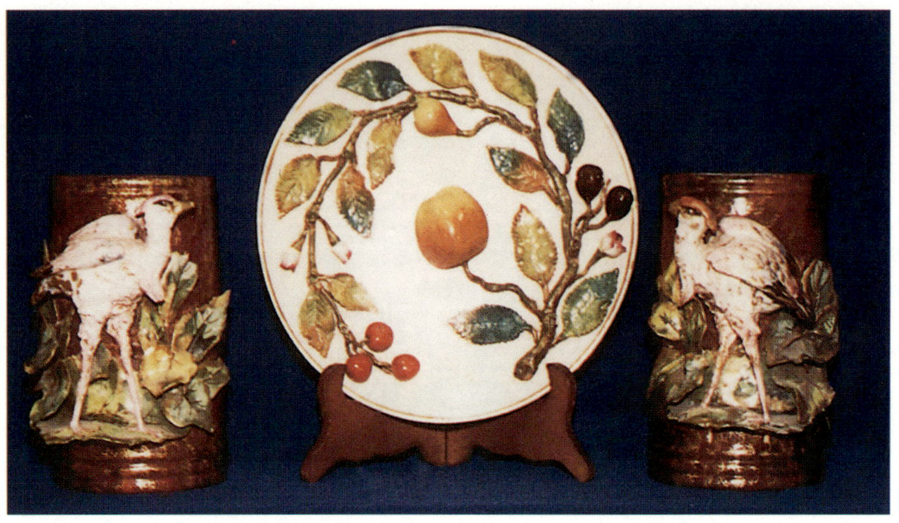

Sides:
Two french bird vases, 8 1/4", marked "EG 152" – **$125**

Middle:
White plaque with applied fruit and leaves – **$50**

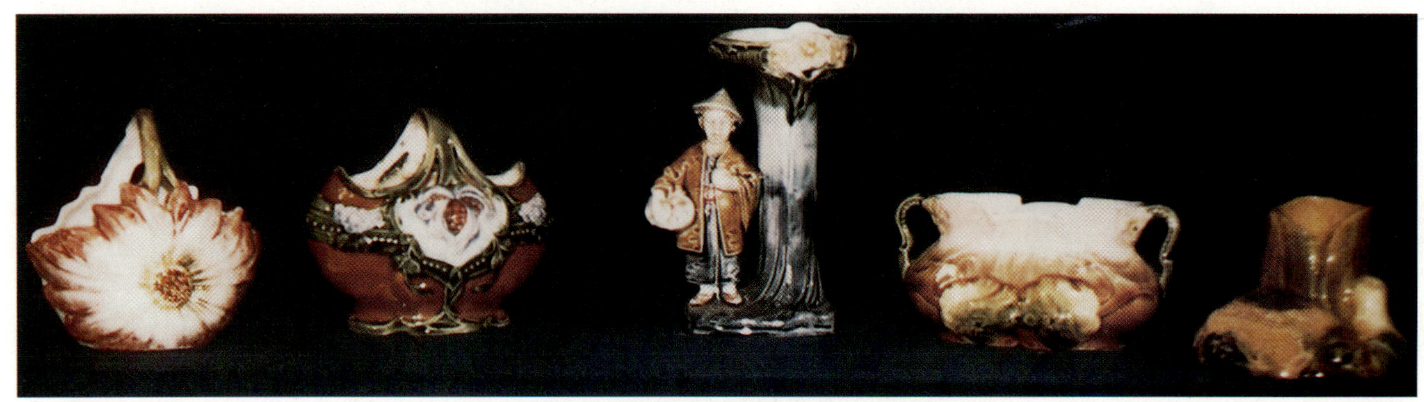

Left to Right:
Continental sunflower basket, 4 1/2" – **$100**

Continental basket – **$100**

Continental figural vase with oriental man at tree – **$100**

Continental planter – **$100**

Tree stump toothpick holder – **$100**

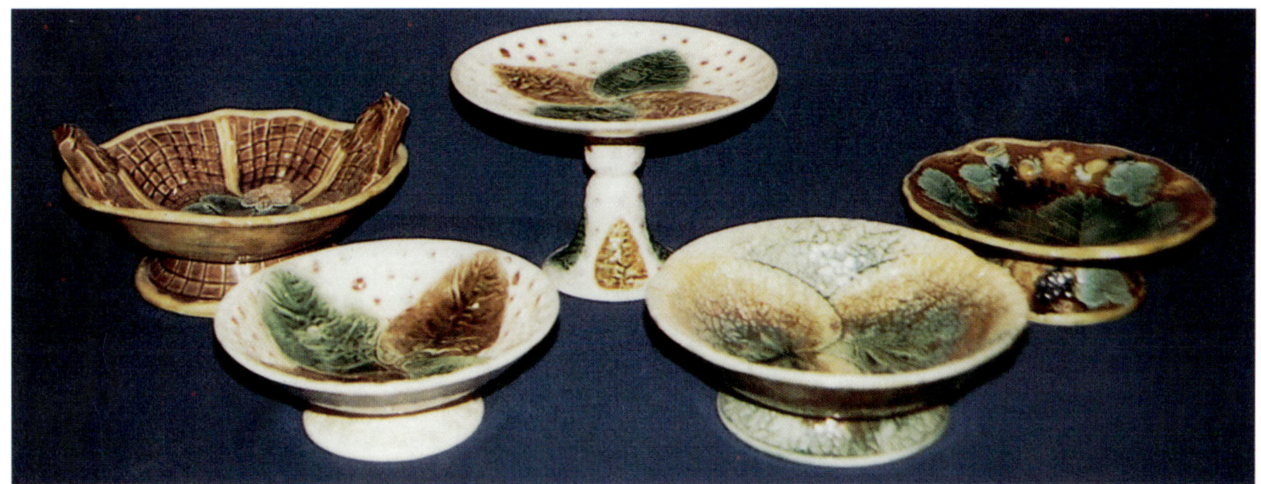

Front Row – Left to Right:
Tobacco leaf with rosettes, low compote bowl, 8 1/2" – **$75**

Overlapping begonia footed bowl – **$100**

Back Row – Left to Right:
Twig handled footed bowl – **$100**

Tobacco leaf cake stand, 6" h x 9 1/4" d – **$75**

Grape leaf platter, 11 1/4" – **$225**

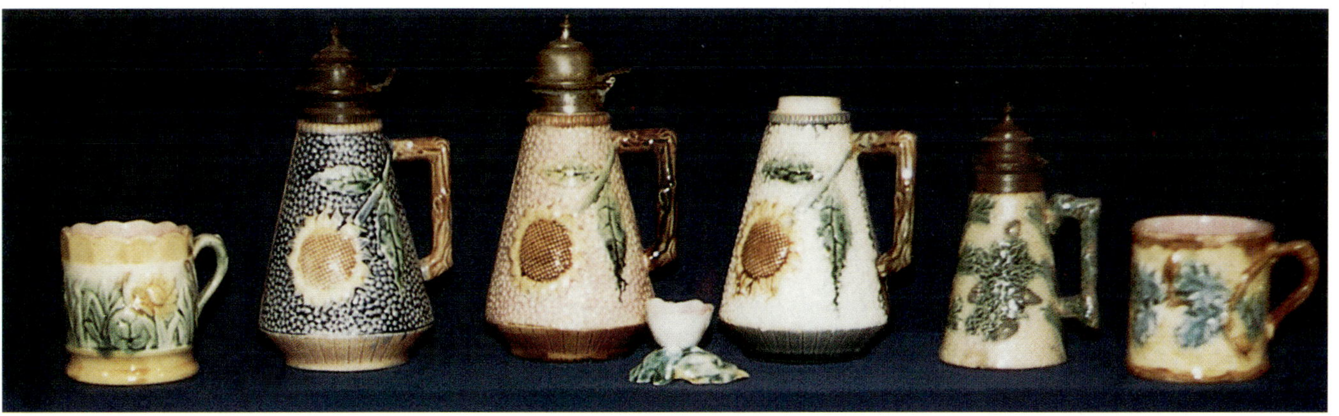

Front Row:
Etruscan lily salt dip – **$50**

Back Row – Left to Right:
Etruscan lily mug – **$50**
Etruscan cobalt sunflower syrup – **$650**
Etruscan pink sunflower syrup – **$375**
Etruscan white sunflower syrup – **$150**
Etruscan acorn mug – **$150**
Etruscan bamboo mug – **$100**

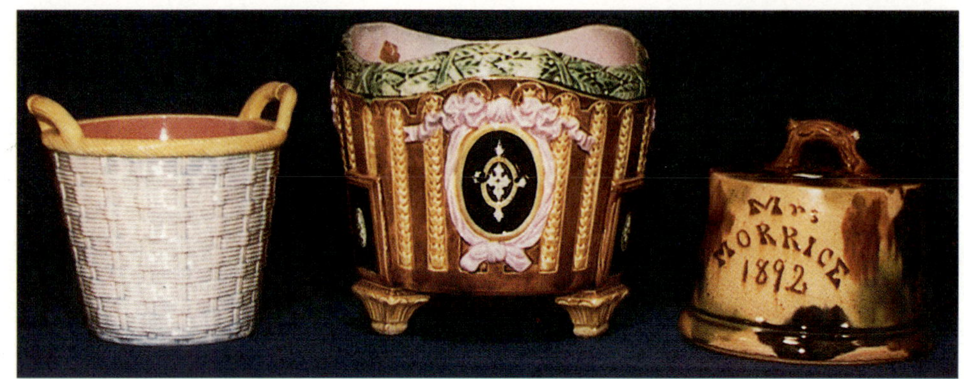

Two handled basket, 6 1/2" tall – **$250**

Jardiniere with medallion in center – **$350**

Cheese bell, mottled, marked Mrs. Morrice 1892 – **$225**

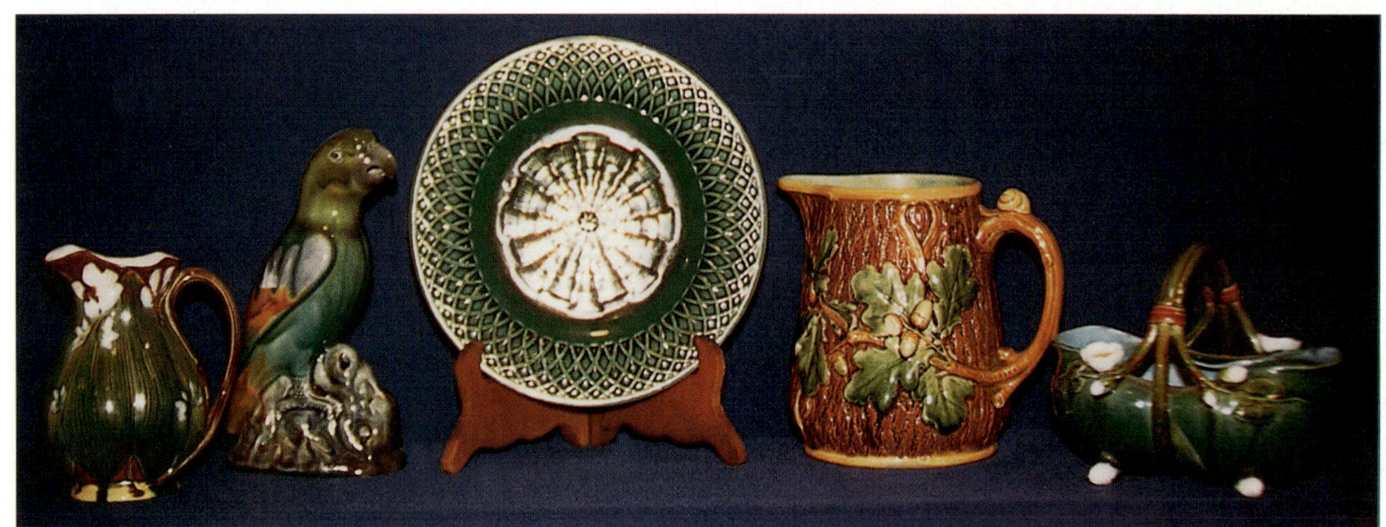

Green leaf and floral pitcher, 6" – **$375**

Minton English parrot, 8 1/2" – **$450**

Minton basketweave dark green plate, 9" – **$100**

Minton oak leaf and acorn on tree bark pitcher with snail finial on handle, date mark 1861, 6 3/4" – **$550**

Minton pond lily basket, 7"w – **$825**

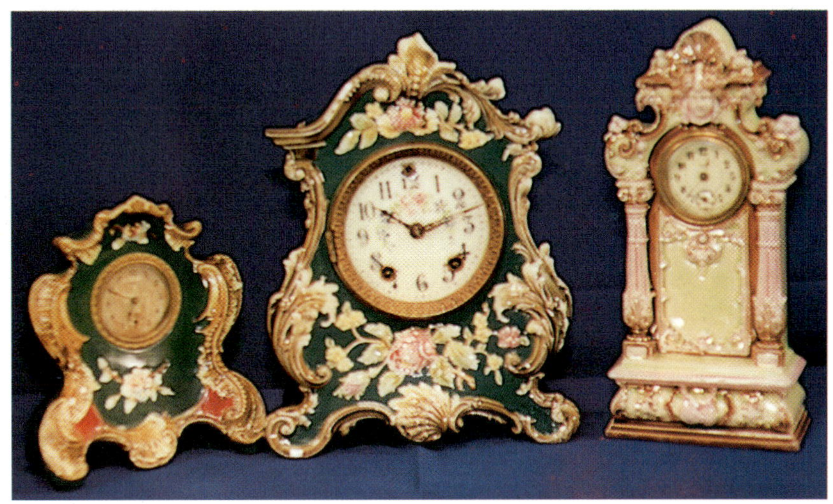

Left to Right:
French majolica clock marked New Haven Clock Works, 7" tall. **$375**

French mantle clock marked Gilbert Works, handpainted face, 11" tall. **$400**

Clock marked New Haven Works, 10 1/2" – **$400**

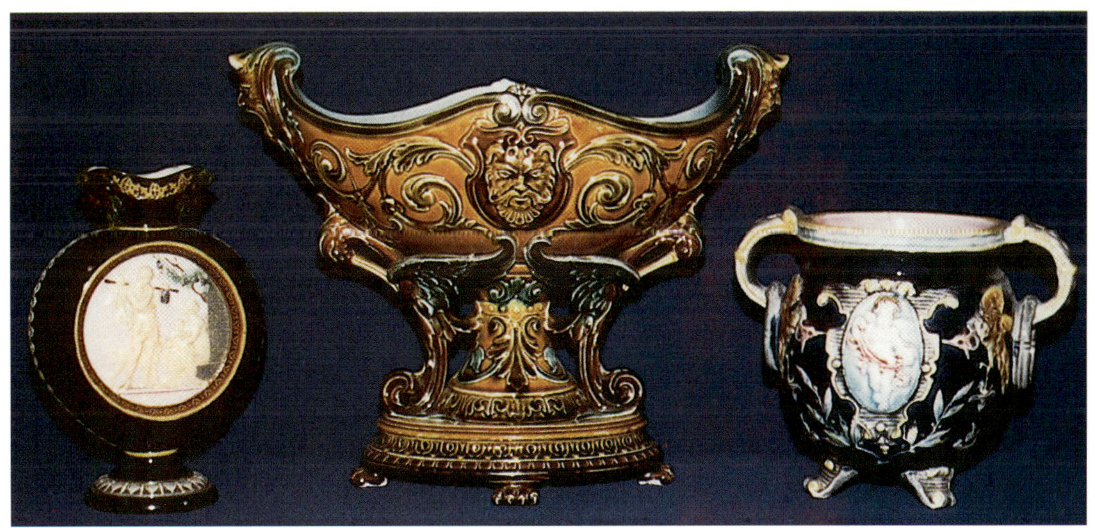

Left to Right:
G. & St. #2018 cobalt flat sided vase with mythological figures in relief and a ram's head on the rim, 9" tall – **$125**

Rorstrand large centerpiece supported by two winged ducks, 9 1/2" d x 12 1/2"h x 16"w. **$450**

Cobalt footed, two handled jardiniere with a cherub on one side and a portrait in relief on the other, and four flying cranes, 8"h. **$325**

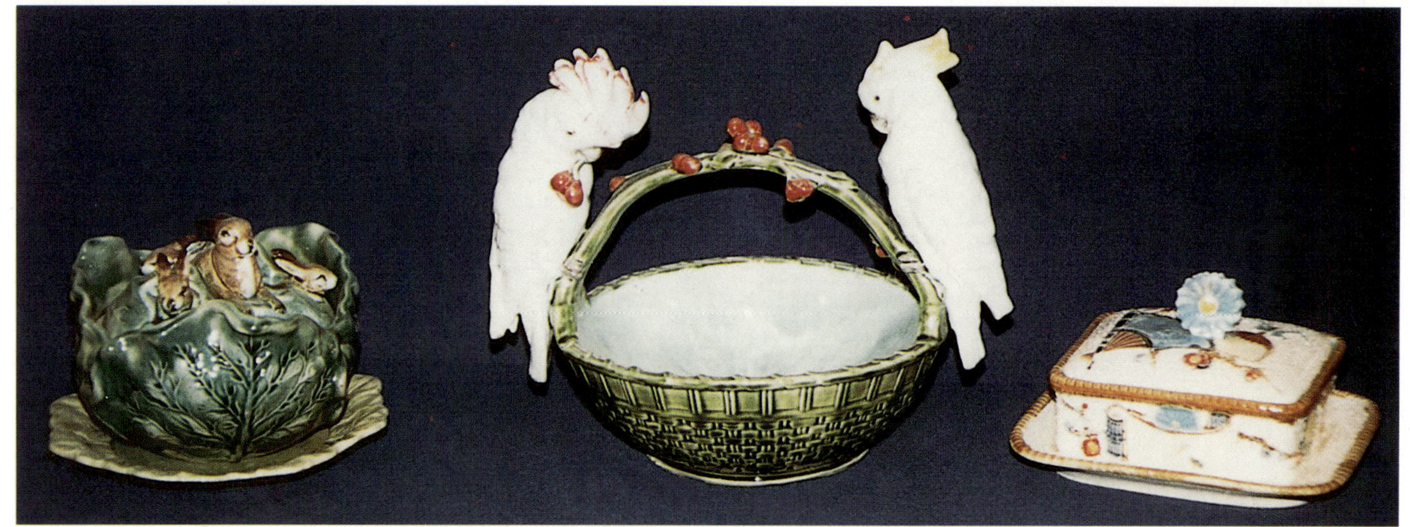

Rabbits in a cabbage head covered dish with cabbage leaf underplate – **$1100**

Czechoslavakian basket with two cockateils on the handle, 9 1/2" x 11 1/2" w – **$500**

Fielding fan and scroll covered sardine box – **$400**

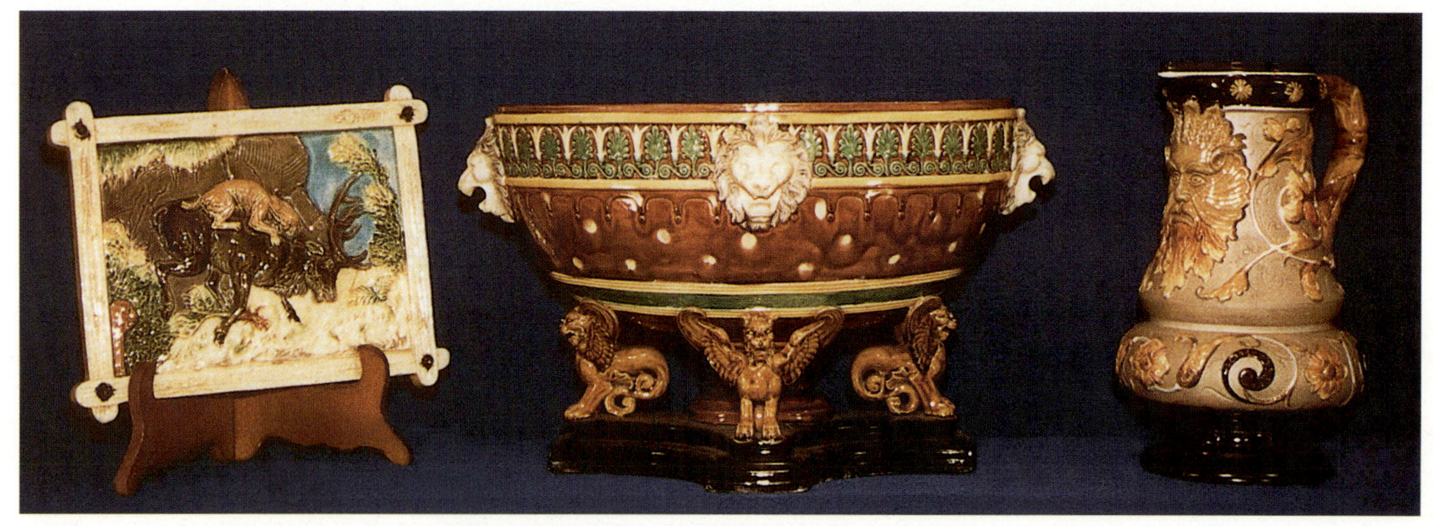

WS & S plaque with a dog on a stag in relief, 8" x 10" – **$475**

WS & S centerpiece bowl with four lion's heads supported by four winged griffons, 9 1/4" h x 15 1/4" l – **$1000**

WS & S pitcher with face spout, foliage in relief, turquoise interior, 10 1/2", #5412 – **$3300**

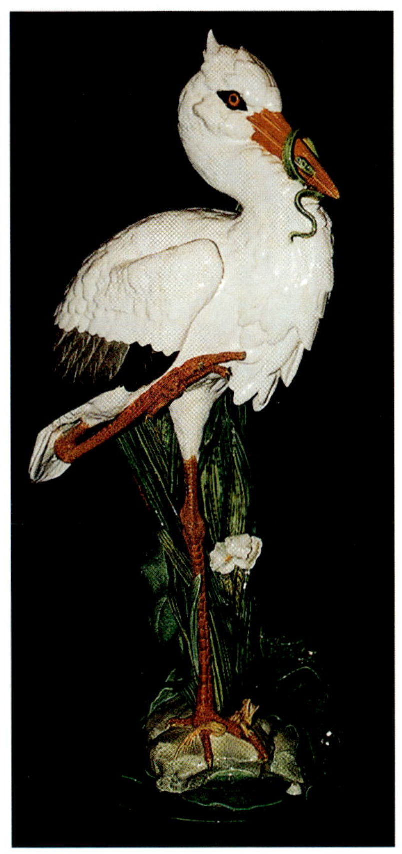

Minton Walking Stick Stand, stork in cattails and a marsh, 40", circa 1875.
$12,500

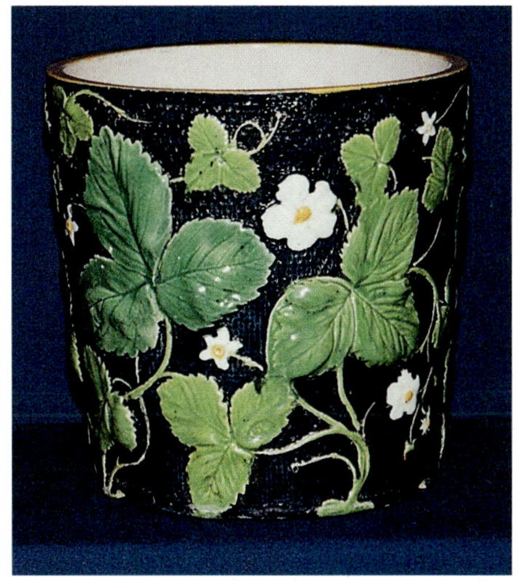

Minton strawberry cachepot, 8" h x 8" d.
$1250

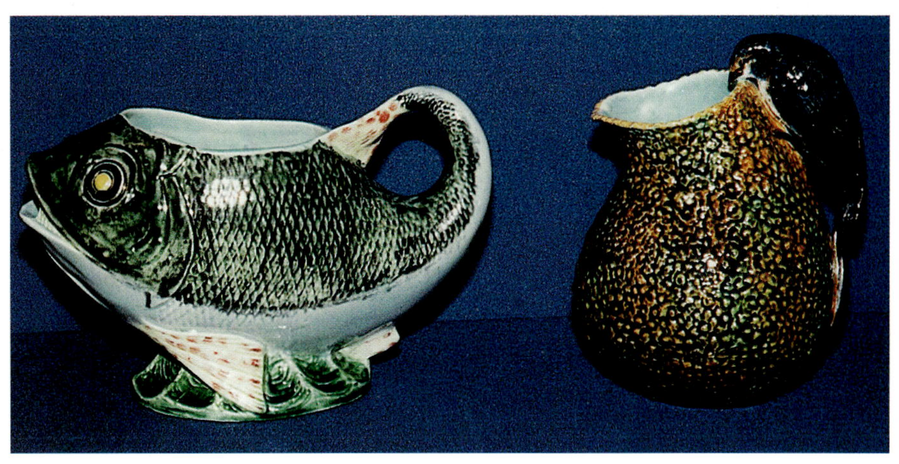

Left to Right:
Minton or Holdcroft Sauce Boat, designed as a fish on waves, 8" l x 5" h – **$1000**

Gourd Pitcher with bird handle, George Jones, mottled color, the bird is cobalt and black, 6 1/2".
$1000